Dance Stories

Dance
Stories

Edited by
Felicity Trotman

Illustrated by
Anna Leplar

Robinson Children's Books

Robinson Publishing Ltd.
7 Kensington Church Court
London W8 4SP

First published in the UK by Robinson
Children's Books, an imprint of Robinson
Publishing Ltd 1996

Illustrations by Anna Leplar

Copyright details for individual stories
appear under Acknowledgements,
pages 405–6

A copy of the British Library Cataloguing in
Publications data is available from the British
Library

ISBN 1 85487 453 5

Printed and bound in the EC

1 3 5 7 9 10 8 6 4 2

Contents

Contents

Introduction

'I could have danced all night' sings the heroine of the musical *My Fair Lady*, and there are times in life – lots of them if you're lucky – when everyone knows that wonderful feeling of joy and happiness when he or she really does seem to have wings. Add a little music, a waltz, the dance of the little swans, rock 'n' roll, a hit by the latest group, and you're away. Dancing.

Dancing is walking gone mad, everyday movements transformed into something extraordinary, showy, magical, affectionate, sexy, highly disciplined or wild and impetuous. And there are stories about all these different aspects of dancing in this collection.

If the first kind of dancing you think of is ballet, there are plenty of stories about that, from a postscript to the most famous of all theatre stories, Noel Streatfeild's *Ballet Shoes*, to stories about auditions, training, making it on stage – even falling over. But ballet isn't just about taking part, but also about the pleasure of being in the audience, of watching great dancers and wonderful ballets like *The Sleeping Beauty*, *The Nutcracker*, *Petrushka* and *The Firebird*, all of which started life as strange, magical stories.

But the urge to dance is much older and more primitive than ballet. It's the ingredient of many a folk tale, from the Grimm brothers' story of the twelve princesses who mysteriously danced their shoes into holes every night, and Patricia Lynch's tale of the Irish boy who finds himself playing his fiddle for the fairy folk, to modern fairy stories like Margaret Mahy's 'The Hookywalker Dancers' – can you guess who they are? – and Joan Aiken's 'The Rose of Puddle Fratrum', in which a retired ballerina who has slipped on a banana skin puts a curse on a ballet.

There are cats and dogs who dance – and why not? – and a dancing bear, and there are stories too about people more like you and me, who dance, sometimes not very well, at parties. Everyone knows Tom, the boy who tramples on girls' feet in Louisa Alcott's 'Polly's Farewell Party'. Sooner or later, we all dance with someone wonderful who then lets us down in the light of day, as happens to Dorothy in Berlie Doherty's 'The Cutlers' Ball', but we also have our unexpected successes, like Jessica in Jane Gardam's 'Dear Florence'.

Whether you're aiming to balance on pointes, have got rhythm or two left feet, I hope you'll dance your way through these stories.

Jean Richardson

Chicken Alley

CAROLYN SLOAN

What do you do when your relatives embarrass you horribly? Diana felt she couldn't let her zany grandmother down, even though she couldn't tell her friends what was going on, but there was an unexpected bonus for her.

Diana felt a rush of excitement. Saudi Arabia! Pictures of deserts and camels and mysterious eastern bazaars ran through her mind. Her dad's office were sending him there for a whole month! And if her mother was going then . . .

Then the shocking truth came out.

'And you're going to stay with Granny Nellie!'

'Oh no! That's not fair! Not for my whole holidays! Mum? Mum!'

'Stop moaning, Di,' said her mother. 'You'll like it when you get there. She's good fun. Besides, she's lonely . . .'

'I'm not surprised!' muttered Diana. She hunched over her homework thinking about Nellie, who didn't like being called a granny, though she was quite an old one. She had to be the most embarrassing person to be with *ever!* It wasn't just her clothes; wearing a baseball cap with her old hippie caftan and odd wellies was normal to her. But the things she did and said . . .

And *they* wouldn't be so bad if she lived on an oil rig in the North Sea – but she lived two streets away. And Diana's friends would see them! They might even *meet* in the supermarket when Nellie was doing her impressions for the check-out queue!

When Diana got to Nellie's she was painting. Not painting dainty little watercolours in the house. She was painting enormous canvases propped up against trees in her garden. One was a messy brown thing called 'Gravy' and another was brown as well and called 'Puddles'. Garbage, the goat, was starting to eat it.

'Diana! It's lovely to see you!' said Nellie, hugging her and covering her in paint. 'What a time we'll have together! I've got a terrific surprise for you!'

Diana felt a shiver of dread. A surprise from Nellie was often a nasty shock. A Terrific Surprise could be fatal. She went up to unpack in the attic bedroom she loved. It was old-fashioned, with rosy wallpaper, and a fat, bungy eiderdown . . . It was a refuge; somewhere that stayed comfortingly the same in a house that didn't.

Or it used to. Was this the surprise? The friendly roses had been painted over in whirls of purple and green and orange. Clashing colours shouted and argued from wall to wall. The bed now had a patchwork quilt in which Diana recognized bits of her grandmother's old clothes and curtains.

'I don't believe this!' She was angry at first, and then amused, and then she felt guilty because Nellie had gone to a lot of trouble making it look so awful specially for her.

She was sticking up her Chicken Alley posters and playing one of their tapes when Nellie came in.

'Oh! Chicken Alley,' she said, 'I like them!'

'Do you?' Diana was amazed she'd even heard of them.

'And why not? I'm not a centurion yet, you know! I watch Top of the Pops sometimes!'

'They're playing at the Arena, here, this month!' Diana said, and then hopefully, 'Did you know that?'

'Are they?' said Nellie, rather oddly. 'How do you like the room?'

'It's . . . absolutely . . . well . . . *brilliant*!' said Diana, truthfully.

Nellie was pleased and went off to concrete the cellar floor. Diana sat on the bed wondering if it was just possible Nellie knew she was a Chicken fan, and had got tickets for their gig as the Terrific Surprise.

Sandra and Gemma had just bought theirs when she met them the next day.

'I think my gran's got some too,' she said rashly.

'Your gran? The one that dropped you off on that funny tricycle?'

'You *can't* go to a gig with that weirdo!'

'She's not weird!' said Diana, angry because they had seen her and were sending her up. 'She's real cool for a gran!'

'I've seen her before,' said Gemma, 'and she is seriously out of her tree!' They soon forgot about grannies, deciding what to wear for the concert and drooling over Rick Boom, Chicken Alley's lead singer.

Diana drooled about him, too, all the way to the Old People's Day Centre, where she was to meet Nellie. She could see her through the window, singing merrily as she sloshed out stew and custard for the 'old' people, most of whom were much younger than she was.

Diana wondered why Nellie couldn't be like one of them. A tidy granny who came to the Centre and had her lunch quietly, and only wore funny hats at Christmas . . .

Nellie's face lit up like a sunrise when she saw Diana come in.

'Here she is!' she said unnecessarily. 'I've just been telling everyone about my surprise for you!'

'Oh?' Diana said. 'You haven't told *me* what it is yet!'

'My tap-dancing class is putting on a show at the Civic Centre . . . '

'*Tap-dancing*?' Diana felt a nightmare coming on . . .

'Yes! We've made up a Dance Story! And you're going to be in it!'

'How sweet,' said an old lady, as Diana tried to hide behind the tea urn.

Diana seethed with indignation all the way home; and then she found that Garbage had got into the house while they were out and eaten the legs off her new jeans.

'Bless him, he was hungry,' said Nellie patting Garbage while Diana felt like kicking him into next week.

'I'll make you some new ones,' said Nellie brightly.

'Now! My tap-dancing class! We're called The Goldies. That's short for golden oldies . . . '

'Why did you say I'd be in it? In front of all those people!'

Nellie grinned wickedly, and Diana knew why.

'Oh come now, Di!' she said. 'Don't pretend to be shy . . . '

'But I *am* shy! I'm not like you! You don't mind what you do or what anyone says about you . . . '

'That's the way to be! Do your own thing, girl!'

'But if I'm in this thing . . . People will *see* me!'

'That's the whole point, silly muffins! They're going to *pay* to see you! And the money's all going to special charities.'

'Do I *have* to?' Diana wailed.

'You're such a good little dancer I thought you'd want to . . . '

'But I've only been doing tap for two terms . . . '

'That's more than we have! It's only a short routine . . . '

'I couldn't . . . I can't . . . '

Nellie smiled, sweetly. 'You don't have to do anything you don't want to, dear,' she said and ne smothered her with a hug.

Diana went up to her room, relieved Chicken Alley tape and danced d she noticed what was on the with crimson frills an grandmother had made and the hem was uneven.

smugly on the floor – expensive ones. At least Nellie hadn't tried to make *those* herself.

They fitted her perfectly. She tried a few taps. It was so easy with good shoes ... They almost danced by themselves. Brilliant! Nellie was making a curry for Garbage when she heard dancing steps echoing down the stairs. She stopped and nodded, pleased with herself.

'So? What do I have to do?' Diana asked after tea.

'Well!' Nellie started to explain excitedly, 'it's a Senior Citizens' Gala Night. There'll be singing and comic sketches and ... Oh! Lots of acts. The Goldies are doing a routine called "Memories".'

'Memories of what?' asked Diana suspiciously.

'Things that happened to us in the past – our first dates, going to dances, a Spanish holiday. The rhythms keep changing ... And then we slow down, knowing how long ago it was, and we're getting old.'

'And probably tired by then,' said Diana thoughtfully.

'Yes. Well, there's that too ... So we stop, and you come on!'

'I do?'

'Yes!' said Nellie firmly. 'You spring through us, like dancing through a curtain! It's a lively little dance, you're Youth and Hope, all the things we once were! it?'

es.' Diana thought it was rather sad and sweet; it be quite good. If only she didn't have to be nd Hope.

'So? That's OK with you, then?' Nellie asked anxiously.

'OK,' Diana sighed, 'but if I've got to be Hope, can I wear my own clothes?'

'Sure!' Nellie was ready to bargain. 'Let's practise some steps.'

The next time Diana met Gemma and Sandra, she had been rehearsing with The Goldies, and was beginning to enjoy it.

'So?' asked Gemma. 'Was your Gran's surprise Chicken Alley?'

'No. Something at the Civic Centre,' Diana said vaguely, 'but it's the same day as the Chicken gig, so I can't go.'

'But that's the oldies' concert night,' said Sandra. 'My mum's doing the coffee bar. You can't go to that!'

'It'll be dead funny with those old wrinklies, imagine!'

'Shut up, Gemma! You'll be old one day!' Diana snapped suddenly. 'And I bet you won't have the guts to tap-dance for charity like my gran!'

'Your gran's *tap-dancing*?' Gemma and Sandra burst into such hysterical giggles that Diana stormed home. She put on her tap shoes and danced, going faster and faster until she had tapped all her anger away.

'Feel better?' asked Nellie, understanding. 'It's great, isn't it, dancing to your own rhythm. Like being a drum and a drummer all at once.'

The day before the show, The Goldies turned up at the

stage door of the Civic Centre, nervously clutching their shoes in plastic bags. They watched the other acts rehearse, but the show really came alive with 'Memories'. Even the Centre staff applauded. A man appeared from the back.

'I'm Chicken Alley's manager,' he said. 'They're playing the Arena tomorrow. Rick Boom's looking for some . . . some mature tap–dancers for his Christmas video . . . If you ladies would do your "Memories" routine, it would be ace!'

'Where's Pickle Valley?' asked The Goldies coach, who never listened to anyone properly. 'Who's Mick Doom?'

'It's a band,' said Diana excitedly. 'I'm a fan, so's Nellie. Oh please say you'll do it! Video! Wow! You'd make a fortune for the charities! You'll all be famous!'

They all gathered round the manager. It was simple. Rick Boom ·had to shoot a short sequence for the video, a song called 'Once Upon a Winter'. He wanted to do it with a background of tapping grannies, wearing hats and coats in a snowstorm.

'But it's summer . . . ' said one of them sensibly.

'Don't worry! We'll bring the snow. Just bring some winter clothes . . . Start at ten and we can wrap it up by lunch-time. Are you on, ladies?' The ladies decided that they were

They were there early the next morning, sweating in winter woollies. The hall was full of machinery and lights and snaking with cables. Rick's manager soon had them dancing, nervously to begin with, and then with increasing skill and enthusiasm.

Everyone forgot about Diana. She was glad, and sat apart, waiting for the magic moment when . . . And then he was there! Rick Boom! Smaller than he looked on television . . . But *there*! Live! Diana felt dizzy with the thrill of being in the same room, breathing the same air . . .

He chatted up the ladies, changed a few lights and ran through his song a few times while they tapped away behind him.

'OK, take a break,' said Rick and went towards the stairs to the circle. He stopped when he saw Diana. 'You the kid who does the final sequence?' he said. 'I hear you're good!'

'Oh no, I . . . I just . . . '

'Sorry we won't be needing you, love. It's just the grans, see? They're supposed to make *me* look young.' He laughed easily and Diana protested that she didn't mind *at all* . . .

'Come up and watch the monitor,' Rick said, 'see how it looks and then we'll go for a take. With snow!' Diana followed him up the stairs and sat next to him and could barely believe it was all happening.

'Aren't these old girls just great?' he said, watching the screen. 'Especially the character in the red hat!'

'That's my grandma,' said Diana proudly.

'Love her!' said Rick.

It all happened too quickly after that, Diana thought, when it was over and a small man with huge cans on his ears said 'Got it!' and Rick was going round thanking the dancers. He spotted Diana again on his way out and smiled and called out to her.

'Coming to our show at the Arena tonight?'

'No . . . I mean, I wanted to. But we're doing this, you see.'

''Course! Good on you, love! Tell you what, I'll get you a rough of this tape, OK? Don't show anyone else, we have to edit and remix it! Good luck for tonight!'

'Thanks,' said Diana, weakly, and she thought, I'll dance my socks off for you tonight, Rick! And for Nellie. For her!

She did. 'Memories' stopped the show, and The Goldies had to do two encores. It was late when Diana and Nellie got home, and Garbage had got into the house again and eaten their supper and the door mat.

'I'll make us some toasted sarnies,' said Diana, because Nellie had sunk, exhausted into a chair. As she grated cheese and chopped bacon, she realized she had never seen Nellie tired before. Never seen her sitting and doing nothing, looking old. She wondered if she sometimes looked like that when she was alone. And whether all the wildly over-the-top things she did were to keep her loneliness away

Nellie woke up with a little grunt when Diana took the tray in.

'What a day it's been!' she sighed, 'and it was the Chicken Alley gig tonight! You should have gone to it!'

'Today was a hundred times better than any gig,' said Diana dreamily. 'And Rick gave me a copy of your video!' She produced her surprise, 'It's just for us to see, and it's signed!'

11

'Put it on then!' said Nellie, and then, softly, 'Oh Diana!'

Sandra and Gemma couldn't wait to gloat to Diana about the Chicken concert, and how they had made eye contact with the drummer and got one of Rick's empty mineral water bottles afterwards.

'Wow!' said Diana, 'lucky you!'

'Coming to see The Beasts on Saturday?'

'No. We're going on a night picnic, Gran and I,' said Diana, 'and I won't see you for the rest of the week. We've got lots to do!'

'You and your gran!' said Gemma. 'You're so sad! What a dead boring holiday for you. Oh well. Rick Boom's got a new video coming out at Christmas. At least you'll be able to see that!'

'That's lucky for me, isn't it?' Diana said pleasantly, and went off with a jaunty wave.

Poppy Smith – Prima Ballerina

JEAN URE

Pippa Smith's ambition to dance in the school display will be recognized by many readers. So will the way her teachers think her efforts to dance well are just showing-off!

One morning Miss Hardcastle said to her class, 'Does anyone here learn ballet? Do we have any little dancers in our midst?'

There was a silence while everyone looked at everyone else. Not a hand went up. Pippa Smith's almost did, but at the last moment she wasn't quite brave enough. Practising ballet in her bedroom every night (and sometimes every morning, too) wasn't really the same as learning from a proper ballet teacher.

Miss Hardcastle obviously hadn't noticed Pippa's hand wavering and then collapsing. She said, 'That's a pity! Miss Wilson up at the big school is looking for four little dancers for the Christmas pantomime. I was hoping we might be able to help. Never mind! I'm sure she'll find someone from somewhere.'

Pippa's heart thudded and banged against her ribs. Why hadn't she put her hand up? After all, she *was* learning ballet – sort of. It was just that she was learning it by herself.

Last year Pippa had been taken to see a ballet called *Swan Lake* with a famous ballerina called Bianca White, and ever since then she had dreamed of becoming a famous ballerina herself, wearing a white frilly dress (known as a tutu) and dancing on her toes in pink satin shoes, only every time she asked her mum if she could have ballet lessons her mum said, 'We'll have to think about it.'

The truth was that Pippa's mum couldn't afford to pay for Pippa to take proper lessons. That was why Pippa had to practise in her bedroom, in front of a large photograph of Bianca White which she had stuck on her bedroom wall. And now she had missed an opportunity to star in the big school's pantomime, all because she was such a *coward*. She was sure Bianca White wouldn't have been a coward.

Next day Miss Wilson came down from the big school to take Miss Hardcastle's class for a special dancing lesson. (The boys were told they could either dance or play football: every single one of them went off to play football. Silly, boys were.)

'What I'm looking for,' said Miss Wilson, 'are four little princesses.'

Pippa immediately drew herself up straight and tall and did her best to look like Princess Diana. It wasn't easy, because Pippa was rather tiny and thin, with raggedy red hair and a snub nose; not a bit like Princess Diana, or indeed any other princess.

'Don't worry if you've never learned ballet,' said Miss Wilson. 'Don't let that stop you.'

Pippa didn't. Nothing would have stopped Bianca White and nothing was going to stop Pippa. By the end of the class she had almost forgotten she was raggedy-haired and snub-nosed. She wouldn't have been at all surprised if someone had curtsied and called her 'Your Royal Highness'.

Miss Wilson was murmuring to Miss Hardcastle. Miss Hardcastle nodded.

'Angela Phillips!' she said. 'Ayesha Khan! Joyce Chan! Hannah Whitbread! Four little princesses, to dance in the pantomime!'

Pippa's freckledy face turned bright scarlet like a blood orange. Whatever was Miss Wilson thinking of? Angela Phillips was the only one who looked in the least like Princess Diana. Hannah was tall, but she wasn't fair, in fact she was black, and Ayesha Khan was just as tiny as Pippa and Joyce Chan was even tinier than either of them. Miss Wilson must be *mad*.

There was only one thing for it: Pippa would have to show her that in spite of having freckles and a snub nose she was a better princess than any of them!

Once a week, the girls of Pippa's class gathered in the PE hall to learn the dance of the four princesses with Miss Wilson.

'I want everyone to learn,' said Miss Wilson, 'just in case any of my four should go down with the flu.'

Pippa at once started praying: please, please let one of Miss Wilson's four go down with the flu . . .

Unfortunately, they all stayed horribly healthy. In the meanwhile, Pippa did her best to be noticed.

'Glide, glide!' chanted Miss Wilson, as the music for the dance came from the cassette player. 'Slowly, slowly . . . slow and graceful . . . remember, you are princesses!'

Slowly and gracefully, arms held before her, Pippa glided. She was so busy being a princess that she didn't notice Mandy Harris coming towards her in the opposite direction. It was Mandy's fault: Miss Wilson had said turn left and Mandy had turned right. (She always had trouble with left and right.) *Crash!* went

Pippa, gliding straight into her.

'*Ow!*' screeched Mandy. 'Watch where you're going!'

Pippa was cross: Mandy had gone and spoilt her flow.

'Watch yourself, you idiot!'

'Now, now!' said Miss Wilson. She looked at Pippa, sternly. 'We'll have less of that.'

The next week they learned the steps for 'Princesses' Playtime'. Each of the princesses had to toss an imaginary ball into the air and catch it as she danced. Pippa tossed and caught, and caught and tossed, and danced just as hard as she could. Her imaginary ball flew far higher than anyone else's, her feet moved far faster. When she leapt she was more vigorous, when she turned she was almost dizzying. Mandy Harris had just better keep out of her way!

'That girl there,' said Miss Wilson, pointing at Pippa. 'Come here, will you, please!'

Proudly, Pippa wiggled her way out to the front. This was the moment she had been waiting for . . . the moment when Miss Wilson said that Pippa Smith must take the place of one of the other princesses!

'What is your name?' said Miss Wilson.

Pippa grinned, broadly. 'Pippa Smith,' said Pippa.

'Pippy Smith?' said Miss Wilson. 'I can see I shall have to keep an eye on you.'

After that, Miss Wilson made Pippa stay at the front where she could see her. And every week, she called her by a different name.

'Pansy Smith, stay in line! Polly Smith, stop showing off!'

She was Pansy and Polly and Petal and Patsy, but she was never asked to be a princess.

On the day of the pantomime, which was a Saturday, Pippa came in to school early. The show didn't start until two o'clock, but Pippa was there by half-past one. Just in case. (In case one of the princesses should suddenly go down with the flu.)

As she walked along the empty corridors of the big school she heard a strange banging sound coming from behind a door marked 'Girls' Cloakroom'. Pippa crept up and listened. She opened the door and peered round.

'Hello?' said Pippa. 'Is anyone there?'

'Help!' squealed a voice. 'I can't get out!'

Someone was locked in a lavatory! It was Ayesha Khan!

Hooray! This was it – Pippa's big chance! She knew what Bianca White would do. Bianca White wouldn't hesitate.

Pippa turned. She was just about to close the door and tiptoe away – 'Thank goodness Pippa is here!' Miss Wilson would say, as she handed Pippa her princess costume – when from behind her locked door Ayesha started to sob.

Pippa hesitated. Ayesha sobbed pitifully.

'Oh, *bother!* said Pippa, as she raced off to get help.

Miss Wilson didn't even say thank you; she was too busy rushing Ayesha to the sickroom. Poor Ayesha! She couldn't possibly dance in that state.

'We'll just have to go on with only three,' said Miss Wilson, looking straight through Pippa as she spoke.

Miss Wilson went off with Ayesha. The curtain was

due to go up in ten minutes. What would Bianca White do? Pippa knew what Bianca White would do.

Boldly, Pippa marched into the dressing room.

'I've got to dance in place of Ayesha,' she said.

And she did! By the time Miss Wilson arrived back it was too late to stop her: Pippa was already on stage.

Next week in the local paper there was a photograph of the princesses doing their playtime dance. Underneath the photograph it said, 'Four little prima ballerinas'. And then it gave their names: 'Angela Phillips, Hannah Whitbread, Joyce Chan and Poppy Smith'.

Pippa didn't mind that she had become Poppy. Nobody ever went on the stage using their real name. She thought that when she became famous that was what she would call herself: Poppy Smith.

She took the scissors and she took the newspaper and she carefully snipped off all the bits she didn't want (which were all the bits that weren't about Poppy Smith) and then she stuck her photograph on the bedroom wall next to Bianca White, and she stuck her new name underneath it.

Bianca White and Poppy Smith . . . prima ballerinas!

The Cat and the Fiddle

ALISON UTTLEY

Alison Uttley's most famous stories are probably the ones she wrote about Little Grey Rabbit and her woodland friends. She wrote many others, too, including this delightful romp, which explains the goings-on behind a well-known song!

Shutters were fastened, doors locked, the rug was rolled back from the hearth, the groaning weights were pulled up to the top of the grandfather clock, and the lamp was extinguished. The family picked up their candlesticks and walked up the wooden stairs to bed, leaving the kitchen to the silence of the night.

The fire flickered with little points of flame, the clock ticked solemnly as it listened to the sounds which came from upstairs, the thump of bare feet on the floor above, the scrape of a chair and then a thud as somebody got into bed.

Tick! Tock! went the old clock, louder and louder, and his brass face shone in the falling light of the fire. There was a scurry of little feet across the floor as a couple of mice came dancing through a hole in the wainscot, and raced to the flour-bag which stood wide open to the pantry bench.

The cat roused herself and looked after them.

'Never mind,' said she. 'Not tonight. I've something better to do than to chase two skinny mice. Tomorrow they will be fatter. Besides, I had a good basin of bread and milk.'

She sighed happily, and stretched her legs in the warmth of the hearthstone. Then she yawned, listened intently to the snores in the room above, and stood up. She crept under the old settle in the corner of the room, and walked about among the boots and shoes which lay scattered there. Sometimes a mouse moved in the toe of one of the farm boots, but she turned aside from temptation, and peered into the stick box. From a pile of kindling chips she lifted out a curiously shaped piece of wood, and carried it back to the hearth. It wasn't a stick at all, it was a fiddle, a roughly shaped little fiddle with four strings of horsehair drawn tightly across the tiny wooden bridge.

She held it under her furry chin, and twanged with her claws, but the noise did not please her, so she went under the settle again and brought out a slim stick for a bow. She tuned the four strings, holding her fiddle to her ear, and then she began. She played a little odd air, a queer jumpy kind of tune, and the clock stared down and ticked louder than ever.

The lading-can shuffled its tin sides, as it lay on the sink, and slowly rocked like a boat at sea, clanging softly on the stone. The wooden milk bowl beat its sides. The nutmeg grater scraped and sawed with a nutmeg, the blow-bellows puffed, and the egg beater began to whirr, as the music from the little fiddle welled through the kitchen and waked all the sleeping pots and pans.

On the hob the great copper kettle sang a shrill high song, and the water began to boil. As the steam came out, the lid rattled up and down like a dancing ninny. Saucepan lids jingled like tambourines as they hung in a row on the wall, and the walking sticks in the corner rapped with little feet and tripped out into the middle of the floor.

The cat glanced round and nodded approvingly. It was better than she expected. She changed her tune to a merry jig, a country dance of long ago. Down leaped the saucepan lids, and down sprang the gleaming silvery dish covers. They could hang there no longer, and they clattered round the blue and red tiled floor with the pewter salt pot and the pepper box.

'Do keep still, pepper,' sneezed the cat. 'I can't play when you dance.' So the pepper box stood in a far corner near the big milk cans and beat time with his round little head.

The eyes of the clock were agoggle, and he held his hands in front of his face in amazement at the capers of some of the kitchen things. He had thought they were so quiet and modest, and here they were, jigging up and down like morris dancers at the fair. He had seen nothing like it since he was born.

The flat-irons burst open the door of the ironing cupboard, and joined in the dance. Everyone kept away from their heavy feet, but the tiniest crimping iron was a great favourite, she was so lively.

There was a movement on the high mantelpiece, and all the brass candlesticks leaned forward, peeping down at the commotion below. The kitchen floor was like a ballroom, and they longed to join the fun, There wasn't room to dance on the narrow ledge where they stood, but it was a long way down to the ground. Could they jump it? They stooped and held out their flat brazen skirts. The copper pestle and mortar in the middle of the mantelpiece counted for the jump. Three hundred years is a great age, and he was content to look on.

'One to be ready! Two to be steady! Three to be *off*!' he shouted, and down they all fell with a great clatter, and danced more gaily than anyone in their shining brass petticoats and their tall extinguisher hats. They knew all the old country dances, for they had watched them in bygone days, and they showed the younger members the stately measures of Queen Bess's reign.

The cat played 'Greensleeves', and 'Here we go round the Mulberry Bush', and 'Over the Hills and Far Away', and all the tunes you have ever heard. She was a musical cat. She had listened to the songs the children sang when they sat with their mother at the piano in the parlour. They didn't know she took any notice, for she lay on the broad window-sill, with her green eyes fixed on the birds in the garden. But her ears twitched, and the little songs went into them, and there they stayed, waiting in her memory till she could make music herself.

Now, all the time she played, there was a subdued squeaking and a muffled whispering on the oak dresser.

It came from the long wooden box which lay near the open knife box. The knives had gone long ago, and were hopping on the floor in glittering rows, but this finely polished oaken box had a heavy lid. Sometimes it moved up a little, and then it sank down again. Evidently something was trying to get out, for bright eyes peered through the crack, and then disappeared, and the struggle began again.

'All together! Heave! Heave-O!' cried a tiny tinkling voice, and the lid shot up. Out scrambled a company of spoons and forks, with a clitter-clatter, and soon they scampered across the dresser. They swarmed down the carved legs, and joined the assembly on the floor. They were the best dancers of all, and they twirled round with each other, with the nutmeg grater, the egg beater, and the toasting fork. One big wooden spoon, used for stirring the jam in the enormous brass pan, actually danced with the frying pan!

Pussy played a waltz, so sweet and dreamy that the willow pattern dishes from the dresser shelf, and the blue cups and lustre jugs hanging on the hooks, stepped lightly down with never a crack, and whirled round in rapture. Even the great iron key of the door waltzed round in the lock and then fell to the floor with a clang.

'Oh!' it cried. 'Do let me join in this lovely whirligig' – for that was the name it gave the waltz, which was new in those days – and it whirled round with the key of the stable door, which had jumped from the end of the dresser where the stable boy had put it for the night.

When the door-key turned in the lock, the door

came open, and little cold night winds slipped into the kitchen, sending the dying flames roaring up the chimney afresh, blowing the little dancers here and there. The cat looked up, and walked to the doorway, playing her fiddle as she went.

'Shut the door! Shut the door!' cried the candlesticks. 'We don't like draughts!'

'Hush!' whispered the cat, softly. 'Hush! Come and look out of doors, all of you. Come and look at the full moon.'

So the crowd of little pots and pans, dishes and jugs, spoons and knives and forks, swayed to the doorway, and gazed up into the sky. There, high up in the blue starry night sky, above the stables and cowsheds and weathercock, hung a great yellow moon, a moon of gold, looking down and actually smiling at them!

They all waved to the moon, and bowed three times over their left shoulder, for it was the first time some of them had ever seen her, and they wished to pay her homage in the ancient way.

'We see her very often from the attic windows,' boasted the candlesticks, but they bowed just the same. The little crimping iron was much impressed by her glory, and touched the ground with her nose, and the cat laid her paw on her heart, and bent down with her fiddle sweeping the earth. She knew the moon very well. She could almost call herself a personal friend of the moon's!

In the orchard stood Sally the cow, and at that moment she, too, raised her head and stared at the golden moon. Rover the house dog came out of his kennel to see what was the matter.

'Hush!' whispered the cat again. 'Look yonder!'

Sally the cow suddenly tossed her head, flicked her tail, and galloped across the orchard. Then she took a leap, and flew up in the air, higher than the apple trees, higher than the weathercock on the barn end. Up she sailed, and all the pots and pans cried, 'Oh-oo-oo-oh!' and opened wide their eyes.

Over the moon went Sally, and then she came spinning down to earth again, and dropped among the apple trees where she started. She went on eating as if nothing had happened, but Rover the dog laughed and laughed as if he would never stop, and all the little dancers clapped their tiny hands.

The cat took up her fiddle and began to play, when, through the open door, down the path to the wicket gate, and across the cobbled yard, ran an odd couple.

'Now's our chance,' whispered the willow pattern dish. 'Will you come with me, beautiful one? Will you run away in the moonshine? It's the one chance in our lives. Never again will the door be open and the way clear as it is tonight.'

'I'll go to the world's end,' sighed the loving spoon, and hand in hand they pattered over the grass to freedom. Down the steps by the orchard they ran, and across the field into the lane, and away.

The moon drew a cloud over her face. Rover crept into his kennel. The cow lay down on the dewy grass and composed herself to much needed sleep. The cat put her fiddle under her arm and returned to the kitchen. All the pots and pans and tins climbed sedately and silently back to their places. The candlesticks clambered up the wall and clasped the mantelpiece to swing themselves up on to it. The spoons, with many a struggle, managed to lift the lid of the spoon box, and slipped inside whispering of their missing sister. The flat-irons opened the cupboard door and went inside to the darkness, with the little crimping iron whose heart thumped with excitement.

'What a romance!' she cried; but 'Hush! What a disgrace!' said the other irons.

'It all comes of dancing,' exclaimed the pestle and mortar, when the candlesticks told him about it, but he wished he had seen the elopement, all the same. It reminded him of the time when the pretty young daughter of the house slipped away at midnight with the squire's son, exactly two hundred years ago.

But the key returned to the lock, and the fire died down. Pussy fell asleep, and slept so soundly that the two little mice, who had been eating in the flour bag during the great dance, now came out again, and boldly jigged round the tired animal!

As they jigged, they heard a little song, a tiny coppery song, which came from the mantelpiece. They looked up and saw the ancient pestle and mortar, with open mouth, chanting this lay:

> 'Hey diddle diddle!
> The cat and the fiddle.
> The cow jumped over the moon.
> The little dog laughed to see such fun,
> And the dish ran away with the spoon!'

But alas! the dish and the spoon didn't go far. John, the farmer's son, found them at the bottom of the lane the next day. The poor dish was broken by the rough stones, and the spoon was bent. It was a sad ending to a honeymoon, but they had their romance.

The Dancing Display

ADÈLE GERAS

The Fantora family all have unusual talents: their grandmother Filomena, for example, who can tell the future from her knitting, or the children – Bianca can make things come to life, and Marco can make himself invisible. When Dilys makes a nuisance of herself at the dancing display, Francesca's talent comes in very useful ... This story comes from The Fantora Family Photographs, *which is narrated by the Guardian of the Family History, Ozymandias the cat.*

In March, after Francesca had been going to classes for nearly two months, our mealtimes began to be filled with the Dancing Display Saga. First of all, Francesca objected strongly to the dance that had been chosen for her class.

'Everyone else's dance is nicer,' she grumbled. 'Some people are doing the Sailors' Hornpipe, and the big girls are doing a proper dance in real tutus to some *Swan Lake* music, and all we're doing is "Mary, Mary, quite contrary".'

'I expect it'll be all right,' said Auntie Varvara soothingly, 'on the night. Are you Mary Mary?'

'No,' said Francesca. 'Polly's a Silver Bell, and I'm a Cockle Shell. I have to wear this ridiculous pink thing on my head.'

'Well,' said Rosie, 'never mind. I'm sure you'll look lovely, dear.'

'They could have made us Pretty Maids all in a Row. Ugly Frilly Dilys is Mary Mary. That's really stupid. She's going to be terrible.'

'Why did Madame Vera choose her?' asked Bianca.

'Polly and I think it's because her dad's a gangster. We think it's because he knows some dreadful secret about Madame Vera, and if she doesn't put his daughter in the main part, then he'll tell everyone.'

'I know her awful secret,' said Filomena. 'She comes from Barnsley.'

Everyone laughed and at last we calmed Francesca down.

Rehearsals began. Auntie Varvara, who had done Home Dressmaking at Evening Class three years ago, said that she would make the pinkish silky tunic that Madame Vera had decided was what every Cockle Shell should wear. Francesca practised her steps. Polly practised hers. The day of the dancing display was coming closer. When it actually arrived, Francesca was so excited that she insisted on being the first person to get to the secondary school Madame Vera was using as a theatre.

Rosie took her in the car, and Bianca went with her to keep her company.

'I'll drop you girls off, and come back later,' Rosie said. 'We've all still got to get dressed, so we'll see you at 6.30. I shall have my work cut out getting Filomena out of her tracksuit.'

Very soon, the dressing room was crowded with Silver

Bells, Cockle Shells and Pretty Maids, not to mention Sailors and Swans of all shapes and sizes. Then, just as Polly was beginning to think *she* might be chosen to stand in for her, Frilly Dilys arrived at last.

Her first action was to spot a place she fancied at the mirror, and then push aside everyone else's make-up, combs and brushes to make room for her own. Then she pushed all the costumes on the costume rail to one side and hung up her ballooning and billowy blue skirt.

'She's just as horrible,' Bianca whispered to Francesca, 'as you said she was.'

'Horribler,' Francesca said, trying to fix her rigid pink shell-thingie, as she called it, on to her head like a gigantic pink snail.

'I'm going to sit down now,' Bianca said. 'Good luck. I bet it'll be lovely.'

It wasn't lovely. It was about as far from lovely as a dance could be. Had you been in the audience, you would not have realized that any choreography had taken place at all. To be sure, the Silver Bells, Cockle Shells and Pretty Maids tried to go through their pre-arranged paces as decreed by Madame Vera, but Frilly Dilys, dazzled by the bright lights, decided to do, as they say, her own thing. This mainly involved galumphing around the stage, more or less in time to the music. When she did not galumph, Frilly Dilys careered, and when that became tiresome, she took to whirling. Madame Vera stood in the wings, she and her pearls together frozen into silent horror.

In the audience, Eddie whispered to Rosie, 'Is that

what's meant to be happening?'

Rosie shook her head, and Auntie Varvara, who knew about matters balletic, winced and winced again.

'I'm never going to be able to take a proper photograph of Francesca in her costume at this rate,' said Eddie. He had brought his camera, and was all ready to take artistic shots of Francesca's dancing début.

Filomena whispered to Bianca, 'I should have known. I've been doing slip stitches all afternoon, in a very feverish shade of orange. That always means things getting out of control.'

'It's not fair,' said Marco. 'You can't see any of the others. I can hardly see Francesca.'

'There she is,' said Bianca. 'She looks surprisingly happy. Can you see that sunflower, painted on the screen thing, over there?'

Marco looked. Sure enough, there was a tiny piece of scenery right at the back of the stage. It was painted to look like a garden, complete with three or four charmingly fuzzy-looking bees. One should not, of course, blame the painters of the scenery for what happened. They were not to know that Bianca would be tampering with their handiwork. The galumphing continued. It was so loud that only Marco noticed the buzzing at first.

'The bees have come to life, Bianca!' he whispered. 'Is that you?'

'Who else could it be?' Bianca answered.

'You don't know Frilly Dilys is afraid of bees.'

'Bet she is though,' Bianca smiled.

She was.

Later, no one could agree about exactly what happened. Which came first, the bees or the wind? Opinion is divided. Perhaps (and this, as a Narrator, is the version I favour) three things happened at once:

1) The dance came to an end and the girls lined up at the front of the stage to take their bow, with Francesca standing on Frilly Dilys's left.

2) Four bees arrived simultaneously in the neighbourhood of Frilly Dilys.

3) A little wind of about Force 6 whipped up from the footlights region and ran to hide in Frilly Dilys's ballooning, billowy blue skirt.

The result of all this was:

a) Frilly Dilys's skirt blew up over her head, covering her face.

b) Frilly Dilys was stung on the arm by a fuzzy little bee.

c) the applause was deafening.

Later, as the girls were changing into their ordinary clothes, Francesca spoke to Dilys.

'That was me,' she said. 'I made the wind blow, the one that lifted your skirt over your head.' She giggled. 'And my sister brought those bees to life. I bet you didn't know she could do that!'

'I don't believe you . . . ' said Dilys. 'That was an accident.'

'Would you like me to show you?' Francesca smiled. 'Look at that face powder . . . you really ought to keep

things like that covered up with me around, you know.'

She waved her fingers over Dilys's open box of powder and a sprightly little breeze blew up.

'I can make it stronger if you like,' said Francesca. 'I can make it blow that stuff all over your frock.'

'No,' said Dilys. 'I believe you now. Do stop. Please.'

'OK,' said Francesca. 'I will. I'm going home now.'

Francesca stalked out, leaving the other girls staring after her.

*   *   *

I am looking again at one of the photographs Eddie took on that occasion. Francesca likes it so much that she made him enlarge it and put it on the Family Wall. It shows her looking charming in her Cockle Shell outfit, and looking happy, too. She is smiling with what one can only call 'glee'. Beside her is a creature, a shape covered in blue silk. All you can see of this person is chubby legs in lace-trimmed pantaloons. It is Frilly Dilys. Eddie refused to make copies of the photograph for Francesca to distribute to others in her dancing class.

'Frilly Dilys has been punished enough,' he said.

Still, Francesca continues to invite friends into the house all the time, so of course, everyone has seen it.

Frilly Dilys is very polite to Francesca these days. She has even invited her for a ride in the shiny car.

The Dancing Princesses

WALTER DE LA MARE

The story of the twelve dancing princesses is a very old one. It's one of the folk-tales collected in Germany by the brothers Grimm in the early part of the last century. There's an English version, Kate Crackernuts, *in which brave Kate rescues a prince! This version of the story is beautifully told by a well-known writer and poet.*

There was a king of old who had twelve daughters. Some of them were fair as swans in spring, some dark as trees on a mountainside, and all were beautiful. And because the king wished to keep their beauty to himself only, they slept at night in twelve beds in one long stone chamber whose doors were closely barred and bolted.

Yet, in spite of this, as soon as the year came round to May again, and the stars and cold of winter were gone and the world was merry, at morning and every morning the soles of the twelve princesses' slippers were found to be worn through to the very welts. It was as if they must have been dancing in them all the night long.

News of this being brought to the king, he marvelled.

Unless they had wings, how could they have flown out of the palace? There was neither crevice nor cranny in the heavy doors. He spied. He set watch. It made no difference. Brand-new though the princesses' gold and silver slippers were overnight, they were worn out at morning. He was in rage and despair.

At last this king made a decree. He decreed that anyone who, by waking and watching, by wisdom or magic, should reveal this strange secret, and where and how and when the twelve princesses' slippers went of nights to get so worn, he should have the hand in marriage of whichever one of the princesses he chose, and should be made the heir to the throne. As for anyone foolish enough to be so bold as to attempt such a task and fail in it, he should be whipped out of the kingdom and maybe lose his ears into the bargain. But such was the beauty of these princesses, many a high-born stranger lost not only his heart but his ears also; and the king grew ever more moody and morose.

Now, beyond the walls of the royal house where lived the twelve princesses was a forest; and one summer's evening an old soldier who was travelling home from the wars met there, on his way, a beldame with a pig. This old beldame had brought her pig to the forest to feed on the beech mast and truffles, but now, try as she might, she could not prevail upon it to be caught and to return home with her to its sty. She would steal up behind it with its cord in her hand, but as soon as she drew near and all but in touch of it, the pig, that meanwhile had been busily rooting in the cool loose loam, with a flick of its ears and twinkle of its tail would scamper off out of her reach. It was almost as if its little sharp glass-green eyes could see through the pink shutters of its ears.

The old soldier watched the pig (and the red sunlight was glinting in the young green leaves of the beeches), and at last he said: 'If I may make so bold, Grannie, I know a little secret about pigs. And if, as I take it, you want to catch *that* particular pig, it's yours and welcome.'

The beldame, who had fingers like birds' claws and eyes black as sloes, thanked the old soldier. Fetching out a scrap of some secret root from the bottom of his knapsack, he first slowly turned his back on the pig, then stooped down and, with the bit of root between his teeth, stared earnestly at the pig from between his legs.

Presently, either by reason of the savour of the root or drawn by curiosity, the pig edged closer and closer to the old soldier until at last it actually came nosing and sidling in underneath him, as if under a bridge. Then in a trice the old soldier snatched him up by ear and tail and slipped the noose of the cord fast. The pig squealed like forty demons, but more as if in fun than in real rage.

'There we are, Grannie,' said the old soldier, giving the old beldame her pig, 'and here's a scrap of the root, too. There's no pig all the world over, white, black or piebald, but after he gets one sniff of it comes for more. *That* I'll warrant you, and I'm sure you're very welcome.'

The beldame, with her pig now safely at the rope's end and the scrap of root between her fingers, thanked the old soldier and asked him of his journey and whither he was going; and it was just as if, with its snout uplifted, its ears drawn forward, the nimble young pig was also listening for his answer.

The old soldier told her he was returning from the wars. 'But as for where *to*, Grannie, or what for, I hardly know. For wife or children have I none, and most of my old friends must have long ago forgotten me. Not that I'm meaning to say, Grannie,' says the soldier, 'that *that* much matters, me being come so far and no turning back. Still, there's just *one* thing I'd like to find out before I go, and that is where the twelve young daughters of the mad old king yonder dance of nights. If I knew that, Grannie, they say I might some day sit on a throne.' With that he burst out laughing, at which the pig, with a twist of its jaws (as though recalling the sweet savour of the root), flung up its three-cornered head and laughed too.

The beldame, eyeing the old soldier closely, said that what he had asked was not a hard or dangerous matter if only he would promise to do exactly what she told him. The old soldier found *that* easy enough.

'Well,' said the beldame, 'when you come to the palace, you'll be set to watch, and you'll be tempted to sleep. Vow a vow, then, to taste not even a crumb of the sweet cake or sip so much as a sip of the wine the princesses will bring to you before they go to bed. Wake and watch; then follow where they lead; and here is a cloak which, come fair or foul, will make you invisible.' At this the beldame took a cloak finer than spider silk from out of a small bag or pouch she wore, and gave it him.

'That hide me!' said the soldier. 'Old coat, brass buttons and all?'

'Ay,' said the beldame, and thanked him again for his help; and the pig coughed, and so they parted.

When she was out of sight the old soldier had another look at the magic cloak and thought over what the beldame had told him. Being by nature bold and brave, and having nothing better to do, he went off at once to the king.

The king looked at the old soldier, listened to what he said and then, with a grim smile half hidden under his beard, bade him follow him to a little stone closet hard by the long chamber where the princesses slept. 'Watch here,' he said, 'and if you can discover this secret, then the reward I have decreed shall be yours. If not—' He glanced up under his brows at the brave old soldier (who had no more fear in his heart than he had money in his pocket), but did not finish his sentence.

A little before nightfall, the old soldier sat himself down on a bench in the stone closet and by the light of a stub of candle began to mend his shoe.

By and by the eldest of the princesses knocked softly on his door, smiled on him and brought him a cup of wine and a dish of sweet cakes. He thanked her. But as soon as she was gone he dribbled out the wine drip by drip into a hole between the flagstones and made crumbs of the cakes for the mice. Then he lay down and pretended to be asleep. He snored and snored, but even while he snored he was busy with his cobbler's awl boring a little hole for a peephole between the stone of the wall where he lay and the princesses' room. At midnight all was still.

But hardly had the little owl of midnight called, *Ahoo! Ahoo! Ahoo!* when the old soldier, hearing a gentle stirring in the next room, peeped through the tiny hole he had bored in the wall. His eyes dazzled; a wondrous sight was to be seen. For the princesses in the filmy silver of the moon were now dressing and attiring themselves in clothes that seemed not of this world but from some strange otherwhere, which they none the less took out of their own coffers and wardrobes. They seemed to be as happy as larks in the morning or like swallows chittering before they fly, laughing and whispering together while they put on these bright garments and made ready. Only one of them, the youngest, had withdrawn herself a little apart and delayed to join them, and now kept silent. Seeing this, her sisters made merry at her and asked her what ailed her.

'The others,' she said, 'whom our father set to watch us were young and foolish. But that old soldier has wandered all over the world and has seen many things, and it seems to me he is crafty and wise. That, sisters, is why I say, Beware!'

Still they only laughed at her. 'Crafty and wise, forsooth!' said they. 'Listen to his snoring! He has eaten of our sweet cakes and drunken the spiced wine, and now he will sleep sound till morning.' At this the

old soldier, peeping through his little bore hole in the stones, smiled to himself and went on snoring.

When they were all ready to be gone, the eldest of the princesses clapped her hands. At this signal, and as if by magic, in the middle of the floor one wide flagstone wheeled softly upon its neighbour, disclosing an opening there, and beneath it a narrow winding flight of steps. One by one, according to age, the princesses followed the eldest down this secret staircase, and the old soldier knew there was no time to be lost.

He flung the old beldame's cloak over his shoulders, and (as she had foretold) instantly of himself there showed not even so much as a shadow. Then, having noiselessly unbarred the door into the princesses' bedroom, he followed the youngest of them down the stone steps.

It was dark beneath the flagstones, and the old soldier trod clumsily in his heavy shoes. And as he groped down, he stumbled and trod on the hem of the youngest princess's dress.

'Alas, sisters, a hand is clutching at me!' she called out to her sisters.

'A hand!' mocked the eldest. 'You must have caught your sleeve on a nail!'

On and down they went and out of a narrow corridor at last emerged and came full into the open air, and, following a faint track in the green turf, reached at last a wood where the trees (their bark, branches, twigs and leaves) were all of silver and softly shimmering in a gentle light that seemed to be neither of sun nor moon nor stars. Anon they came to a second wood, and here the trees shone softly too, but these were of gold. Anon they came to a third wood, and here the trees were in fruit and the fruits upon them were precious stones – green, blue and amber, and burning orange.

When the princesses had all passed through this third wood, they broke out upon a hillside, and, looking down from out the leaf-fringed trees, the old soldier saw the calm waters of a lake beyond yellow sands, and drawn up on its strand twelve swan-shaped boats. And there, standing as if in wait beside them, were twelve young men that looked to be princes. Noble and handsome young men they were.

The princesses, having hastened down to the strand, greeted these young men one and all, and at once embarked into the twelve swan-shaped boats, the old soldier smuggling himself as gingerly as he could into the boat of the youngest. Then the princes rowed away softly across the water towards an island that was in the midst of the lake, where was a palace, its windows shining like crystal in the wan light that bathed sky and water.

Only the last of the boats lagged far behind the others, for the old soldier sitting there invisible on the thwart, though little else but bones and sinews, weighed as heavy as a sack of stones in the boat. At last the youngest of the princes leaned on his oars to recover his breath. 'What,' he sighed, 'can be amiss with this boat tonight? It never rowed so heavily.'

The youngest of the princesses looked askance at him with fear in her eyes, for the boat was atilt with the weight of the old soldier and not trimmed true. Whereupon she turned her small head and looked towards that part of the boat where sat the old soldier, for there it dipped deepest in the water. In so doing, she gazed straight into his eyes, yet perceived nothing but the green water beyond. He smiled at her, and – though she knew not why – she was comforted. 'Maybe,' she said, turning to the prince again and answering what he had said, 'maybe you are wearied because of the heat of the evening.' And he rowed on.

When they were come to the island and into the palace there, the old soldier could hardly believe his eyes, it was a scene so fair and strange and unearthly. All the long night through, to music of harp and tambour and pipe, the princesses danced with the princes. Danced, too, the fountains at play, with an endless singing of birds, trees with flowers blossoming, and no one seemed to weary. But as soon as the scarlet shafts of morning showed beyond these skies, they returned at once to the boats, and the princesses were soon back safely under the king's roof again, and so fast asleep in their beds that they looked as if they had never stirred or even sighed in them the whole night long. They might be lovely images of stone.

But the old soldier slept like a hare – with one eye open. When he awoke, which was soon, he began to think over all that he had seen and heard. The longer he pondered on it, the more he was filled with astonishment. Every now and then, as if to make sure of the land of the living, he peeped with his eye through the hole in the wall, for he was almost of a

mind to believe that his journey of the night before –
the enchanted woods, the lake, the palace and the
music – was nothing more than the make-believe of a
dream.

So, being a man of caution, he determined to say
nothing at all of what had passed this first night, but
to watch again a second night. When dark drew on, he
once more dribbled out the spiced wine into the
crannies of the stones and crumbled the sweet cakes
into morsels for the mice, himself eating nothing but
a crust or two of rye bread and a rind of cheese that he
had in his haversack.

All happened as before. Midnight came. The
princesses rose up out of their beds, gay and brisk as
fish leaping at evening out of their haunts, and soon
had made ready and were gone to their trysting place
at the lakeside. All was as before.

The old soldier – to make sure even surer – watched
for the third night. But this night, as he followed the
princesses, first through the wood where the leaves
were of silver and next where they resembled fine
gold, and last where the fruits on the boughs were
all of precious stones, he broke off in each a twig. As
he did so the third time, the tree faintly sighed, and
the youngest princess heard the tree sigh. Her fears
of the first night, far from being lulled and at rest,
had only grown sharper. She stayed a moment in the
wood, looking back, and cried, 'Sisters! Sisters! We are
being watched. We are being followed. I heard this
tree sigh, and it was in warning.' But they only laughed
at her.

'Sigh, forsooth!' they said. 'So, too, would you, sister, if you were clad in leaves as trees are, and a little wind went through your branches.'

Hearing this, in hope to reassure her, the old soldier softly wafted the three twigs he carried in the air at a little distance from the youngest's face. Sweet was the scent of them, and she smiled. That night, too, for further proof, the old soldier stole one of the gold drinking cups in the princes' palace and hid it away with the twigs in his haversack. Then for the last time he watched the dancing and listened to the night birds' music and the noise of the fountains. But, being tired, he sat down and yawned, for he had no great wish to be young again and was happy in being himself.

Indeed, as he looked in at the princesses, fast, fast asleep that third early morning, their dreamless faces lying waxen and placid amid the braids of their long hair upon their pillows, he even pitied them.

That very day he asked to be taken before the king and, when he was come into his presence, entreated for him a favour.

'Say on!' said the king. The old soldier then besought the king to promise that if he told the secret thing he had discovered, he would forgive the princesses all that had gone before.

'I'd rather,' he said, 'be whipped three times round Your Majesty's kingdom than open my mouth else.'

The king promised. Then the old soldier brought from his haversack the three twigs of the trees – the silver and the gold and the be-gemmed – and the gold cup from the banqueting hall; and he told the king all

50

that had befallen him.

On first hearing of this, the king fell into a rage at the thought of how his daughters had deceived him. But he remembered his promise and was pacified. He remembered, too, the decree he had made, and sent word that his daughters should be bidden into his presence. When they were come, the dark and the fair together, he frowned on them, then turned to the old soldier: 'Now choose which of these deceivers you will have for wife, for such was my decree.'

The old soldier, looking at them each in turn, and smiling at the youngest, waved his great hand and said: 'My liege, there is this to be said: Never lived any man high or low that *deserved* a wife as gentle and fair as one of these. But in the place of enchantment I have told of, there were twelve young princes. Well-spoken and soldierly young men they were; and if it was choosing sons I was, such are the sons I would choose. As for myself, now – if I may be so bold, and if it would be any ease to Your Majesty's mind – it being a promise, in a manner of speaking – there's one thing, me having roved the world over all my life, I'm mortal anxious to *know*—' and here he paused.

'Say on,' said the king.

'Why,' replied the old soldier, 'what sort of thing it feels like to sit, even though but for the mite of a moment, on a throne.'

On hearing this, the king grasped his beard and laughed heartily. 'Easily done,' he cried. 'The task is to stay there.'

With his own hand he led the old soldier to the

throne, placed his usual crown upon his head, the royal sceptre in his hand, and with a gesture presented him to all assembled there. There sat the old soldier, with his war-worn face, great bony hands and lean shanks, smiling under the jewelled crown at the company. A merry scene it was.

Then the king earnestly asked the old soldier if he had anything in mind for the future, whereby he might show him his favour. Almost as if by magic, it seemed, the memory of the beldame in the forest came back into the old soldier's head, and he said: 'Well, truth's truth, Your Majesty, and if there *was* such a thing in my mind, it was pigs.'

'Pigs!' cried the king. 'So be it, and so be it, and so be it! Pigs you shall have in plenty,' said he. 'And, by the walls of Jerusalem, of all the animals on God's earth there's none better – fresh, smoked or salted.'

'Ay, sir,' said the old soldier, 'and even better still with their plump-chapped noddles still on their shoulders and the breath of life in their bodies!'

Then the king sent for his Lord Steward and bade that seven changes of raiment should be prepared for the old soldier, and two mules saddled and bridled, and a fat purse of money put in his hand. Besides these, the king commanded that out of the countless multitude of the royal pigs should be chosen threescore of the comeliest, liveliest and best, with two lads for their charge.

And when towards sundown a day or two after, the old soldier set out from the royal house into the forest with his laden mules, his pigs and his pig lads, besides the gifts that had been bestowed on him by the twelve noble young princes and princesses, he was a glad man indeed. But most he prized a worn-out gold and silver slipper which he had asked of the youngest princess for a keepsake. This he kept in his knapsack with his magic scrap of root and other such treasures, as if for a charm.

A Competition is Announced

JAHNNA N. MALCOLM

Rocky, McGee, Zan, Mary and Gwen meet at the ballet class which, for different reasons, they've all had to join. When they find out they all hate ballet, the girls become good friends. Part of the reason they don't like their classes is the presence of the Bunheads. This is the nickname they give Courtney Clay and her friends, all good dancers, but mean and spiteful. This extract comes from the second book in the 'Scrambled Legs' series, The Battle of the Bunheads.

Several girls were already in the ballet studio limbering up, when the gang entered the big light-filled room. One whole wall was covered with mirrors and rows of ballet *barres* lined the other. Mrs Bruce, the accompanist, was already in her seat at the piano, shuffling through her sheet music.

The gang took their positions at the end of the room, as far from the piano and teacher as possible. They didn't want to seem too enthusiastic about taking ballet lessons. After all, they were only taking the class to be together.

Page and Alice threw back the door to the studio

and Courtney swept in, holding the roll book like a badge of office. She walked up to the piano and nodded at the accompanist.

'Hello, Mrs Bruce, it's good to see you again.'

Mrs Bruce looked up from her music with a vague smile.

'Class!' Courtney clapped her hands together. 'May I have your attention, please?'

Several girls whispering by the mirrors turned and focused their attention on her curiously.

'I have been asked to call roll and start the class for today,' Courtney announced in a clear, precise voice.

'Get a load of her,' Gwen whispered. 'She acts like she's the teacher.'

'Several of you look new to the Academy,' Courtney continued, 'so I'd like to welcome you.'

'Give me a break,' Rocky groaned.

Courtney shot Rocky a warning look. 'The Academy is for serious ballerinas, but every now and then some misfits get in.' Her lips narrowed into a thin, tight smile. 'But they always get weeded out.'

As she called the roll, Courtney kept her eyes focused on the gang. She made a big deal about calling McGee by her proper name, Kathryn, which made McGee grind her teeth. When she called Rocky, Rochelle, Rocky didn't even answer. Courtney quickly went on through the rest of the class.

'Now everyone will please line up at the *barre*,' Courtney announced. 'We will begin with *pliés*.' She made a grand gesture to Mrs Bruce to begin to play. The plump old lady completely missed the signal. She was too busy rifling through her huge leather bag for a tissue.

McGee was the first to get the giggles. She tried to stifle them behind her hand, but that only made them more obvious. Courtney's eyes flashed angrily and she ordered, 'Silence!' Mrs Bruce, who had finally found a Kleenex, answered her with a loud honk.

Gwen and Rocky laughed out loud. Zan and Mary Bubnik couldn't control themselves and collapsed into titters. Soon all of the girls on their side of the studio were in hysterics.

Courtney slammed the roll book down on the piano, causing a startled Mrs Bruce to toss her Kleenex up in the air in fright. That set off a whole new eruption of laughter.

'Silence, right this minute!' Courtney shouted. Her voice could hardly be heard above the din. Even Page, Alice, and a few other Bunheads were snickering.

Suddenly, the studio door opened, and a beautiful, dark-haired girl glided into the room. Everyone fell silent at the sight of her. She wore a long-sleeved black leotard with a low-cut back. The matching black nylon dance skirt that was wrapped round her waist swirled gracefully as she walked. Her hair was parted in the middle and swept into a coil at the nape of her neck.

'Why, it's the Sugar Plum Fairy!' Mary Bubnik cried, recognizing the dancer from her role in the holiday production of *The Nutcracker*. 'Annie Springer.'

The lovely ballerina turned to Mary and smiled, revealing a tiny dimple in her cheek. 'That's right. How sweet of you to remember.'

Mary Bubnik blushed a deep red. 'Who could forget you?'

McGee, Gwen and Rocky pressed forward to meet the ballerina. Zan, who was usually shy, heard herself gush, 'You were perfectly wonderful!'

Rocky nodded. 'The best.'

'Why, thank you.' The dancer tilted her head slightly. 'You five look very familiar to me.'

'We were with you in *The Nutcracker*,' Gwen announced proudly.

Miss Springer put one delicate finger to her lips and studied the girls. 'What parts did you dance?'

Suddenly they all felt tongue-tied. None of them wanted to be the one to tell their lovely new teacher what they had actually played. It was too embarrassing.

Courtney did it for them. 'They played the lowly rats.'

'Oh, yes.' Annie Springer raised a knowing eyebrow. 'You were certainly a big hit with the audience.'

'Thanks, Miss Springer,' Mary Bubnik murmured.

'Well, since we've danced together,' the slender brunette said, 'please, call me Annie.'

'The audience really seemed to like our dance, too,' Page Tuttle burst in. She gestured grandly to the Bunheads.

Annie turned to look at the other girls. 'And what did you dance?'

Page's face fell. Alice Wescott piped up in her high, nasal voice, 'We were the flowers.'

'Oh, of course, I'm sorry.' Annie graced them with a smile, then faced the room and clapped her hands

together. 'Well, we should really get started. I have a lot to cover today. Let's begin with roll call.'

'I've already done that,' Courtney said, strutting up to join the teacher at the front of the class. When Miss Springer cocked her head in confusion, Courtney explained, 'I was asked to by Miss Delacorte. You see, I'm Courtney Clay.'

Courtney waited patiently for her to be impressed. Annie simply nodded pleasantly. Courtney hinted,

'My mother is on the board of directors.'

'Oh, Cornelia Clay?'

Courtney nodded. She smiled smugly out at the roomful of girls, satisfied that she had regained her proper position.

'Well, I've just been meeting with your mother and the rest of the company.' Annie perched lightly on a bench by the window and said, 'Gather round, everyone. I have some terrific news.'

'Great,' Gwen whispered to Rocky. 'The more time she kills on this stuff, the less time we'll have to spend doing those awful warm-ups.'

'Let's sit close,' Zan said, hurrying to grab a spot on the floor right in front of the ballerina.

'I still can't believe we have the Sugar Plum Fairy for our very own teacher,' Mary Bubnik replied, her voice breathless with excitement.

Annie delicately folded her hands in her lap as she waited for the class to get comfortable. Then she smiled and announced, 'The International Ballet is coming to America!'

Most of the class responded with a loud 'Oooh!' Rocky and McGee and a few of the others just stared blankly back at their teacher.

Mary Bubnik shyly raised her hand. 'Excuse me for asking, but what's the International Ballet?'

Page Tuttle leaned over to Courtney and hissed, loud enough for the whole class to hear, 'What would a hick from Oklahoma know?'

Mary's eyes clouded with hurt as Courtney and her friends snickered. Mary quickly recovered, saying, 'I know it's a dumb question, but I'm kind of new to this whole ballet thing.'

'It's not a dumb question at all,' Annie reassured Mary. 'The International Ballet is one of the finest ballet companies in the world. They're from Paris, France.'

'Does that mean they speak French?' Mary asked, blinking her big blue eyes.

'Well, of course, they speak French,' Courtney spoke up. 'What did you think – Russian?'

Annie shot Courtney a reprimanding look. 'Some of the dancers do speak Russian, Mary. And Italian and German and, of course, French. That's what makes them so very special. They're the best dancers from all around the world.'

'And they're coming to America,' Zan sighed.

Annie nodded. 'Not only are they coming to the United States, but they will be giving a performance here in Deerfield!'

The class applauded happily.

'Whatever for?' Gwen wondered out loud. When the class turned to stare at her, she shrugged and said, 'I mean, let's face it, Deerfield is not the most exciting place in the world.'

'Well, their director is an old friend of Mr Anton and Miss Jo, our company directors,' Annie explained. 'They all toured together in their younger days.'

Page Tuttle raised her hand. 'Didn't Mr Anton used to be the dance partner for their prima ballerina, Alexandra Petrovna?'

'Alexandra Petrovna!' Zan sat straight up. 'I've heard of her!'

'Everyone has,' Annie said, her eyes glowing brightly. 'She is the best ballerina alive today.' Her voice grew low and hushed. 'I saw her dance a few years ago, and I'll never forget it. It gives me chills just thinking about it.'

This time Zan raised her hand. 'I remember reading that she escaped from Romania on a train and it was really terrifying.'

'That's right,' Annie replied with a nod. 'She hid in a suitcase.'

'What is she, a midget?' McGee asked.

'No, no!' Annie laughed. 'It was really more of a steamer trunk than a suitcase. They're a lot larger. But *this* suitcase had a removable back, just big enough to hide a person.'

Gwen shook her head in wonder. 'Just the same, I don't think I could get my head in a suitcase, let alone my whole body.'

'That's the truth,' Page whispered to Courtney. Gwen shot them her best dirty look.

'She nearly got caught at the border because the guards were inspecting everyone's luggage,' Zan said, continuing the tale. 'Luckily, a friend riding in the next compartment pretended to get terribly sick and in the confusion, the guards skipped the bag she was hiding in. It saved Alexandra Petrovna's life.'

'That is amazing,' Mary Bubnik said to Zan, shaking her head with awe.

Zan nodded. 'It is, isn't it.'

'No, no, I mean that you can know all that stuff.'

'I read about it in a book called *Great Escapes.*'

Mary Bubnik turned to the rest of the girls and announced proudly, 'Zan is like a walking encyclopedia. She knows everything. Go ahead, ask her something.'

Before Zan could protest, Page Tuttle sang out, 'What is the role Alexandra Petrovna is most famous for?'

'I don't know.' Zan looked confused. 'The book I read wasn't about ballet.'

'Well *everybody* knows that her *Giselle* is the best ever,' Courtney replied smugly.

'I cried when I saw her dance it,' Annie said softly. 'Which brings me to the next, and most important, part of my announcement.'

An excited murmur ran around the room as the girls crowded in closer.

'Alexandra Petrovna will be dancing *Giselle* here for one performance only. The board has decided that one lucky student from this academy will be chosen to present a bouquet of roses to her at the curtain call.'

'Oh, I wish it were me!' Mary Bubnik cried. McGee never would have admitted it out loud, but she secretly hoped she might be picked, too. Gwen, Rocky, and Zan were all feeling the same way.

'This is a great honour and privilege,' Annie reminded them. 'And a bit of a problem. We spent the better part of that meeting trying to decide how to pick our flower bearer.'

'Miss Springer?' Courtney raised her hand again. 'My mother told me that the older dancers will get to take a master class with Miss Petrovna.'

'That's right,' the ballerina agreed. 'And the younger students are still too little to appreciate the honour. So . . . '

Mary Bubnik held her breath.

'We decided the flower bearer should come from the fifth and sixth grade classes.'

A cheer went up from the girls in the room. Annie held up her hand. 'Those are the Monday, Wednesday and Saturday classes.'

'Three classes.' McGee added them up. 'Hey, that gives us a fighting chance.'

Zan squeezed Mary Bubnik's hand. 'Wouldn't it be great if it were one of us?'

'Two girls from each class will be nominated,' Annie said.

Every student in the class raised her hand.

'And on the morning of the ballet,' Annie went on, 'they will dance for Miss Petrovna.'

'*Dance*?' Gwen shouted. She and her four friends dropped their hands on to their laps.

'Yes, dance,' Annie repeated. 'Then Miss Petrovna will personally choose the lucky girl.'

'I don't see why we have to dance,' McGee grumbled loudly.

'Yeah,' Rocky agreed, 'especially if all we have to do is walk out three feet and hand her flowers. I mean, how hard is that?'

'This *is* a ballet academy, remember?' Page Tuttle drawled, rolling her eyes at Courtney.

'That's right,' Courtney declared. 'The flower bearer

should be the best dancer in the class. It's only proper.'

'No one should be nervous,' Annie said. 'The steps are very simple. You can learn them in a few minutes.'

'How are you going to choose the two girls from this class?' Mary Bubnik asked.

'Well, I thought we should be democratic about it,' the pretty ballerina replied. 'I'll give you all a few minutes to think about it, then we'll take nominations and vote.'

Courtney immediately gathered Page, Alice, and several other girls around her. They pulled together without a backward glance at the rest of the class. Other groups formed near the window.

Mary Bubnik and Zan joined McGee, Rocky, and Gwen in a huddle at the back of the class.

'OK,' McGee said in low whisper. 'We need to make sure that two of us are picked. So who should we nominate?'

Mary Bubnik raised one finger. 'I nominate Zan and Gwen, because Zan knew all about Miss Petrovna's daring escape and Gwen is the oldest.'

Zan smiled gratefully but shook her head. 'I could never dance in front of Miss Petrovna. I'd be so terribly nervous that I 'd lose.'

'And you can count me out,' Gwen said firmly. 'Solo dancing is just not my style.' She didn't want to mention that getting up in front of dozens of people in her leotard sounded like the worst possible torture she could imagine. It made her stomach ache just thinking about it.

'Well, I think our nominees ought to be Rocky and

McGee,' Mary Bubnik whispered. 'McGee was such a good leader in our mouse dance.'

'Thanks, Mary,' McGee said, blushing a bright pink that showed her freckles.

'And Rocky is our best actress, ' Mary continued.

'Thanks.' Rocky punched Mary lightly on the shoulder. She had taken a six-week course in acting at the recreation centre on Curtiss-Dobbs Air Force Base. Rocky had learned how to make terrific faces and could even make herself cry when she wanted to. A thoughtful look crossed her face. 'I wonder how I should act when I dance for this Petrovna lady?'

'You should definitely act sad,' Zan said. 'The ballet *Giselle* is a really tragic story. It's about a peasant girl who falls in love with a prince who asks her to be his wife.'

'That's tragic?' Gwen asked. 'It sounds romantic to me.'

'It is, at first,' Zan agreed. 'Then Giselle finds out that he is already engaged to marry someone else.'

'Why, that low-down, two-timin' sneak!' Mary Bubnik drawled, putting her hands on her hips. 'So what does this Giselle do?'

'She goes crazy and kills herself.'

'Kills herself?' Rocky repeated in disbelief. 'I'd kill *him.*'

'Me, too!' Gwen agreed.

'Oh, no,' Zan said shocked. 'She loves him too much. You see, after she dies, she's transported to this strange world filled with the spirits of all the women who have been unhappy in love.'

'And *they* kill him?' Rocky asked hopefully.

Zan smiled. 'They try to.'

'How?' McGee leaned closer to catch all the gory details.

'By making him dance to death.'

Mary Bubnik cocked her head. 'How could anyone get danced to death?'

'Well, they couldn't very well shoot him,' Gwen said sensibly. 'The audience paid a lot of money to see him dance.'

'Besides, it'd be a pretty short ballet, wouldn't it?' McGee said with a grin.

'So how does it end?' Rocky asked.

'Well, Giselle keeps the prince dancing all night long,' Zan explained. 'Just when he's about to drop dead, dawn comes and the spirits have to depart. Giselle returns to her grave, and the prince is left alone, broken-hearted.'

'Serves him right,' Gwen declared.

Mrs Bruce struck a resounding chord on the piano to get everyone's attention.

'Are we ready?' Annie asked the class.

The gang nodded and the rest of the girls murmured, 'Yes.'

'Then let's have the nominations.'

Before anyone could open her mouth, Alice Wescott was on her feet, calling out in her loud, nasal voice, 'I nominate Courtney Clay—'

'Surprise, surprise,' Gwen muttered under her breath.

'And . . . ' Alice paused for dramatic effect and looked around the room. 'Mary Bubnik.'

'What?' McGee blurted out, then quickly covered her mouth.

'Me?' Mary Bubnik cried, clapping her hands together with glee. 'Y'all really want me?'

Courtney and her friends nodded, with huge grins on their faces. 'All right,' Annie said, 'Courtney Clay and Mary, uh . . . Bubnik.' She repeated Mary's name slowly to make sure she had it right. Then Annie looked up and asked, 'Any more nominations?'

Gwen was about to nominate Rocky and McGee when she saw the look of pure joy on Mary Bubnik's face. She lowered her hand and said nothing.

When no one else spoke up, Annie said, 'Well that makes it easy, then. Our class representatives will be Courtney Clay and Mary Bubnik.'

Mary squealed with delight, then turned to her friends. 'I knew the Bunheads would come around and start liking us. Oh, you guys, I am *so* happy! Can't wait to tell my mother.'

'Courtney and Mary?' Annie called out. 'Will you come up here and I'll fill you in on the details.'

Mary skipped up to the front of the room. Rocky turned to the rest of the gang and whispered, 'Those Bunheads are up to something.'

McGee nodded. 'And we'd better find out what it is – *fast.*'

And Olly Did Too

JAMILA GAVIN

Many children have known what it is like to have a younger brother or sister who copies what they do – or, perhaps, have been a younger brother or sister, wanting to show that they are just as good at doing something as an older member of the family! In this story, Olly's copying leads to a happy ending for him, and for his older sister.

Jenny said, 'When I grow up, I'm going to be a ballet dancer.'

Her younger brother Olly said, 'I will too,' but everyone laughed and took no notice.

Jenny tried to look like a ballet dancer. She always wore her hair swept tightly back into a bun; she always stood with a very straight back; she always held her head up high to show off her long neck; and when she walked, she turned her feet out, just like ballet dancers do.

Olly rushed about like a wild thing, wearing his track suit and trainers. He kept jumping and leaping and kicking his legs in the air, like a frisky horse.

'Are you trying to be a footballer, Olly?' people asked.

'No,' said Olly, 'I'm going to be a ballet dancer!'

Everyone roared with laughter, because Olly was such a little toughie with his spiky hair and rough and tumbling body.

Every Wednesday after school, Mum took Jenny to her ballet lesson. Olly went too, but only to watch because Mum couldn't leave him at home on his own.

Olly used to fidget. He watched Jenny in her black leotard and pink, fluffy, cross-over cardigan. He kicked his feet against the chair while she put on her shining pink ballet shoes and criss-crossed the pink satin ribbons round her ankles.

Mum had to rap Olly across the knees and tell him to keep still. In the end, she would send him right away to the back of the hall with a box of action toys, to keep him out of mischief. But as soon as the piano started thumping out the tunes for the dancers to do their exercises, Olly did them too where no one could see them.

Every day, Jenny practised her ballet movements in the kitchen. She would hold the back of a chair and then call out the French words for each position:

'Première position . . . pliez . . . jetez . . . attitude . . .'

Olly did too. He pointed his toes and bent his knees and lifted his leg forwards and backwards; he raised his arm and curved his hands and always remembered to look in whatever direction his fingers went. But nobody noticed. They thought he was fooling about.

Having a ballet dancer in the family was such hard work. There always seemed to be a show to rehearse or an exam to prepare. Father couldn't count the number

of times he had driven Jenny to and from draughty
church halls; and Mother couldn't remember how
many costumes she'd made. Olly had never known a
time when the house wasn't scattered with bits of stiff
net for tutus, satin and silks for bodices and ribbons,
or when every surface wasn't covered with boxes of
pins and buttons and sequins.

Olly liked dressing up too, but everyone thought he

was just messing around. He would grab the old green velvet curtains Mum had kept for cutting up, and swing them round his shoulders like a cloak; and how everybody laughed when he put on his mother's black leather boots which almost went up to his thighs.

'What on earth do you think you look like in those!' exclaimed Jenny, scornfully.

'That's what princes wear, isn't it?' retorted Olly.

When it was Jenny's birthday, they took her to the ballet. Olly went too, because Granny couldn't babysit that night. Everyone thought Olly would hate going to the theatre and they hoped he wouldn't wriggle and keep asking to go to the toilet. Mum said he would probably be bored and fall asleep.

When they arrived at the theatre, there were lots and lots of girls wearing velvet dresses with broad sashes. All had their hair swept under Alice-bands or twisted into net buns; and all were standing like swans, holding their heads up very high and with their feet turned out. There were many boys too, trying to look grand and grown-up, but Olly didn't notice. He couldn't stand still long enough to notice. He was so excited. He couldn't wait to get inside and see the dancers.

'One day,' whispered Mum proudly to Jenny, 'everyone will be queuing to see you!'

Olly said, 'Will they come and see me too?' But everyone laughed.

They went in through the glass doors into the foyer with the red velvet plush carpet. Those who hadn't already bought tickets were queueing hopefully, while others, like Dad, fumbled in jackets and pockets for theirs.

'You're in the upper circle,' said a man in black and white evening dress examining their tickets. 'You take the left staircase.'

Jenny walked sedately up the stairs, sliding her hand along the gold banister like a princess. She didn't look to the right or the left, but straight ahead, as though a handsome prince was waiting for her at the top.

Olly hopped and jumped and would have raced up two at a time if his legs had been long enough. He couldn't wait to get inside.

'Hurry up, Jenny! Hurry up!' he begged.

'Behave yourself, Olly. We're going to the ballet, not a football match,' said Mum sternly.

At last they were inside. At last they found their seats. They were rather high up, but had a perfect view right down to the stage. Dad turned, to warn Olly to sit still and not to dare make a noise, but he didn't need to. Olly was leaning forward watching the musicians coming into the dark orchestral pit below the stage. First the harpist came in, because he took the longest to tune all those strings; then came a horn player, because she wanted to practise a difficult bit; and one by one, the violinists and cellists, the clarinettists and flautists and all the other players came in with their instruments.

The leader of the orchestra entered with his violin under his arm. The audience clapped and when he had bowed and sat down, the oboist played an A and all the players tuned into it.

Finally, the conductor made his entrance. He climbed up on to a rostrum and bowed to the audience while everybody clapped. Then the conductor faced his players.

The lights went down. There was a huge hush, and with a wave of a baton the music started. The great, heavy curtain rose slowly upwards.

Olly never moved a muscle; he might have been a statue, his body was so still, and his eyes so fixed. But his soul heaved like an ocean. His spirit flew like a bird. It soared across the darkened auditorium; it wafted among the white, billowing skirts of the girls, and sprang up, up, up with the shining princes in their glittering jackets. The dancers no longer seemed to be ordinary human beings, but enchanted people; magic people; the way their bodies created changing shapes and patterns, sometimes moving like one body; arms lifting and falling, legs bending and stretching, backs arching and heads turning, all at the same time. And the way the stage was no longer just a wooden stage, but in one scene it was brilliantly lit as a magnificent royal palace, and in the next, it was a dark, menacing forest. If it was real, then Olly wanted to be up there with them, dancing and leaping to the lilting rhythms of the music; but if it was a dream, and it seemed to be a dream, then he never, never, never wanted to wake up.

After that, Olly was always dreaming: day dreams and night dreams. Sometimes he dreamed in school, when he should have been doing his sums, but instead, he found himself floating up to the ceiling. Suddenly he was astride a black horse and galloping across the night sky; a bejewelled turban of silk was wound round his head, and a cloak of darkness whirled behind him. Then he was a hunter, stalking through a forest hung with diamonds and pearls, where long-legged spiders spun webs of silver, and strange-winged gnomes sprang through the air. Sometimes he was a magician or a king, or simply just a dancer spinning through space.

Most of all, he dreamed he was up on that stage, where the lights glittered above him like stars; where he could hear the squeak of the ballet shoes as the dancers pirouetted and twirled, the swish of costumes and the clouds of music which rose from the pit below, flowing into his arms and legs.

One day, Mum and Dad took Jenny to an audition. It was to choose the best dancers to go to a special ballet school. Jenny didn't really want to go because it meant she would have to miss her riding lesson. All of a sudden, Jenny had become mad about horses, and wasn't so sure now that she wanted to be a dancer.

'Of course you must go, Jenny,' said Mother with a frown. 'You've always wanted to be a ballet dancer, and this may be your one big chance.'

Olly went too, because he couldn't be left on his own.

An ancient lady, who looked about a hundred years old, leaned her chin on a silver-tipped cane and watched every child with the eye of a hawk. Olly had been told to sit quietly at the back, but though he was quiet, he couldn't sit still. When the children were

75

told to stand, he stood; when they were told to walk, he walked; he walked just as the princes had walked that day at the ballet, with heads held proudly and one arm lifted out before him, making a noble gesture.

He walked down the side aisle, until he was nearly at the front. Nobody had noticed, because all eyes were fixed on the children who were auditioning – except the old lady. Somehow, she noticed. Perhaps she had eyes at the back of her head. Perhaps she was a witch, and her back tingled when somebody danced. She seemed to see everything, though no one knew. Suddenly she got up – or did she spring? For as she got to her feet, she was no longer just an old lady, she was a dancer. Olly stopped, and shrank, watching, into the shadows.

She walked along the line of children, pointing with her silver cane. She studied their fronts and their backs; their thighs and their legs; their knees and their ankles, and she even made them walk barefoot, so that she could examine their toes.

'You may have to look as delicate as flowers, but you have to be as strong as tigers,' she muttered.

'I'm strong!' exclaimed Olly, suddenly stepping out boldly before her. 'Olly!' hissed his mother, very shocked. 'Don't be rude. Go and play with your cars at the back of the hall.'

But the old, old lady waved her silver cane at him.

'Yes, I've been watching you. Let me have a look at you, my boy. Strip off down to your underpants.'

Some children giggled, but Olly did as he was asked.

'Walk across the stage!' she ordered. Olly walked.

'Point your toes, bend your knees, stand on one leg, jump in the air.' Olly did all those things.

About fifty children had come to the audition that day, but they knew that only six could be chosen. At the end of every session, a person with a large notebook would say to the parents of each child, 'We'll let you know.'

So they had to go home and wait. They waited and waited. Mum was longing to know whether Jenny had been chosen, and watched for the post every day. But Jenny hardly noticed the time going by. She was clamouring for a pair of riding boots and jodhpurs and she was asking if she could go to pony camp in the summer.

At last, one day, a letter came through the door. It was from the ballet school. Mother opened it with trembling fingers.

'Well,' exclaimed Dad with breathless impatience, 'has Jenny got in?'

Mum didn't answer. She read the letter once, then she read it again.

'For goodness sake, tell me!' begged Dad. 'What do they say?'

Finally, Mum replied in a small voice, 'They say they want Olly!'

'Oh, good!' yelled Olly, leaping into the air. 'I always wanted to be a dancer!'

'Does that mean I don't have to go to ballet classes any more?' cried Jenny with a grin. 'Oh good! I'd much rather go horse-riding instead!'

Olly shut his eyes tight. He imagined himself up on

the stage. He could feel the warmth of the lights and the smell of the face paints; he could hear the music casting its spell over him, so that his feet began to twitch. Before him was a wide, empty space. With a whoop of joy, he gave a giant leap. With his arms and legs outstretched, he was like a tiger in full flight.

That year, a specially chosen group of children went to the ballet school to train as dancers. Olly went too.

The Audition

CAROLINE PLAISTED

For many young people learning ballet, an audition for the Royal Ballet School is something they can only dream of. Some dancers do get that far – but what is the audition like? This story is based on personal experience.

'Number seventy-two, please! Seventy-two? Are you here?'

Suzy was startled from the conversation she was having with a girl called Anna from Birmingham.

'Yes! Yes – I'm here!' Suzy squeaked.

'Join this group, please. You'll be needed for class in about ten minutes.'

And, after all of the others in her group had been called, Suzy was whisked along with them to the studio. They all took their positions at the *barre* and the class began, as usual, with *pliés*. Suzy made sure that she remembered everything Miss Nancy, her ballet teacher, had told her – 'shoulders down and relaxed, tuck your bottom in and pull in your tummy muscles'. Suzy concentrated so hard that, before she knew it, the girls were being asked to do centre work.

'. . . *chassé* and close. Now, everyone got that?' the teacher at the front asked. 'OK, let's begin! Music please . . . one two three, two two three, three two three, four!'

Some of the girls were so nervous that they got their feet muddled up and did things wrong. But Suzy was lucky, she somehow managed to concentrate long enough. She even occasionally managed to smile like Miss Nancy had told her to. On the other side of the studio, Suzy spotted her new friend Anna, who was trying so hard to look her best she was biting her bottom lip.

'Goodness, she's really good,' thought Suzy as she watched whilst the first twelve girls, one of them Anna, put all the energy they could muster into the routine they had just learned. Anna performed the exercise faultlessly. If this was the kind of talent that Suzy was up against, what hope did she have?

Suzy Stephens was ten years old and, for as long as she could remember, she had wanted to be a ballerina. Every Friday, after school, Suzy had a private lesson with her teacher, Miss Nancy, and on Tuesdays and Saturdays she attended a ballet class with eleven other little girls at Miss Nancy's studio. On every other day of the week, Suzy practised on her own in her bedroom at the special *barre* which her daddy had attached to the wall.

Soon after her eighth birthday, Suzy had seen a television programme about the Royal Ballet School – she was entranced by it. She had seen boys and girls, aged from eleven to eighteen, who were being given some of the best ballet training in the world. They had ballet lessons every day, special music teaching and ordinary school lessons, all at the same place. Suzy had decided, there and then, that she absolutely had to go there. So she started a campaign to persuade her parents to let her go.

And it had taken a lot of persuading! 'Think of the cost,' her dad had said. 'Think of how difficult it must be to get in – children from all over the world apply to go there,' her mum had said. But when Suzy had spoken to Miss Nancy about it, she had agreed that she thought it was at least worth applying for an audition when Suzy was old enough.

It had seemed to take for ever before that time came, but it finally did. Suzy's mum had to fill in all sorts of forms which asked how tall Suzy was and also other members of her family. Then she'd had to go along to a photographer's studio to have special photographs taken showing Suzy from the front, the back and the side. The photographs were sent to the Royal Ballet School with her application form a long time before Christmas.

In January, Suzy's parents received a letter. 'Please bring Suzy to a first audition on 1 February,' it said. Suzy's chance had come at last and, after a trip to buy a new pair of shiny satin ballet shoes, Suzy went along to the Royal Ballet School.

Suzy hadn't really known what to expect but, as it turned out, the audition was just like doing an ordinary ballet class. The difference was that she was given a number (forty-one) to attach to the front and back of her leotard and the 'class' consisted of about thirty girls and two boys who were being watched by four people at the front of the studio with clipboards. Throughout the audition the four people (three women and a man) wrote notes. At the end, everyone was asked to stand quite still and face the front, then the back and finally both sides of the studio. (Miss Nancy told her afterwards that this was to check that their bodies were in good proportion and that they didn't have curvature of the spine.)

Back in the changing room afterwards, Suzy told her mum all about it. What would she do if they didn't think she was good enough? 'Try not to worry about it, Suzy love,' her mum said. 'They said they'd write to us by the end of the week to let us know. Anyway, the most that can happen at this stage is for you to be asked to come along for another audition.'

Which is exactly why Suzy now found herself, just over six weeks later, standing amongst about two hundred other girls, with another number attached to her. This time she was seventy-two. Everyone was gathered in the huge changing room and it was very noisy as the little girls and their mothers chattered nervously about the day ahead of them. A young lady, herself an older student at the Royal Ballet School, had explained to everyone that the girls would be called in groups of about forty to a studio to do a ballet class. After the first one, some girls would be asked to stay to attend a second class later on. Eventually, only about twenty to thirty boys and girls would be left. And these were the ones who would be lucky enough to be asked to attend the Royal Ballet School the following September.

Everyone was back in the changing room and Suzy was relieved to see her mum.

'How was it, love?' she asked her anxiously.

'Oh, much harder than last time, Mum. All the routines were much longer,' Suzy said, sitting down on the changing bench.

'You were in there nearly an hour!' her mum exclaimed. 'Oh, look, here comes the young lady again.'

'Can I have everyone's attention, please?' called out the girl. 'Thank you to everyone who has come along today. We're very sorry, but only the following people will be required for the next stage: numbers three, eight . . . '

Suzy had butterflies in her stomach and began to feel a bit sick. Supposing her number wasn't called? She looked at her mother and gripped her hand. The girl carried on calling out numbers.

'Sixty-two, sixty-three, seventy, seventy-two, seventy-five . . . '

Suzy couldn't believe it! Seventy-two – that was her! Suzy was being asked to attend a further class!

The girl continued to call out numbers: '. . . seventy-nine, eighty-two, eighty-three, eighty-seven, ninety . . . ' Suzy wondered if Anna, the girl she had met earlier, would be called. She knew her number was ninety-something. '. . . ninety-one, ninety-three, ninety-four, ninety-five . . . '

Yes – that was Anna, Suzy knew, because she could

see Anna's mother giving her a hug, just like she had received from her mum only a few moments before.

The following hour passed very slowly and Suzy's mother made her put on some leg-warmers and the cross-over her granny had knitted her to make sure that her muscles didn't get cold. Seeing as she'd got this far, Suzy's mum didn't want her chances ruined because she'd gone stiff whilst waiting.

But although the tense atmosphere hung over all the girls in the dressing room, Suzy was pleased when Anna came back over to sit next to her.

'Well done. I watched you whilst your line did the exercise with all those *jetés*. It was really complicated but you managed it first time,' Anna said. 'Some of the other girls in your group only got half of it right.'

'Oh thanks. Miss Nancy – that's my ballet teacher – says that I'm not bad at jumping,' Suzy pulled at the ties on her cross-over. 'But it's *barre* work that I fall down on – Miss Nancy is always telling me off for holding on to the *barre* as if I'm superglued to it. She says that my fingers should only be resting on it, light as a feather. I spotted you right at the beginning of the class. You looked so confident, almost as if you'd done this before.'

'I suppose I sort of have,' Anna said pulling her knees up under her chin. 'I auditioned for Elmhurst as well a few weeks ago.'

'Oh, you're so lucky. My mum said it was the Royal Ballet School or nothing,' Suzy said, looking quickly over her shoulder to see if her mum had heard. (She hadn't because she was busy talking to Anna's mum.) 'How did you get on?'

'Well, they offered me a place. Mum's accepted it – just in case I don't do well today. Of course, I'd much rather go here. How long have you been doing ballet then?'

And with that, the two girls jabbered away, nineteen to the dozen, talking about the one subject that they both rated number one – ballet. Eventually, the girl was back and both Suzy and Anna were ushered along to do another class. This one was very similar to the first one and didn't last as long.

Back in the changing room, numbers were called out again: 'twenty-three, twenty-four . . . ' Would Suzy and Anna be lucky again? 'Sixty-three, seventy-two . . .' YES!

'Oh, please call out Anna's number,' Suzy thought anxiously. The two seemed to be getting on so well, Suzy didn't want to go on to the next stage without her.

'. . . ninety-four, ninety-six . . . ' Oh no, Anna was out! Suzy couldn't believe it. How could they have chosen her and not Anna?

'. . . er, er, . . . sorry, I've made a mistake,' the girl's forehead was creased as she went back up the piece of paper she had in her hand with her finger. 'Ninety-four, ninety-five, ninety-six . . . ' Brilliant! Anna had done it too.

But before the two girls had a chance to congratulate each other, the girl was telling them all something else.

'Now,' she said, 'will everyone left here please put their clothes on? I need you all to follow me to the classroom. It's time for you to do a general knowledge test.'

General knowledge? This was a bit of a shock to everyone. None of them had realized that they would be tested for anything other than their ballet. But the test turned out not to be too bad (except for the maths – Suzy and Anna agreed on that) and soon they were all back in the changing room again. For another wait . . .

'Mrs Stephens? Is Mr Stephens with you?' a lady with grey hair asked, interrupting Suzy and her mother's silent, nervous trance.

'Er, yes. He's outside – do you need to speak to him?'

'Well, we'd like to talk to both of you – and Suzy too. Will you all come this way?' The lady walked briskly along the corridor before disappearing through a door – which the Stephens family scurried through a few seconds later.

'Do sit down, all of you,' the lady said, as she settled down herself behind a desk. 'Now, I'm the Ballet Principal of the Royal Ballet School and I'd like to thank you very much for coming in to see us today. Suzy, you must be very tired after such a long day. How are you feeling?'

'Um, fine thank you,' Suzy said, anxious to please despite the fact that the butterflies had returned to her stomach and she was suddenly feeling sick.

'Well, that's good. But what do you think of everything you've seen about the Royal Ballet School today? Do you think you'd like to be one of its students?' the lady asked.

'Oh, I think it's wonderful! I'd love to come here!' Suzy almost bounced off her seat as she said it.

'Excellent. You see, Mr and Mrs Stephens, we'd like to offer Suzy a place here . . . '

Suzy was beside herself with joy! She was so excited that she didn't hear anything else that her parents or the lady talked about. All she could think about was next September, when she would be at the Royal Ballet School at last! Ballet lessons every day! Special leotards! Maybe even the chance to perform on stage at the Royal Opera House with the dancers of the Royal Ballet! Would Suzy be able to wait until September?

'Thank you again, Suzy,' the lady said to her as she

saw Suzy and her parents out of the room. 'And see you again in September!'

'Oh, yes, 'bye!' said Suzy.

Suzy was grinning from ear to ear as she walked excitedly back along the corridor with her parents. She'd done it. But despite her excitement and happiness, Suzy couldn't stop wondering about Anna. They'd left her and her mother back in the dressing room – they hadn't had a chance to speak to them, they were so flustered by the briskness of the Ballet Principal.

'Your dad will go and get the car, Suzy, whilst we go back to the changing room to fetch your ballet things,' said Suzy's mum as she led her daughter back to the room where they seemed to have spent almost the entire day.

When they went in, Suzy looked around eagerly for Anna, but neither she nor her mother were anywhere to be seen. Had they gone home already, Suzy wondered? Had Anna not been asked to come back next September like her?

'Come on, Suzy love,' Mrs Stephens said. She knew that her daughter had made a new friend in Anna. 'Your dad will be waiting . . . you never know – perhaps Anna's popped to the loo. Come on, we've got a long journey to get home. You'll find out what's happened to Anna in September.'

Except that September's ages away, thought Suzy as she picked up her ballet bag and followed her mum back along the corridor. They were soon back to the main hallway which was very busy with older students, who were standing chatting, and dancers from the Royal Ballet Company, who were checking the notices pinned to the enormous board by the door. (One of the many things Suzy had discovered was that the dancers from the Royal Ballet had rehearsal rooms at the School. In fact, Suzy was certain that she'd seen Darcey Bussell coming out of the canteen earlier that day.)

Mrs Stephens pushed open the heavy black front door and she and Suzy stepped out into the darkness of the noisy London street.

'There's your dad in the car, Suzy. Quickly, or we'll cause a traffic jam.'

But, just as they were climbing into the car, they heard shouting behind them: 'Suzy! Suzy!' Suzy turned around quickly – it was Anna.

'Suzy – it's brilliant! I'm going too! They've offered me a place.' Anna was so happy she was almost giggling.

'Oh Anna – it *is* brilliant.'

'Come on,' said Mr Stephens. 'We've got to get going – *now*. Say goodbye.'

Suzy hopped in to the car and leant out of its open window. She waved ecstatically to her new friend.

'Bye, Anna! Well done – and see you in September!'

The Concert Party

FELICITY THOMPSON

This is a most unusual ballet story – with a very unexpected narrator. How many people would have been as imaginative as Flora? The author has worked in the world of ballet, and written for adults, but this is one of her first stories for children.

They're standing up and clapping. Everyone.

And it's only a week ago I heard her arguing.

'But Mum, the ballet concert—'

'There'll be plenty of other concerts, Flora. And anyway you couldn't have stayed at home by yourself.'

'Why not?'

'Stop being ridiculous, Flora. You're twelve!'

'I could have stayed with a friend. I'm sure I could have.'

'For Suzie's sake just make the best of it and unpack your clothes.'

For my sake. Quarrelling.

But my cousin Flora is lucky. I would give anything to learn dancing. She goes on about the kind of dedication it takes, how important it is to her, how it's wonderful to do. But listening to them then, I was glad she'd had to give it up for me. I wanted her here. It was my birthday, wasn't it?

'Did anyone ask *me* if I wanted to come? Surely Suzie has friends of her own. What can we do together except sit down all week?'

'Flora!'

At dinner time Flora looked at the delicious meal my mother had dished up and said: 'I'm watching my figure, Aunt Dorothy. I can't possibly eat this.'

My mother had spent hours preparing the food. She looked as if she might burst into tears.

'I'll eat it,' said David. That's her younger brother. He's a total couch potato.

'No, you won't.' Uncle Jack's voice was low and threatening. 'Eat your dinner, Flora!'

Yes, I thought, eat your dinner, Flora. Get fat like me. Well, I'm not fat really. It's just I can't get enough exercise to digest my food properly, so I'm always having to watch what I eat, but Mum had given me that night off, and cooked all sorts of lovely things. I could eat anything I wanted, and there was Flora taking the pleasure away.

Eventually she excused herself from the table, and wandered out into the garden. I followed her to the door. Outside the sun was setting and the air was cold, and I think it was to cheer herself up that Flora did a few ballet steps, then several more. How I wanted to feel that wonderful sensation of energy, waking up inside the muscles and surging through the body, that she was always talking about. She twirled round the fish pond and leaped over it a couple of times.

'I wish I could do that!' I called before I could stop myself.

Flora swung round.

'Help me out?'

Flora frowned. 'I'll come inside. It's cold out here.'

'Please?'

It was difficult, her helping me out of my chair. She wasn't quite sure how to let me lean on her without my mother around to instruct her.

'Dance for me again?' I said, sinking down on to the grass beside the fish pond. 'Twirl like you did before.'

'What? *Pirouette*?'

'Is that what it's called?'

Flora whirled around and around.

'More!' I said, excited.

'It's hard without music,' she said breathlessly, stopping for a moment. 'Could you sing, do you think?'

So I hummed and Flora timed her steps to the song. Eventually she too collapsed down on the grass.

'You make it look so easy,' I said enviously.

'It's very hard work learning to dance. One day I want to be as good as Rowena.'

'Who's Rowena?'

'There's a photograph of her in Madame's office. She's Madame's great success and now she's leading ballerina with the American Ballet Theatre.' Then she told me all about the dancing school, and her friend Linda and the others, and how there was a summer concert planned.

'Rehearsals started today and I might have been given a solo this time. Madame – Miss Pearson is her name, but we have to call her Madame – Madame has just begun to notice me. "Higher, get that *arabesque*

93

higher!" she said to me last week. Well, she doesn't say, she sort of over-dramatizes in a kind of rasping hysterical scream, but when I did, she got all excited and said, "Nice line, darling." And you just don't get compliments from Madame ever, not unless she has plans for you. And now, I won't be there. Linda always gets a solo, always the dance I would give anything to do and when I get back I'll be so out of practice that Madame will stick me in the back row and ignore me.'

I felt sorry for her. 'You're missing it for my birthday.'

Flora looked embarrassed. 'Well,' she said, trying hard to sound enthusiastic, 'your birthday will be nice.'

'Suzie!'

My mother was striding towards us. 'Flora! How dare you entice this child out to sit on the damp grass?'

'I'm not a child, Mum!'

'I—' Flora began.

But Mum didn't want explanations. She was too busy bundling me back to my chair. 'You should be more considerate, Flora,' she shouted angrily over her shoulder as she took me inside.

'I don't see why we can't watch telly,' David was muttering when I came into the living-room. He gave me a filthy look, probably certain he would die without his constant diet of television. He was sprawled on the sofa drawing a huge dragon on his arm with a blue felt tip pen. 'Tattoo,' he explained when Flora came in.

Flora glanced at him in disgust and flopped into a chair. 'Want to play cards or something?'

She didn't want to, I could tell.

'Oh, neat!' moaned David. 'Really brilliant!'

'Well, what else is there?' asked Flora.

'I know!' I said suddenly. 'Let's have a concert here!'

David stared at me. 'A what?'

'A concert! Flora can dance for us.'

'Wow,' moaned David. 'Just what we always wanted!'

'A concert!' breathed Flora, looking at me with delight. 'Do you really think we could?'

'Why not? But it has to be good!' I said. 'Costumes. Everything!'

'Where?'

Flora looked at the folding doors which divide my bedroom off from the sitting-room. 'We could put a row of chairs in your room and use those doors as a sort of curtain. We can turn the lights on after we open them just like a real stage.'

'Great!'

'When?'

'Friday night?'

'Count me out!' said David.

'No,' said Flora. 'You like telling jokes, don't you?'

'Is that sensible?' I said, remembering my mother's face when David had told a joke once.

'We'll censor him. He has to help, and if that's all he can do—'

'OK, David's the joker.'

'And you—' said Flora.

'I'm part of the audience,' I said quickly.

The white crêpe paper rustled as I folded it all the way down the centre. It was Tuesday and Flora and I had been down to the shops.

'Now the pink one! Needle and cotton. Elastic! Where?' demanded Flora.

'Mum's sewing table.'

She ran to find them.

When she came back she had two of her pretty vests too. 'These are for tops.'

The crêpe paper gathered up into two pretty tutus. 'One pink, one white, and the vests will match. You'll look lovely,' I said admiringly.

'Which do you like best?' she asked, holding them up against her.

'Pink,' I said. 'Yes, the pink.' She put it on my lap and I rustled it with my fingers. 'It's so lovely,' I said, wishing it could be mine.

'I hope you don't expect *me* to dress up,' said David.

'Oh yes,' said Flora, 'but you have to invent your own outfit. We're too busy.'

'Anything?'

'Anything!'

'We did buy you a joke book,' I said.

'Yes,' said Flora, 'so there's no excuse for awful jokes.'

'Magic,' said David, and he went off to study it.

'Music! We need music!'

It was Thursday. We had the music. We had the costumes. Flora had been practising like mad, getting me to sit in the middle and watch to see what I thought. Sometimes she asked me to hold up my arms in a position to see what it would look like. 'Remember that for me,' she'd say. How could I forget? I felt really part of her dance and when the piece of music came I'd do the movement to remind her. And then she had me try another position with my arms. 'I never thought I'd be doing choreography this week,' she said. 'Making up the steps is really interesting, getting them to flow and blend into one another.'

David was being rather secretive about his act.

'What's your costume like?' Flora wanted to know. 'I hope you're going to look decent.'

'You wait!' said David.

'What is it?' I asked. 'A clown? A wizard maybe?'

'Not on your life,' he said. 'It's a surprise.'

We spent the last hours rehearsing again and making programmes and decorating them. Flora put my name in it as well. 'You're part of it,' she said, when I protested.

I asked Mum if she'd make a little tea party for us all for afterwards.

'All good concerts should have a reception afterwards for the artists,' said Flora approvingly.

Late in the afternoon Flora set up my room like a theatre with chairs for Mum, and Flora's parents and a space for my chair, and we decorated my bed with some flowers, and put a programme out on each seat.

'Where's David? Why isn't he helping?' Flora said crossly.

We soon saw why when he appeared just before we were ready to start. He had on black leggings and he had decorated the upper half of his body with felt tips – butterflies, dragons, birds. He looked amazing!

'Wait till you hear my jokes,' he said.

But I never did, because what Flora said next took my breath away.

The doors open slowly. It's dark and the music begins, those sweet high notes Flora and I listened to and thought about. I'm sitting on Mum's desk stool alone when the light comes on. Centre stage. Me! I can see surprise on my mother's face, then a little puzzled frown. I'm the last person she expected to see.

I lift my arms and sway them a little, just like Flora showed me, then I lower them slowly, first one and then the other, and again, and the beautiful tutu I'm wearing rustles. The music speeds up and Flora comes on! I lift my arms, framing my face, while Flora spins right round the stage, leaning in, facing her *arabesques* and *attitudes* in towards me, using me as the centre point of her dance. Then we sway together lifting our arms as she planned, floating our hands gracefully to the music. Flora does an *arabesque* while I lift my arm to match her line and then she twirls around me again, twirling, twirling. How beautifully she moves. I'm almost dizzy with delight watching her, being part of her dance. The melody rises and she circles me again. Now she's taking my hands and as she points her toes and runs gracefully round in a circle, I am *pirouetting* too, *pirouetting*, turning on my stool. She lets go and I turn and turn and turn. Look at me! I'm dancing and everyone's clapping and I know what it feels like, at last I know what it feels like, Flora. I want to cry out, I'm alive! I know what it means, that wonderful sensation of energy flowing through me. But now the music's finishing, and I remember I have to fold my hands across to my shoulders. Flora balances in a beautiful *arabesque* behind me as the last note fades away. Then everything is still.

The audience stands up and starts clapping and my mother rushes over to me with tears in her eyes, and hugs me, and then she hugs Flora. And then Flora's mother is hugging her!

And Flora, my darling cousin Flora, whispers in my ear: 'Tonight, Suzie, *you're* the dancing star.'

The Mega-Nuisance

GERALDINE KAYE

Like Flora in the last story, Rosalind suffers a great disappointment. In a completely different way, she finds out that she values her family – even her little brother Paddy. You'll find the tale mentioned in this story, 'The Tin Soldier', on page 261.

'Paddy, you should shut your mouth when you're eating,' Rosalind said crossly. 'I don't want to see all your chewed-up liver and bacon, thanks very much.'

'You know he finds it difficult, Rozzy,' Mum said gently. 'Especially now with this awful cold and his nose stuffed up, poor little chap.'

Rosalind said nothing. A seven-year-old brother like Paddy who was all hugs and kisses, *who needed it?* she thought.

'Your audition tomorrow, isn't it?' Daddy said as if her bad mood needed explaining. 'Don't let it get to you, poppet. It's not the end of the world if you don't get in.'

'I know,' Rosalind said out loud but secretly she thought it *would* be the end of the world. She had been thinking about the audition, working towards it, ever since she done her first ballet exam and Miss Reid had put her into the acceleration class for gifted pupils. In

October she had got through the preliminary audition for entrance to White Lodge, the Royal Ballet School at Richmond. Now it was February and tomorrow was the *final* audition. They lived too far away for daily travel. She would have to board and the best thing about that was she would only have to put up with Paddy at half-term and holidays. If she got into White Lodge.

'Wozzy?' Paddy said, smiling widely as Mum wiped his face and hands and let him get down from his chair. He couldn't say his 'r's properly. 'Wozzy?' he was beside her now, pulling at her skirt and staring up at her with his eyes like grey marbles. 'Wozzy wead . . . ? Wozzy wead . . . ?'

'Sorry,' Rosalind said getting up. She kicked off her shoes and gripped the back of her chair and raised one leg to illustrate. 'I'm busy, Paddy. I've got to do a *barre* tonight.' She had to see to her *pointes* and her ribbons and practise her *pliés* but you couldn't explain things like that to Paddy.

Miss Reid had said her *pliés* could let down her whole *enchaînement*. Even the greatest dancers had stronger and weaker parts to their dancing, Miss Reid said.

'Wozzy wead . . . ? Wozzy wead . . . ?' Paddy said batting the book against her.

'Oh, read to him for a minute while we wash up, there's a love,' Mum said. 'You're his favourite person, you know.'

'Big deal,' Rosalind said. He certainly wasn't hers and she couldn't pretend. She wasn't good at pretending.

'Wozzy wead . . . ?'

'Oh, all right, mega-nuisance,' Rosalind said, walking off to the sitting-room. 'Bring your book then.'

How could you be fond of somebody you don't like looking at, she wondered as he scrambled on to her lap and put his arms lovingly round her neck. A long time ago, alone in the sitting-room with Paddy, she had held his lips closed between her fingers as if she could change him. Perhaps Paddy had wanted her to change him too because he hadn't pulled away. He just stared at her with tears running down his face.

He had been four then. She had been four when he was born. 'Why is he so ugly?' she had said, seeing him at the hospital for the first time. She was too young to know it was better not to say things like that. 'Poor little chap, poor little boy,' Mum had said, rocking him tenderly. Had she ever held her like that when she was a baby, Rosalind wondered.

Afterwards, Daddy had explained that Paddy was a Down's syndrome child, some people called it mongol. He would always have some trouble learning to do things, but he should be able to go to school and learn to read and write. Later he might get a job doing simple work. He was delicate too: he had cold after cold. His heart was damaged and his lungs didn't work properly. They would all have to work hard helping Paddy to learn to keep his tongue in and his mouth closed. Daddy said there were many things Paddy would do very well, but he might take a long time to learn.

Rosalind tried hard to be nice to Paddy like Mum was. But it was just too difficult. How could she bring friends home, for instance, with him in the house. Once she had heard girls in the cloakroom whispering, 'Have you seen her brother? Well, he's funny.'

'He's not funny,' she had shouted, erupting through the thicket of coats like an avenging angel. 'He's Down's syndrome, so there.'

They had all gone pink and Tracey's mouth fell open like a parody of Paddy's. Well, it would all be different if she got into White Lodge. All her form were going to Hill Street Comprehensive next year and she need never see any of them again. And nobody from White Lodge need ever see Paddy, if she didn't want them to.

'Wead us . . . wead us . . . ' Paddy had opened the book and was snuggling against her. His fair hair still smelled of liver and bacon.

His favourite story was *The Tin Soldier* by Hans Andersen and that was odd because it had been her favourite story too. The tin soldier was disabled with only one leg, she supposed, but he stood straight and true whatever happened, even when he was swallowed by a big fish. The tin soldier loved the paper dancer, and no wonder, Rosalind thought, she loved her too. The little dancer who stood on the mantelpiece was partly herself of course. But why did Paddy love the story? He wasn't anything like the tin soldier who stood true and steadfast whatever happened, or anybody else in the story unless it was the fish with the big swallowing mouth.

Still it was the story he always wanted read. Not that she really had to read it because she knew it by heart. She recited her way through while Mum and Daddy cleared the table.

'Goodnight, mega-nuisance,' she said as Daddy gave Paddy a piggyback upstairs to bed. They were both so good with Paddy, made such a fuss of him. Once she had tried to say something about it and Mum had said, 'Well, of course . . . they didn't think he'd survive . . . I mean we're lucky to have him . . . we have to make the most of him while . . . because . . . ' She never finished the sentence, just blinked and added, 'Oh, sorry, Rozzy dear . . . ' But it was clear what she meant.

That evening Rosalind darned the toes of her *pointes* with pink silk more carefully than she had ever done before. Everything was ready for the next day but the night was full of restless, anxious dreams. Saturday morning was sunny, the sky a comforting Cambridge blue as Rosalind got dressed. Mum was going to drive her to Richmond.

'Car?' said Paddy, running to the door after breakfast. 'Me come in car?'

'You're not taking him?' Rosalind said.

'Well, he does love the car so,' Mum said apologetically. 'Daddy's going to take him to Richmond Park to see the deer while you're having your audition.'

'No,' said Rosalind. Somebody might see him and nobody from White Lodge was ever going to see Paddy. 'I'm not going then.' She sat down in the chair in the hall. 'If you're taking Paddy, I'm not going.'

There was a pause. Daddy and Mum looked at each other and then Daddy said. 'Tell you what, we'll go to the park here, Paddy, eh? Feed the ducks.'

'Park with Wozzy . . . ?' Paddy said looking from one face to the other uncertainly.

'Better get going, you two,' Daddy said crisply. 'Good luck, poppet, I'm sure you'll do fine.'

'Thanks,' said Rosalind. They set off. It was a two-hour journey and Mum didn't say a word, but her lips pressed together said a silent *selfish*. And Rosalind couldn't get Paddy's disappointed face out of her head which was really unfair, she thought, because she *ought* to be thinking about her *pliés* which Miss Reid said was the one thing which might let her down.

She never really knew what happened. All she heard was a screech of brakes and then a stupendous crash and a jerk which flung her against her seat belt, then the side of the Mini caved in like toffee. A shower of glass and then blackness.

She woke up in hospital. Daddy was there and her leg was hurting badly and so was her head.

'What happened? Where's Mum?'

'Don't worry, love. She's quite all right. She's at home with Paddy. Nothing but a few bruises. It was you who copped it, you've broken your leg.'

'What . . . ?' It was dark outside. 'What time is it?'

'About seven o'clock.'

'The audition . . . ?'

'I'm afraid it was all over long ago,' Daddy said.

'Did I . . . didn't I . . . ?' She still didn't know what had happened. She didn't know anything except there was this terrible pain in her leg. And thousands of bandages.

'The car was hit by a lorry,' Daddy explained, taking her hand. 'You've been concussed. Your leg was badly broken. They had to put a pin in it, bit of metal or plastic or something. But the doctor thinks you'll be quite all right eventually. Probably not even a limp.'

'Eventually?' Rosalind whispered. How long was eventually?

She stared at the pale grey walls of the women's surgical ward. Everybody said she was very brave. At first the woman in the next bed tried to talk but Rosalind turned away. For a bit she wondered if she could have an audition later, next year say, they took people at twelve, didn't they? But then Miss Reid came to see her and she shook her head. 'Such a shame, this setback,' she said, but a lifetime of teaching ballet had accustomed her to setbacks. She smiled at Rosalind kindly. 'I daresay you'll be able to go on with your grades later on,' she said vaguely. She didn't come again.

Daddy or Mum came every day. They brought books and puzzles and things to do but Rosalind took no interest. She had no interest in anything. Going to White Lodge had been the first step to a ballet career and if she couldn't take even the first step, she didn't want to take any step at all.

'You're not dying, you know,' the physiotherapist said quite irritably one day. 'You really must try to work at your exercises or you won't improve.'

'I don't care,' Rosalind said. She couldn't pretend. She had never been good at pretending.

One afternoon Tracey and Holly came from Grove Road Primary. The top class had drawn get-well cards. Nearly all of them had a ballet girl standing on her *pointes*.

'Thanks,' Rosalind said and her eyes filled with tears.

'I don't suppose you'll be going to that school, will you, that posh ballet school? I mean it's great, you'll be coming to Hill Street Comprehensive with the rest of us, eh?' Tracey said, trying to be nice. Rosalind just stared at them with tears streaming down her face until a nurse led them away. 'It's no good being sorry for ourselves,' the same nurse said later that evening. 'You're lucky to be alive, young lady.' Rosalind had stopped crying then. She put the ballet girl cards under her pillow.

'How's Paddy?' she said when Mum came that evening.

'He's all right. Well, he's got a bit of a cold as a matter of fact and a chesty cough. Doctor's put him on antibiotics and he's got to stay in bed. Still he's a good little patient. He talks about you all the time. He'd got Granny reading him *The Tin Soldier* when I left. Nothing ever seems to get him down . . . so brave . . . marvellous really.'

'Mm,' said Rosalind. At first she was glad not to be there, listening to Paddy coughing in the next room. But that night she woke and looked at the moon shining pale through the curtains and she wondered if he was all right.

'Why don't you bring Paddy to see me?' she said that next day. She was sitting in a chair by this time.

'Well . . . we didn't think you . . . '

'I'd really *like* to see him,' she said. 'I mean it's been ages.'

'Well, when he's better … He's still got a temperature, you know.' Mum looked worried when she spoke but Rosalind didn't realize how worried until after she had gone. That night she woke and lying in the ward with quiet breathing all round her, she was sure that something awful was happening to Paddy. And the more she thought about it the more she was sure that he was really sick. Paddy who loved her most in the world was really ill and she might never see him again and they weren't telling her . . . just making excuses . . .

'Where's Paddy?' she said quite loudly when Daddy came next day and several heads turned to look. 'Why didn't you bring him?'

'Paddy? He's all right,' Daddy said. 'He's outside as a matter of fact. Mum thought they'd better wait in the car. Well, his temperature's down but he's still got a bit of a cold.'

'I want to see him,' Rosalind almost shouted.

'Well, okay, poppet,' Daddy said. 'No need to get all het up.' He waved from the window, beckoning.

She could see at once that Paddy was all right when he came running into the ward.

'Wozzy . . . Wozzy . . . Wozzy,' he shouted, scrambling joyfully on to the bed and hugging her, anointing her cheek with two weeks' supply of wet kisses. He was just the same, grey eyes, blond hair. 'Wozzy wead . . . Wozzy wead book.'

'Oh, all right, mega-nuisance,' she said and Paddy grinned hugely at the familiar word. The book fell open at the right page and she began to recite. The woman in the next bed was smiling, whispering to Mum, 'Ever so good with him, isn't she?'

She was like the paper dancer, Rosalind thought, listening to the sound of her own voice, the paper dancer who had been burned up in the fire. That was right. But Paddy wasn't like the big-mouthed fish at all. He was like the tin soldier who stood brave and true on his one leg and went on loving the paper dancer whatever happened.

Paddy *was* the tin soldier, steadfast to the end.

The Greatest

MICHELLE MAGORIAN

*Learning dancing doesn't mean only being a dancer . . . in
this story we see two other careers that could spring from it.
As in the last story, Kevin finds that family is important,
too.*

'Boys' group,' said the teacher.

The second group of girls broke away from the
centre of the dance studio, their faces flushed, their
skin streaming with sweat.

A skinny girl, whose fair hair was scraped up into a
bun, smiled at him, and pretended to collapse with
exhaustion against the *barre*.

'Kevin, aren't you a boy any more?' asked the teacher.

'Oh yes!' he exclaimed. 'Sorry.'

He joined the other three boys in the class. They
were waiting for him opposite the mirror.

'You've been in a dream today,' she said. 'Now I
expect some nice high jumps from you boys, so we'll
take it slower. That doesn't mean flat feet. I want to see
those feet stretched. First position. And one and two.'

Kevin brought his arms up into first in front of him
and out to the side to prepare for the jumps.

He loved the music the pianist chose for them. It
made him feel as if he could leap as high and as

powerfully as Mikhail Barishnikov. He knew that *barre* work was important but he liked the exercises in the centre of the studio best, especially when they had to leap.

But today all the spring had gone out of him. A lead weight seemed to pull him down. Bending his knees in a deep *plié* he thrust himself as high as he could into the air.

'I want to see the effort in your legs, not your faces,' remarked the teacher as he was in mid-spring.

They sprang in first position, their feet together, and out into second with their feet apart, then alternated from one to the other, out in, out in, sixteen times in each position, sixteen times for the changeovers.

'Don't collapse when you've finished,' said the teacher. 'Head up. Tummies in. And hold. Right everyone, back into the centre.'

It was the end of class. The girls made wide sweeping curtsies, the boys stepped to each side with the music and bowed.

'Thank you,' said the teacher.

They clapped to show their appreciation, as if they were in an adult class. Kevin knew that was what they did because in the holidays he was sometimes allowed to attend their Beginners' Classes in Ballet, even though he was only ten. He was more advanced than a beginner but at least the classes kept him fit.

Everyone ran to the corner of the studio to pick up their bags. It wasn't wise to leave any belongings in the changing room. Too many things had been stolen from there.

The teacher stood by the door taking money from those who paid per class, or tickets from those whose parents paid for them ten at a time, which was cheaper.

Martin was standing in front of him, pouring out a handful of loose change into the teacher's tin. His father disapproved of boys or men doing ballet so Martin did it in secret and paid for his classes and fares by doing odd jobs. His only pair of dance tights were in ribbons and his dance shoes were so small that they hurt him.

Kevin handed his ticket to the teacher.

'I saw your father earlier on,' she said. 'Whose class is he taking?'

'He's not doing a class. It's an audition.'

'Is that why your head is full of cotton wool today? Worried for him?'

'Not exactly,' he said slowly.

He tugged at Martin's damp T-shirt.

'Dad gave me extra money today. I have to wait for him. Want some orange juice?'

'Yeah,' said Martin eagerly.

'Let's grab a table.'

They ran down the corridor to the canteen area and flung their bags on to chairs.

'I'm bushed,' said Martin.

'Were you sweeping up Mr Grotowsky's shop this morning?'

'Yeah. And I cleaned cars. Dad thinks I'm working this afternoon, too.'

'What if he checks up?'

'He won't. As long as he doesn't see me he doesn't care where I am.'

'Doesn't he wonder why you don't have any money when you go home?'

'No. I tell him I spend it on Wimpys or fruit machines.'

Although he was only eleven Martin had already decided what he wanted to do with his life. He had it all mapped out. First he'd be a dancer, then a choreographer. His idol was a tall, thin, black American teacher in the Big Studio. He had performed in and choreographed shows in the West End. Professional dancers and students sweated and slaved for him, arching and stretching, moving in fast rhythms, leaping and spinning. There were black ones there too, like Martin. One day one of those black dancers would be him.

Some of the students were afraid of the teacher but they worked hard to be allowed to get into, and stay in, his classes.

'Get a classical training first,' he had told Martin abruptly when Martin had plucked up enough courage to ask his advice. So that's what Martin was doing.

'What's the audition for?'

'A musical.'

Kevin put their beakers of orange on to the table.

'So what's the problem? Don't you think he has a chance?'

Kevin shrugged.

'Which one is it?'

'*Guys and Dolls*. He's going up for an acting part. He

thinks his best chance of getting work as an actor is if he gets into a musical. He says no one will look at him if they know he's a dancer. He says directors think dancers haven't any brains.'

'I'd like to see them try a class.'

'Yes. That's what Dad says.'

'Is it because you're nervous for him? Is that it?'

'No. We had a row this morning. We just ended up shouting at one another. We didn't talk to each other all the way here. Even in the changing room.'

'What was the row about?'

'About him auditioning for this job. I don't want him to get it.'

'Why? He's been going to enough voice classes.'

'Yes, I know,' he mumbled.

For the last year his father had been doing voice exercises every morning, taking singing lessons, working on scenes from plays at the Actors' Centre, practising audition speeches and songs, and reading plays.

'I didn't think he'd have to go away, though. This theatre's a repertory theatre and it's miles away. I'd only see him at the weekend. And even then it'd probably only be Sundays. And if he got it he'd start rehearsing two weeks after I start school.'

'So? You've been there before. Not like me. I start at the Comprehensive in a week's time. It'll be back to Saturday classes only.' He swallowed the last dregs of his orange juice.

'Want another? Dad said it was OK.'

'Yeah. I'll go and get them.'

Kevin handed him the money and pulled on his track-suit top over his T-shirt even though he was still boiling from the class.

He couldn't imagine his father being an actor. But his father had explained that he couldn't be a dancer all his life, that choreographers would eventually turn him down for younger dancers and, in fact, had already done so a couple of times. He had to decide which direction he wanted to go in before that started to become a habit.

For the last two years, since Kevin's mother had died, his father had only accepted work in cabaret in London, or bit parts in films, or had given dance classes. Otherwise he had been on the dole. Kevin was used to him being around now.

When his mother was alive and his parents were touring with a dance company, Kevin used to stay with a friend of the family. Dad said it would be like old times staying with her again. Kevin didn't want it to be like old times. He wanted things to stay just as they were.

He pulled on his track-suit trousers, dumped his holdall on his chair and waved to Martin.

'I'll be back in a minute,' he yelled.

He ran down the two flights of stairs which led to the entrance hall, past two of the studios there and downstairs to the basement where the changing rooms and other studios were.

Outside the studio where the audition was taking place stood a crowd of people peering in at the windows. They were blocking the corridor so that dancers going to and from the changing room had to keep pushing their way through with an urgent, 'Excuse me!'

The door to the studio opened and six disappointed men came out. Kevin's dad wasn't among them.

Kevin squeezed in between two people by one of the windows and peered in.

Inside the steamed-up studio, a group of men of every age, height and shape were listening to a woman director. A man was sitting at a piano.

The director was smiling and waving her arms about.

'Here. Squeeze in here,' said a dancer in a red leotard. 'You can see better. They're auditioning for *Guys and Dolls*. It's the men's turn today.'

Kevin didn't let on that he knew.

'She's really putting them through it,' said the dancer. 'First they have to sing on their own and the MD, that's the man at the piano, decides who's going to stay. Then they have to learn a song together.'

'What's the song?' asked Kevin.

' "Luck Be a Lady Tonight." Know it?'

Kevin nodded.

Know it? As soon as his father had heard he had been given the audition every song from *Guys and Dolls* had been played from breakfast to bedtime.

'Then they have to do an improvisation. The director chooses who to keep out of that lot and then the choreographer teaches them a dance routine.'

The dancing would be kid's stuff for his father, thought Kevin. He wiped the glass. His father was standing listening. So, he'd passed two singing tests. Now it was the acting.

The director was obviously explaining what the scene was about. She was pointing to individual men.

'She's telling them about the characters,' said the dancer.

Kevin felt angry. How could his father go through with it when he knew that Kevin didn't want him to go away? He observed his father's face, watched him grip his arms in front of himself and then quickly drop them and let out a breath.

'Excuse me!' he said fiercely, and he pushed himself out of the crowd and along the corridor to the stairs. And then he stopped. He remembered the look on his father's face and realized it was one of anxiety. It astounded him. He had seen his father upset before, but never scared. Why would he be scared? He was a brilliant dancer. But now, of course, he also needed to be a good actor. He was trying something new in front of actors who had been doing it for years and some of those actors were younger than him. That took guts, as Martin would say.

Kevin hadn't given a thought to how nervous his father might have been feeling. He knew how badly he missed the theatre. To start a new career when you were as old as him must be hard; harder too when he knew that Kevin hoped he would fail.

He turned and ran back down the corridor, ducked his head and pushed his way back into the crowd to where the dancer in the red leotard was standing. He wasn't too late. They hadn't started the improvisation yet. He stared through the glass willing his father to look at him.

The director stopped talking. The men began to move, their heads down in concentration as she backed away.

Please look this way, thought Kevin.

And then he did. He frowned and gazed sadly at him.

Kevin raised his thumb and mouthed, 'Good luck!'

At that his father's face burst into a smile.

'Thanks,' he mouthed back and he winked.

Kevin gave a wave and backed away through the crowd and along the corridor.

It was going to be all right, he thought. If his father did get the acting job he knew he'd be taken backstage and he'd meet lots of new people, and at least he wouldn't be touring so he could stay with him sometimes. And Martin could come too. And Dad would be happy again.

Martin wasn't at the table. Their bags were still there with the two plastic beakers of orange juice.

Kevin knew where to find him. He walked to the corridor. Martin was gazing with admiration through one of the windows into the Big Studio. His idol was giving a class to the professional dancers.

He grinned when he saw Kevin.

'Guess what!' he squeaked. 'I was by the door when he went in and he noticed me. And he spoke to me. He looked at my shoes and he said I ought to swap them for bigger ones at Lost Property and then, you know what he said? He said, "Say I sent you!" '

He turned back to watching the class and sighed.

'Isn't he the greatest?'

'Yes,' agreed Kevin, and he thought of his father. 'Yes, he's the greatest.'

What Happened to Pauline, Petrova and Posy

NOEL STREATFEILD

Noel Streatfeild's story Ballet Shoes *is one of the most famous children's books about ballet ever written. At the end, the three Fossil girls are about to go to different parts of the world to work at the things they are particularly good at. What happened then? Did they ever meet again? Years later, Noel Streatfeild wrote this short story, so we can find out . . .*

The first to leave were Sylvia and Pauline. In a way, although they all hated to say 'goodbye', it was a relief when Pauline was really off.

'There wouldn't be as much fuss if it was royalty moving,' Posy whispered to Petrova.

The film company was determined that as they intended to make a star of Pauline she should travel like one. A lady from the company arrived and for three days took Pauline shopping. Pauline had never worn outgrown clothes as Petrova and Posy had to do because she was the eldest. But during the years when they were poor while Gum was away she had cheap clothes, even for the first night of her film her frock was made at home by Nana. Pauline was now fifteen and the lady from the company made sure she was dressed as the most up-to-date teenager to be found anywhere.

Then there were interviews and photographs.

'They wear me out,' said Posy. 'Here's me chosen to join Manoff's ballet company but nobody cares, but because Pauline is going to Hollywood to make a film, people from papers come all day long.'

However, at last the day of departure came. It was in May, so Pauline, looking lovely in a tweed travelling coat over a lightweight frock, stepped into a huge hire car. Her wonderful matching luggage all marked 'Pauline Fossil' was packed in by the chauffeur and she and Sylvia rolled away.

Nana had the last word:

'Don't forget. Wool next the skin, dear. Warm climates can be treacherous.'

Posy left next. She and Nana in a taxi with their rather shabby suitcases piled beside the driver. Nobody could cry when Posy left, for she was radiant. They had not far to go, only to Victoria Station to join Monsieur Manoff and his ballet.

The final move was when pantechnicons came to fetch all the contents of the house in the Cromwell Road. When everything was gone, Gum, Petrova, cook and Clara got into a car and drove to the Midlands. There, until the house Gum had bought was ready for them, they stayed in an hotel. Petrova was in a daze of excitement, for near the new house was an aerodrome, and at the aerodrome a man called Nobby Clark who had undertaken to train her to be a mechanic. Already a governess called Miss Potter came daily to give her lessons.

'Can't have you going to a school,' Gum explained. 'You see, I'm used to travelling. Now if you want to, you can come too and we'll take the Potter with us.'

Petrova, crooning over the overalls she was to wear when training at the aerodrome, could not imagine ever wanting to go away, but she could understand that Gum might.

'But if he does,' she told cook and Clara, 'we'll see we know where he is. We don't want him going away for years and leaving us with no money.'

The part for which Pauline had been given her Hollywood contract was the girl in an English book. The girl, who was called Sara, had run away from home when she found out that her father and mother no longer loved each other, so were not going to share a home any more. Sara adored both parents and the thought of living first with one and then with the other was more than she could bear. So she ran away to Europe where she got mixed up with extraordinary events. Of course in the end her father and mother, having found Sara, were so happy that they joined together again.

It is not easy to act in a film, as Pauline had found when she made her first. Then she had only played a small part, now she had the leading part. She was, of course, rehearsed by a coach, but that too was difficult. When Pauline understood why she was to say something in a certain way she could do it, but if she did not understand she would go on asking 'Why?' until she did understand. At first the coach thought Pauline a horrible girl, but later she came to see how her mind worked and then she and Pauline became friends. It was in fact largely due to her coach that Pauline made the enormous success in that first film that she did.

Her film being such a success Sylvia signed, on Pauline's behalf, a long contract. They rented a very nice house with a swimming pool on the lawn and bought a car and hired a chauffeur. 'It all sounds very grand,' Sylvia wrote to Petrova, 'but for Hollywood we live very simply.'

Two things Pauline insisted on. She must have a private governess. She would not go to the studio school and every eighteen months she must have time off to visit England and Czechoslovakia.

'After all,' she told Mr Silas B. Shoppenhanger, who owned the film company. 'I have two sisters and I must see them. We're family.'

Meanwhile in the Midlands Petrova too was a success. She had taken examinations in mechanics and passed them with ease, and now she was promoted to studying aeroplane engines.

'You see,' she explained to Nobby on her fourteenth birthday, 'I want, as soon as I can, to get my pilot's licence. Then, the moment I am eighteen, I can fly alone.'

To Gum she said:

'You wait until I'm grown up – then, if you can buy

a little aeroplane, I can fly you anywhere in the world you want to go. And we can visit Czechoslovakia and Hollywood on the way.'

Posy was superbly happy training under Manoff, which well she might be, for Manoff thought her a genius and did not hide how he felt.

'Posy,' he would say, 'soon I am taking this company to America. Before that happens you will be dancing for me. I plan two new ballets written specially for you.'

129

One plan came true. Pauline took a three months' break and did visit both Petrova and Gum and Nana and Posy. This was a great success. Pauline seemed unchanged. She always had been the star performer in the family and of course the eldest, and she still was. Cook and Clara were a bit in awe of her to start with, but they soon got over it when they found she still liked to come into the kitchen and sit on the table and talk to them.

Posy was charmed to see both Sylvia and Pauline again, but with her, dancing was all her life. But Nana was thrilled to see them.

'Oh dear, Miss Sylvia, you wouldn't believe how I've counted the days until you came. Of course I'm glad Posy is doing so nicely at the dancing, but such a language they talk here. And the food! You wouldn't believe the trouble I have to get the simplest things, like oatmeal for porridge and treacle for puddings.'

Sylvia, listening, could see life was hard on Nana. She knew not a word of the language and made no effort to learn. What with school and dancing classes Posy was out all day. It must be a lonely life.

She thought things over and made a suggestion.

'I tell you what we'll do, Nana. We'll change places. You go back to Hollywood with Pauline and I'll stay here and look after Posy. We might at least try it out.'

That was what happened and it was a great success. It was also very fortunate, for the next year the war started which began in 1939.

To take a huge ballet company plus stage staff, wardrobe and scenery across the world takes immense organization at any time, but during a war it is a nightmare. Transport was hard to arrange and the company moved in isolated groups. Nana, without a word of the language, would have found things terribly difficult, but Sylvia took it in her stride and somehow arrived safely in New York with a wildly excited Posy.

For many of the ballet company life was to be very hard, for the war lasted five years and of course no theatre wanted to engage the company for that long. But Posy never suffered: when, having made a huge success in the new ballets, the company divided into small groups and went on tour, she and Sylvia went to stay with Pauline until the next ballet season started in New York.

As soon as she was old enough Petrova joined a flying service which transported new aeroplanes from the factory where they had been built to the air base which was waiting for them.

'I am so lucky,' she would say to Gum. 'I could so easily have been born at a time when girls didn't fly.'

When they were children living in the Cromwell Road the girls had made a vow on their birthdays. It was: 'We three Fossils vow to try and put our name in history books because it's our own and nobody can say it's because of our grandfathers.'

I don't know if the Fossils ever got their name in history books. Pauline certainly didn't – film stars don't. Posy would for ever be part of ballet history, but not I think ordinary history. Petrova? I don't know, but I sometimes wonder.

The Rose of Puddle Fratrum

JOAN AIKEN

When dancers are described as being 'magical' it doesn't usually mean the sort of magic that happens in this story! Joan Aiken has written a wonderfully funny, unexpected story that mixes ballet, banana skins and a blacksmith – not forgetting a computer called Fred!

In this story a ballet called The Nightingale and the Rose *is mentioned. It's based on a story by Oscar Wilde. You'll find the story later in this collection, on page 151.*

Right, then: imagine this little village, not far back from the sea, in the chalk country, Puddle Fratrum is its name. One dusty, narrow street, winding along from the Haymakers' Arms to Mrs Sherborne's Bed and Breakfast (with french marigolds and bachelors' buttons in the front garden): half-way between these two, at an acute bend, an old old, grey stone house, right on the pavement, but with a garden behind hidden from the prying eyes of strangers by a high wall. And the house itself – now here's a queer thing – the house itself covered all over *thick,* doors, windows, and all, by a great climbing rose, fingering its way up to the gutters and over the stone-slabbed roof, sending out tendrils this way and that, round corners, over sills, through crevices, till the place looks not so much like a house, more like a mound of vegetation, a great green thorny thicket.

In front of it, a BBC man, standing and scratching his head.

Presently the BBC man, whose name was Rodney Cushing, walked along to the next building, which was a forge.

TOBIAS PROUT, BLACKSMITH AND FARRIER, said the sign, and there he was, white-haired, leather-aproned, with a pony's bent knee gripped under his elbow, trying on a red-hot shoe for size.

Rodney waited until the fizzling and sizzling and smell of burnt coconut had died down, and then he asked, 'Can you tell me if that was the ballerina's house?' – pointing at the rose-covered clump.

BBC men are used to anything, but Rodney was a bit startled when the blacksmith, never even answering, hurled the red-hot pony shoe at the stone wall of his forge (where it buckled into a figure-eight and sizzled some more), turned his back, and stomped to an inner room where he began angrily working his bellows and blowing up his forge fire.

Rodney, seeing no good was to be had from the blacksmith, walked along to the Haymakers' Arms.

'Can you tell me,' he said to Mr Donn the landlord over a pint of old and mild, 'can you tell me anything about the house with the rose growing over it?'

'Arr,' said the landlord.

'Did it belong to a ballet dancer?'

'Maybe so.'

'Famous thirty years back?'

'Arr.'

'By name Rose Collard?'

'Arr,' said the landlord. 'The Rose of Puddle Fratrum, they did use to call her. And known as far afield as Axminster and Poole.'

'She was known all over the world.'

'That may be. I can only speak for these parts.'

'I'm trying to make a film about her life, for the BBC. I daresay plenty of people in the village remember her?'

'Arr. Maybe.'

'I was asking the blacksmith, but he didn't answer.'

'Deaf. Deaf as an adder.'

'He didn't seem deaf,' Rodney said doubtfully.

'None so deaf as them what won't hear. All he hears is nightingales.'

'Oh. How very curious. Which reminds me, can you put me up for the night?'

'Not I,' said the landlord gladly. 'Old Mrs Sherborne's fule enough for that, though; she'll have ye.'

Mrs Sherborne, wrinkled and tart as a dried apricot, was slightly more prepared to be communicative about the Rose of Puddle Fratrum.

'My second cousin by marriage, poor thing,' she said, clapping down a plate with a meagre slice of Spam, two lettuce leaves, and half a tomato. 'Slipped on a banana-peel, she did ('twas said one of the scene-shifters dropped it on the stage); mortification set in, they had to take her leg off, that was the end of her career.'

'Did she die? Did she retire? What happened to her?'

In his excitement and interest, Rodney swallowed Spam, lettuce, tomato, and all, at one gulp. Mrs Sherborne pressed her lips together and carried away his plate.

'Came back home, went into a decline, never smiled again,' she said, returning with two prunes and half a dollop of junket so thickly powdered over with nutmeg that it looked like sandstone. 'Let the rose grow all over the front of her house, wouldn't answer the door, wouldn't see a soul. Some say she died. Some say she went abroad. Some say she's still there and the nightingales fetch her food. (Wonderful lot of nightingales we do have hereabouts, all the year round.) But one thing they're all agreed on.'

'What's that? ' The prunes and junket had gone the way of the Spam in one mouthful; shaking her head, Mrs Sherborne replaced them with two dry biscuits and a square centimetre of processed cheese wrapped in a seamless piece of foil that defied all attempts to discover its opening.

'When she hurt her leg she was a-dancing in a ballet that was writ for her special. About a rose and a nightingale, it was. They say that for one scene they had to have the stage knee-deep in rose-petals – fresh every night, too! Dear, dear! think of the cost!'

Mrs Sherborne looked sadly at the mangled remains of the cheese (Rodney had managed to haggle his way through the foil somehow) and carried it away.

'Well, and so?' Rodney asked, when she came back into the dark, damp little parlour with a small cup of warm water into which a minute quantity of Dark Tan shoe-polish had almost certainly been dissolved. 'What about this ballet?'

''Twas under all the rose-petals the banana-peel had been dropped. That was how she came to slip on it. So when Rose Collard retired she laid a curse on the ballet – she came of a witch family, there's always been a-plenty witches in these parts, as well as nightingales,' Mrs Sherborne said, nodding dourly, and Rodney thought she might easily qualify for membership of the Puddle Fratrum and District Witches' Institute herself – 'laid a curse on the ballet. "Let no company ever put it on again," says she, a-sitting in her wheelchair, "or, sure as I sit here—"'

'Sure as I sit here, what?' asked Rodney eagerly.

'I disremember exactly. The dancer as took Rose's part would break *her* leg, or the stage'd collapse, or there'd be some other desprat mischance. Anyway, from that day to this, no one's ever dared to do that ballet, not nowhere in the world.'

Rodney nodded gloomily. He already knew this. It had been extremely difficult even to get hold of a copy of the score and choreographic script. *The Nightingale and the Rose* had been based on a version of a story by Oscar Wilde. Music had been specially written by Augustus Irish, choreography by Danny Pashkinski, costumes and scenery designed by Rory el Moro. The original costumes were still laid away in mothballs in the Royal Museum of Ballet. Rodney was having nylon copies made for his film.

'Well, you won't be wanting nothing *more*, I don't suppose,' Mrs Sherborne said, as if Rod might be expected to demand steak tartare and praline ice. 'Here's the bath plug, I daresay you will wish to retire as the TV's out of order. Put the plug back in the kitchen after you've had your bath.'

This was presumably to discourage Rodney from the sin of taking two baths in quick succession, but he had no wish to do so. The water was hardly warmer than the coffee. When he ran it into the tiny bath, a sideways trickle from the base of the tap flowed on to the floor, alarming an enormous spider so much that all the time Rodney was in the bath he could hear it scurrying agitatedly about the linoleum. A notice beside a huge canister of scouring powder said PLEASE LEAVE THIS BATH CLEAN, after which some guest with spirit still unbroken had added WHY USE IT OTHERWISE?

Shivering, Rodney dropped the bath plug in the kitchen sink and went to his room. But the bed had only one thin, damp blanket; he got dressed again, and leaned out of the window. Some nightingales were beginning to tune up in the distance. The summer night was cool and misty, with a great vague moon sailing over the dim silvered roofs of Puddle Fratrum. Due to the extreme curve in the village street, the corner of Mrs Sherborne's back garden touched on another, enclosed by a high wall, which Rod was almost sure was that of the legendary Rose Collard.

He began to ponder. He scratched his head.

Then, going to his suitcase, he extracted a smallish piece of machinery, unfolded it, and set it up. It stood on one leg, with a tripod foot.

Rodney pulled out a kind of drawer on one side of this gadget, revealing a bank of lettered keys. On these he typed the message,

'Hullo, Fred.'

The machine clicked, rumbled, let out one or two long experimental rasping chirrs, not at all unlike the nightingales warming up, and then replied in a loud creaking voice,

'Friday evening June twelve nineteen-seventy, eight-thirty p.m. Good evening, Rodney.'

The door shot open. Mrs Sherborne came boiling in.

'What's this?' she cried indignantly. 'I let the room to *one*, no more. Entertaining visitors in bedrooms is strictly against the—' She stopped, her mouth open. 'What's *that*?'

'My travelling computer,' Rodney replied.

Mrs Sherborne gave the computer a long, doubtful, suspicious glare. But at last she retired, saying, 'Well, all right. But if there's any noise, or bangs, mind, or if neighbours complain, you'll have to leave, immediate!'

'I have problems, Fred,' Rodney typed rapidly as soon as the door closed. 'Data up to the present about Rose Collard are as follows:' and he added a summary of all that he had learned, adding, 'People in the village are unhelpful. What do you advise?'

Fred brooded, digesting the information that had been fed in.

'You should climb over the garden wall,' he said at length.

'I was afraid you'd suggest that,' Rodney typed resignedly. Then he closed Fred's drawer and folded his leg, took a length of rope from a small canvas holdall, and went downstairs. Mrs Sherborne poked her head out of the kitchen when she heard Rodney open the front door.

'I lock up at ten sharp,' she snapped.

'I hope you have fun,' Rodney said amiably, and went out.

He walked a short way, found a narrow alley to his left, and turned down it, finding, as he had hoped, that it circled round behind the walled garden of the rose-covered house. The wall, too, was covered by a climbing rose, very prickly, and although there was a door at the back it was locked, and plainly had not been opened for many years.

Rodney tossed up one end of his rope, which had a grappling-hook attached, and flicked it about until it gripped fast among the gnarled knuckles of the roses.

Inside the wall half a dozen nightingales were singing at the tops of their voices.

'The place sounds like a clock factory,' Rodney thought, pulling himself up and getting badly scratched. Squatting on top of the wall, he noticed that all the nightingales had fallen silent. He presumed that they were staring at him but he could not see them; the garden was full of rose-bushes run riot into massive clumps; no doubt the nightingales were sitting in these. But between the rose thickets were stretches

of silvery grass; first freeing and winding up his rope, Rodney jumped down and began to wander quietly about. The nightingales started tuning up once more.

Rodney had not gone very far when something tapped him on the shoulder.

He almost fell over, so quickly did he spin round.

He had heard nothing, but there was a person behind him, sitting in a wheelchair. Uncommon sight she was, to be sure, the whole of her bundled up in a shawl, with a great bush of moon-silvered white hair (he could see the drops of mist on it) and a long thin black stick (which was what she had tapped him with), ash-white face, thinner than the prow of a Viking ship, and a pair of eyes as dark as holes, steadily regarding him.

'And what do *you* want?' she said coldly.

'I – I'm sorry, miss – ma'am,' Rodney stammered. 'I did knock, but nobody answered the door. Are you – could you be – Miss Rose Collard?'

'If I am,' said she, 'I don't see *that's* a cause for any ex-Boy Scout with a rope and an extra share of impertinence to come climbing into my garden.'

'I'm from the BBC. I – we did write – care of Covent Garden. The letter was returned.'

'Well? I never answer letters. Now you *are* here, what do you want?'

'We are making a film about your life. Childhood in Puddle Fratrum. Career. And scenes from the ballet that was written for you.'

'So?'

'Well, Miss Collard, it's this curse you laid on it. I—'

He hesitated, jabbed his foot into a dew-sodden silvery tussock of grass, and at last said persuasively, 'I don't suppose you could see your way to take the curse *off* again?'

'Why?' she asked with interest. 'Is it working?'

'*Working*! We've had one electrician's strike, two musicians', three studio fires, two cameras exploded, five dancers sprained their ankles. It's getting to be almost impossible to find anyone to take the part now.'

'My part? Who have you got at present?'

'A young dancer called Tessa Porutska. She's pretty inexperienced but – well, no one else would volunteer.'

Rose Collard smiled.

'So – well – couldn't you take the curse off? It's such a long time since it all happened.'

'Why should I take it off? What do I care about your studio fires or your sprained ankles?'

'If I brought Tess to see you? She's so keen to dance the part.'

'So was I keen once,' Rose Collard said, and she quoted dreamily, '"One red rose is all I want," cried the Nightingale.'

'It's such a beautiful ballet,' pleaded Rodney, 'or at least it *would* be, if only the stage didn't keep collapsing, and the props going astray, and the clarinettist getting hiccups—'

'Really? Did all those things happen? I never thought it would work half so well,' Rose Collard said wistfully, as if she rather hoped he would ask her to a rehearsal.

'What exactly were the terms of the curse?'

'Oh, just that some doom or misfortune should

143

prevent the ballet ever being performed right through till Puddle church clock ran backwards, and the man who dropped the banana-peel said he was sorry, and somebody put on the ballet with a company of one-legged dancers.'

Rodney, who had looked moderately hopeful at the beginning of this sentence, let out a yelp of despair.

'We could probably fix the church clock. And surely we could get the chap to say he was sorry – where is he now, by the way?'

'How should I know?'

'But *one-legged* dancers! Have a heart, Miss Collard!'

'*I've* only got one leg!' she snapped. 'And I get along. Anyway it's not so simple to take off a curse.'

'But wouldn't you like to?' he urged her. 'Wouldn't you enjoy seeing the ballet? Doesn't it get a bit boring, sitting in this garden year after year, listening to all those jabbering nightingales?'

There was an indignant silence for a moment, then a chorus of loud, rude jug-jugs.

'Well—' she said at last, looking half convinced, 'I'll think about it. Won't promise anything. At least – I tell you what, I'll make a bargain. You fix about the church clock and the apology, I'll see what I can do about remitting the last bit of the curse.'

'Miss Collard,' said Rodney, 'you're a prime gun!' and he was so pleased that he gave her a hug. The wheelchair shot backwards, Miss Collard looked very much surprised, and the nightingales all exclaimed,

'Phyooo – jug-jug-jug, tereu, tereu!'

Rodney climbed back over the wall with the aid of

his rope. Mrs Sherborne had locked him out, so he spent the night more comfortably than he would have in her guestroom, curled up on a bed of hassocks in the church. The clock woke him by striking every quarter, so he rose at 6.45 and spent an hour and a half tinkering with the works, which hung down like a sporran inside the bell tower and could be reached by means of his rope.

'No breakfasts served after 8.15!' snapped Mrs Sherborne, when Rodney appeared in her chilly parlour. Outside the windows mist lay thick as old-man's-beard.

'It's only quarter to,' he pointed out mildly. 'Hark!'

'That's funny,' she said, listening to the church clock chime. 'Has that thing gone bewitched, or have I?'

Rodney sat down quietly and ate his dollop of cold porridge, bantam's egg, shred of marmalade and thimbleful of tea. Then he went off to the public call-box to telephone his fianceé Miss Tessa Prout (Porutska for professional purposes) who was staying at the White Lion Hotel in Bridport along with some other dancers and a camera team.

'Things aren't going too badly, love,' he told her. 'I think it might be worth your while to come over to Puddle. Tell the others.'

So presently in the Puddle High Street, where the natives were all scratching their heads and wondering what ailed their church clock, two large trucks pulled up and let loose a company of cameramen, prop hands, ballet chorus, and four dancers who were respectively to take the parts of the Student, the Girl, the Nightingale, and the Rose. Miss Tessa Porutska (née

Prout) who was dancing the Nightingale, left her friends doing *battements* against the church wall and strolled along to Mrs Sherborne's, where she found Rodney having a conversation with Fred.

'But Fred,' he was typing, 'I have passed on to you every fact in my possession. Surely from what you have had you ought to be able to locate this banana-peel dropper?'

'Very sorry,' creaked Fred, 'the programming is inadequate,' and he retired into an affronted silence.

'What's all this about banana-peel?' asked Tess, who was a very pretty girl, thin as a ribbon, with her brown hair tied in a knot.

Rodney explained that they needed to find a stage-hand who had dropped a banana-peel on the stage at Covent Garden thirty years before.

'We'll have to advertise,' he said gloomily, 'and it may take months. It's not going to be as simple as I'd hoped.'

'Simple as pie,' corrected Tess. 'That'll be my Great-Uncle Toby. It was on account of him going on all the time about ballet when I was little that I took to a dancer's career.'

'Where does your Uncle Toby live?'

'Just up the street.'

Grabbing Rodney's hand she whisked him along the street to the forge where the surly Mr Prout, ignoring the ballet chorus who were rehearsing a Dorset schottische in the road just outside his forge and holding up the traffic to an uncommon degree, was fettling a set of shoes the size of barrel-hoops for a great grey brewer's drayhorse.

'Uncle Toby!' she said, and planted a kiss among his white whiskers.

'Well, Tess? What brings you back to Puddle, so grand and upstage as you are these days?'

'Uncle Toby, weren't you sorry about the banana-peel you dropped that was the cause of poor Rose Collard breaking her leg?'

'Sorry?' he growled. 'Sorry? Dang it, o' *course* I was sorry. Sorrier about that than anything else I did in my whole life! Followed her up to London parts, I did, seeing she was sot to be a dancer; got a job shifting scenery so's to be near her; ate nowt but a banana for me dinner every day, so's not to miss watching her rehearse; and then the drabbited peel had to goo and fall out through a strent in me britches pocket when we was unloading all they unket rose-leaves on the stage, and the poor mawther had to goo and tread on it and bust her leg. Worst day's job I ever did, that were. Never had the heart to get wed, on account o' that gal, I didn't.'

'Well, but, Uncle Toby, did you ever *tell* her how sorry you were?'

'How could I, when she shut herself up a-grieving and a-laying curses right, left, and rat's ramble?'

'You could have written her a note?'

'Can't write. Never got no schooling,' said Mr Prout, and slammed down with his hammer on the horseshoe, scattering sparks all over.

'Here, leave that shoe, Uncle Toby, do, for goodness' sake, and come next door.'

Very unwilling and suspicious, Mr Prout allowed himself to be dragged, hammer and all, to the back of

Rose Collard's garden wall. Here he flatly refused to climb over on Rodney's rope.

'Dang me if I goo over that willocky way,' he objected. 'I'll goo through the door, fittingly, or not at all.'

'But the door's stuck fast; hasn't been opened for thirty years.'

'Hammer'll soon take care of that,' said Uncle Toby, and burst it open with one powerful thump.

Inside the garden the nightingales were all asleep; sea-mist and silence lay among the thickets. But Uncle Toby soon broke the silence.

'Rose!' he bawled. 'Rosie! I be come to say I'm sorry.'

No answer.

'Rose! Are you in here, gal?'

Rodney and Tess looked at one another doubtfully. She held up a hand. Not far off, among the thickets, they heard a faint sound; it could have been somebody crying.

'*Rosie?* Confound it gal, where are you?' And Uncle Toby stumped purposefully among the thickets.

'Suppose we go and wait at the pub?' suggested Tess. 'Look, the sun's coming out.'

An hour later Mr Prout came pushing Miss Collard's wheelchair along Puddle Fratrum's main street.

'We're a-going to get wed,' he told Rodney and Tess, who were drinking cider in the little front garden of the Haymakers' Arms. (It was not yet opening hours, but since the church clock now registered 5 a.m. and nobody could be sure of the correct time there had been a general agreement to waive all such fiddling rules for the moment.) 'A-going to get wed we are,

Saturday's a fortnight. And now we're a-going to celebrate in cowslip wine and huckle-my-buff, and then my intended would like to watch a rehearsal.'

'What's huckle-my-buff?'

Huckle-my-buff, it seemed was beer, eggs, and brandy, all beaten together; Tess helped Mr Donn (who was another uncle) to prepare it.

The rehearsal was not so easily managed. When the chorus of village maidens and haymakers were half-way through their schottische, a runaway hay-truck, suffering from brake-fade, came careering down the steep hill from Puddle Porcorum and ran slap against the post office, spilling its load all the way up the village street. The dancers only escaped being buried in hay because of their uncommon agility, leaping out of the way in a variety of *jetés*, *caprioles*, and *pas de chamois*, and it was plain that no filming was going to be possible until the hay had somehow been swept, dusted, or vacuumed away from the cobbles, front gardens, doorsteps, and window-sills.

'Perhaps we could do a bit of filming in your garden, Miss Collard?' Rodney suggested hopefully. 'That would make a wonderful setting for the scene where the Nightingale sings all night with the thorn against her heart while Rose slowly becomes crimson.'

'I don't wish to seem disobliging,' said Miss Collard (who had watched the episode of the hay-truck with considerable interest and not a little pride; '*Well,*' she had murmured to her fiancé, 'just fancy my curse working as well as that, after all this time!') 'but I should be really upset if anything – well, troublesome, was to happen in my garden.'

'But surely in that case – couldn't you just be so kind as to remove the curse?'

'Oh,' said Rose Collard, 'I'm afraid there's a bit of a difficulty there.'

'What's that, Auntie Rose?' said Tess.

'As soon as you get engaged to be married you stop being a witch. Soon as you stop being a witch you lose the power to lift the curse.'

They gawped at her.

'That's awkward,' said Rodney at length. He turned to Tess. 'I don't suppose you have any talents in the witchcraft line, have you, lovey, by any chance?'

'Well, I did just have the rudiments,' she said sadly, 'but of course I lost them the minute I got engaged to you. How about Mrs Sherborne?'

'The curse has to be taken off by the one who put it on,' said Rose.

'Oh.' there was another long silence. 'Well,' said Rodney at length, 'maybe Fred will have some suggestion as to what's the best way to put on a ballet with a company of one-legged dancers.'

They drank down the last of their huckle-my-buff and went along to Mrs Sherborne's.

'Hello, Fred? Are you paying attention? We have a little problem for you.'

And that is why, when *The Nightingale and the Rose* was revived last year, it ran for a very successful season at Covent Garden danced by a company of one-legged computers, with Fred taking the part of the nightingale.

The Nightingale and the Rose

OSCAR WILDE

This is the story that Joan Aiken described as turned into a ballet in her story 'The Rose of Puddle Fratrum', on page 133. It's an extremely sad story by a famous Irish playwright and author. One of Oscar Wilde's sons described how when his father got tired of playing with him and his brother, he would invent fairy stories for them – this is one of them. It would make a wonderful ballet, and maybe one day someone will compose music for it.

'She said that she would dance with me if I brought her red roses,' cried the young student, 'but in all my garden there is no red rose.'

From her nest in the holm-oak tree the nightingale heard him, and she looked out through the leaves and wondered.

'No red rose in all my garden!' he cried, and his beautiful eyes filled with tears. 'Ah, on what little things does happiness depend! I have read all that the wise men have written, and all the secrets of philosophy are mine, yet for want of a red rose is my life made wretched.'

'Here at last is a true lover,' said the nightingale.

'Night after night have I sung of him though I knew him not: night after night have I told his story to the stars and now I see him. His hair is dark as the hyacinth-blossom, and his lips are red as the rose of his desire, but passion has made his face like pale ivory and sorrow has set her seal upon his brow.'

'The prince gives a ball tomorrow night,' murmured the young student, 'and my love will be of the company. If I bring her a red rose she will dance with me till dawn. If I bring her a red rose, I shall hold her in my arms, and she will lean her head upon my shoulder and her hand will be clasped in mine. But there is no red rose in my garden, so I shall sit lonely and she will pass me by. She will have no heed of me, and my heart will break.'

'Here, indeed, is the true lover,' said the nightingale. 'What I sing of; he suffers: what is joy to me, to him is pain. Surely love is a wonderful thing. It is more precious than emeralds and dearer than fine opals. Pearls and pomegranates cannot buy it, nor is it set forth in the market-place. It may not be purchased of the merchants, nor can it be weighed out in the balance for gold.'

'The musicians will sit in their gallery,' said the young student, 'and play upon their stringed instruments, and my love will dance to the sound of the harp and the violin. She will dance so lightly that her feet will not touch the floor, and the courtiers in their gay dresses will throng round her. But with me she will not dance, for I have no red rose to give her;' and he flung himself down on the grass, and buried his face in his hands, and wept.

'Why is he weeping?' asked a little green lizard, as he ran past him with his tail in the air.

'Why, indeed?' said a butterfly, who was fluttering about after a sunbeam.

'Why, indeed?' whispered a daisy to his neighbour, in a soft, low voice.

'He is weeping for a red rose,' said the nightingale.

'For a red rose?' they cried. 'How very ridiculous!' and the little lizard, who was something of a cynic, laughed outright.

But the nightingale understood the secret of the student's sorrow, and she sat silent in the oak tree, and thought about the mystery of love.

Suddenly she spread her brown wings for flight, and soared into the air. She passed through the grove like a shadow and like a shadow she sailed across the garden.

In the centre of the grass plot was standing a beautiful rose tree, and when she saw it she flew over to it, and lit upon a spray.

'Give me a red rose,' she cried, 'and I will sing you my sweetest song.'

But the tree shook its head.

'My roses are white,' it answered; 'as white as the foam of the sea, and whiter than the snow on the mountain. But go to my brother who grows round the old sundial, and perhaps he will give you what you want.'

So the nightingale flew over to the rose tree that was growing round the old sundial.

'Give me a red rose,' she cried, 'and I will sing you my sweetest song.'

But the tree shook its head.

'My roses are yellow,' it answered; 'as yellow as the hair of the mermaiden who sits upon an amber throne, and yellower than the daffodil that blooms in the meadow before the mower comes with his scythe. But go to my brother who grows beneath the student's window, and perhaps he will give you what you want.'

So the nightingale flew over to the rose tree that was growing beneath the student's window. 'Give me a red rose,' she cried, 'and I will sing you my sweetest song.'

But the tree shook its head.

'My roses are red,' it answered; 'as red as the feet of the dove, and redder than the great fans of coral that wave and wave in the ocean-cavern. But the winter has chilled my veins, and the frost has nipped my buds, and the storm has broken my branches, and I shall have no roses at all this year.'

'One red rose is all I want,' cried the nightingale, 'only one red rose! Is there no way by which I can get it?'

'There is a way,' answered the tree, 'but it is so terrible that I dare not tell it to you.'

'Tell it to me,' said the nightingale, 'I am not afraid.'

'If you want a red rose,' said the tree, 'you must build it out of music by moonlight, and stain it with your own heart's blood. You must sing to me with your breast against a thorn. All night long you must sing to me, and the thorn must pierce your heart, and your life-blood must flow into my veins, and become mine.'

'Death is a great price to pay for a red rose,' cried the nightingale, 'and life is very dear to all. It is pleasant to sit in the green wood, and to watch the sun in his chariot of gold, and the moon in her chariot of pearl. Sweet is the scent of the hawthorn, and sweet are the bluebells that hide in the valley, and the heather that blows on the hill. Yet love is better than life, and what is the heart of a bird compared to the heart of a man?'

So she spread her brown wings for flight and soared into the air. She swept over the garden like a shadow, and like a shadow she sailed through the grove.

The young student was still lying on the grass, where she had left him, and the tears were not yet dry in his beautiful eyes.

'Be happy,' cried the nightingale, 'be happy; you shall have your red rose. I will build it out of music by moonlight, and stain it with my own heart's blood. All that I ask of you in return is that you will be a true lover, for Love is wiser than Philosophy, though he is wise, and mightier than Power, though he is mighty. Flame-coloured are his wings, and coloured like flame is his body. His lips are sweet as honey, and his breath is like frankincense.'

The student looked up from the grass, and listened, but he could not understand what the nightingale was saying to him, for he only knew the things that are written down in books.

But the oak tree understood, and felt sad, for he was very fond of the little nightingale who had built her nest in his branches.

'Sing me one last song,' he whispered; 'I shall feel lonely when you are gone.'

So the nightingale sang to the oak tree, and her voice was like water bubbling from a silver jar.

When she had finished her song, the student got up, and pulled a notebook and a lead pencil out of his pocket.

'She has form,' he said to himself, as he walked away through the grove – 'that cannot be denied to her; but has she got feeling? I am afraid not. In fact, she is like most artists; she is all style without any sincerity. She would not sacrifice herself for others. She thinks merely of music, and everybody knows that the arts are selfish. Still, it must be admitted that she has some beautiful notes in her voice. What a pity it is that they do not mean anything, or do any practical good!' And he went into his room, and lay down on his little pallet bed, and began to think of his love; and, after a time, he fell asleep.

And when the moon shone in the heavens the nightingale flew to the rose tree, and set her breast against the thorn. All night long she sang, with her breast against the thorn, and the cold crystal moon leaned down and listened. All night long she sang, and the thorn went deeper and deeper into her breast, and her life-blood ebbed away from her.

She sang first of the birth of love in the heart of a boy and a girl. And on the topmost spray of the rose tree there blossomed a marvellous rose, petal following petal, as song followed song. Pale was it, at first, as the

mist that hangs over the river – pale as the feet of the morning, and silver as the wings of the dawn. As the shadow of a rose in a mirror of silver, as the shadow of a rose in a water-pool, so was the rose that blossomed on the topmost spray of the tree.

But the tree cried to the nightingale to press closer against the thorn, and louder and louder grew her song, for she sang of the birth of passion in the soul of a man and a maid.

And a delicate flush of pink came into the leaves of the rose, like the flush in the face of the bridegroom when he kisses the lips of the bride. But the thorn had not yet reached her heart, so the rose's heart remained white, for only a nightingale's heart's blood can crimson the heart of a rose.

And the tree cried to the nightingale to press closer against the thorn. 'Press closer, little nightingale,' cried the tree, 'or the day will come before the rose is finished.'

So the nightingale pressed closer against the thorn, and the thorn touched her heart, and a fierce pang of pain shot through her. Bitter, bitter was the pain, and wilder and wilder grew her song, for she sang of the love that is perfected by death, of the love that dies not in the tomb.

And the marvellous rose became crimson, like the rose of the eastern sky. Crimson was the girdle of petals, and crimson as a ruby was the heart.

But the nightingale's voice grew fainter, and her little wings began to beat, and a film came over her eyes. Fainter and fainter grew her song, and she felt something choking in her throat.

Then she gave one last burst of music. The white moon heard it, and she forgot the dawn, and lingered in the sky. The red rose heard it, and it trembled all over with ecstasy, and opened its petals to the cold morning air. Echo bore it to her purple cavern in the hills, and woke the sleeping shepherds from their dreams. It floated through the reeds of the river, and they carried its message to the sea.

'Look, look!' cried the tree, 'the rose is finished now,' but the nightingale made no answer, for she was lying dead in the long grass, with the thorn in her heart.

And at noon the student opened his window and looked out.

'Why, what a wonderful piece of luck!' he cried; 'Here is a red rose! I have never seen any rose like it in all my life. It is so beautiful that I am sure it has a long Latin name,' and he leaned down and plucked it.

Then he put on his hat, and ran up to the professor's house with the rose in his hand.

The daughter of the professor was sitting in the doorway winding blue silk on a reel, and her little dog was lying at her feet.

'You said that you would dance with me if I brought you a red rose,' cried the student. 'Here is the reddest rose in all the world. You will wear it tonight next your heart, and as we dance together it will tell you how I love you.'

But the girl frowned.

'I am afraid it will not go with my dress,' she answered; 'and, besides, the chamberlain's nephew has sent me some real jewels, and everybody knows the jewels cost far more than flowers.'

'Well, upon my word, you are very ungrateful,' said the student angrily and he threw the rose into the street, where it fell into the gutter, and a cart-wheel went over it.

'Ungrateful!' said the girl. 'I tell you what, you are very rude; and, after all, who are you? Only a student. Why, I don't believe you have even got silver buckles to your shoes as the chamberlain's nephew has,' and she got up from her chair and went into the house.

'What a silly thing love is!' said the student as he walked away. 'It is not half as useful as logic, for it does not prove anything, and it is always telling one of things that are not going to happen, and making one believe things that are not true. In fact, it is quite unpractical, and, as in this age to be practical is everything, I shall go back to philosophy and study metaphysics.'

So he returned to his room and pulled out a great dusty book and began to read.

Petrushka

Retold by Troy Alexander

Petrushka is another very sad story – or is it? The story told in the ballet was made up specially by Alexandre Benois to accompany music by Igor Stravinsky, but Petrushka himself is a well-known figure in Russian folk tales. One important thing about him is that he never dies! Petrushka means Little Peter in Russian.

It was a bright day at the end of the fierce Russian winter, and the big square in the heart of St Petersburg was full of life. Soldiers and servant girls, cooks and coachmen, nursemaids and nobles had all come out into the sunshine to enjoy the Shrove Tuesday fair. They strolled about, colourful in their best clothes. They bought cakes and sweets and glasses of tea from the stalls. They chatted with their friends and laughed at the entertainers and the sideshows. Tomorrow was the start of the season of Lent, and they would be serious. Today was for pleasure!

Laughter and music rang in the air as the crowd enjoyed their day's holiday. A dancer on one side of the square began to compete with a dancer on the other side, and the crowd turned from one to the other as the two tried to outdo each other. When both dancers fell exhausted to the ground, the spectators clapped and cheered them both, throwing coins as a reward, which the dancers scooped up eagerly.

Suddenly the crowd were startled by the sound of loud drumbeats. At the back of the fair was a booth, decorated in bright colours and with thick blue curtains pulled shut across the front. As people turned at the loud noise, two drummers appeared from behind the curtains. They marched into the square, pushing the crowd back to make a space in front of the booth.

Then from behind the curtain came a strange figure. It was an old man, with beady eyes and a closed-in, cruel face, covered in wrinkles. He wore a long, dark robe, covered with magical signs. This old man was a magician. He owned the booth, and whatever was to be shown there. Many fair-goers remembered clever and mysterious tricks he had offered in past years. The magician stared at the people, who were waiting expectantly, and took a flute out of his pocket. He started to play on his flute, a high, sweet, strange tune, which he repeated several times. Suddenly the curtains in front of the booth swept apart!

On the stage, three life-sized puppets were displayed. In the middle there was a very pretty dancer, with big bright eyes, red cheeks and a pert little four-cornered hat with a fur edge. She looked as though she would break into a dance at any minute. On the left, ready for anything, there was a dark and dashing Moorish soldier, strong and confident in a splendid gold-laced uniform. On the right was the drooping figure of a clown. His clothes seemed far too big for him, his face

was white, and his mouth seemed to be twisted in pain. His name was Petrushka.

The magician blew some notes on his flute – and the puppets started to dance. They moved stiffly at first, as puppets do. But after a few minutes they jumped down from the stage of the booth, and came down into the square. Here they began to act out a story in dance.

The Moor and Petrushka were both in love with the dancer. She liked the Moor best, which made the poor clown very angry. He attacked his rival, but the Moor defended himself easily, giving Petrushka a good beating.

As the three puppets enacted the story the spectators gradually realized that it wasn't simply make-believe. It seemed as though the three weren't puppets at all, but real people, who had been imprisoned by the old magician, and made to do his will. What was going on was not a play – it was deadly serious! The watchers began to feel afraid. Some of them quietly crept away.

The old magician realized what was happening. He waved his hands in the air, and the puppets stopped their performance at once. They moved jerkily back on to the stage of the booth, then stopped moving completely, frozen into place. The curtains closed.

Behind the curtain, the magician threw Petrushka back into his cell. He lay in the dark on the floor of his small room. It had no windows, or furniture, and the only decoration was a portrait of the magician, which seemed to lean down from the wall and mock the poor clown. Petrushka was utterly miserable. He was completely at the mercy of the magician, he had been thrashed by the Moor, and he was madly in love with the dancer – but she wouldn't look at him.

Then, just as he was feeling more unhappy than he had ever been before, the door of his room opened – and in came the dancer! Petrushka could hardly believe it. He was so full of excitement and joy that he threw himself at her feet and poured out his love for her – but all he did was frighten her. Being scared made her feel angry. Why should she waste her time with this ridiculous clown? He must be mad! She ran off, slamming the door behind her.

Petrushka was in despair. If only he could escape!
He beat against the walls in his misery, ramming his
fist so hard against one wall that he broke right through
it – but there was nothing on the other side of the
hole! He was trapped.

The Moor had gone back to his room, too. It was big,
well-lit and magnificently decorated in exotic colours
and patterns. The Moor found a coconut, and started to
play with it. He threw it up and caught it, sometimes
with his hands, sometimes with his feet. Then he heard
the milk splashing about inside the nut. He put it down
on the floor, and picked up his great scimitar. Raising
the sword above his head, he brought it down hard on
the coconut – but to his amazement the blade bounced
back, and the nut did not break!

The Moor was not just surprised. He was frightened,
too. The coconut should not have been able to resist
his fierce blow. Perhaps it was magical? Perhaps it was
even a god? He dropped to his knees, bowed to the
mysterious coconut, and started to say some prayers.

As he knelt, the door of his room opened. With a
merry blast on the tin trumpet she was holding, the
dancer came skipping in. The Moor watched, smiling
with pleasure as she danced around his room. He stood
up, and moved over to the dancer, taking his place as
her partner in her dance. She was delighted! She loved
the Moor's colourful appearance, and lapped up all his
attentions. She was too heartless and silly to see that he
was completely selfish under his brilliant surface. When
the Moor stopped dancing and pulled the dancer down

on to his couch, she did not resist very hard. She liked the idea of sitting beside the handsome soldier!

Suddenly the door burst open. Petrushka had heard the noise, and had come to see what was happening. When he saw the dancer and the Moor sitting together, he was overwhelmed with jealousy and rage. He rushed at the Moor, lashing out with his fists in an attempt to drive his rival away. The Moor, surprised by Petrushka's attack, lost his temper. Snatching up his scimitar, he flourished it in the air, and chased Petrushka round the room, slashing the razor-sharp blade at him in a determined attempt to get rid of the annoying clown. To avoid the blade crashing down on his head, Petrushka had at last to spring through the door. He only just managed it.

Out in the square the holiday-makers had been enjoying the fair. A dancing bear was a popular attraction. Then, as the snow started to fall again, many people in the busy square had started to dance, and nursemaids, coachmen and gypsies had led lively performances.

As the light faded, and the lamps were lit, there were sudden and unexpected noises from the booth with blue curtains. The throng of people heard the noises, and turned to look. From behind the curtains, Petrushka came running, with a terrified look on his face as he looked over his shoulder. Hard on the clown's heels came the Moor brandishing his scimitar.

Petrushka dodged this way and that, trying to escape. They charged straight into the crowd, scattering them on every side. As the onlookers gazed in horror, the

Moor caught up with the clown, and struck him down. Petrushka tried once to get up, then he fell lifeless to the ground.

The dancer had followed Petrushka and the Moor into the square. Now the victorious Moor took her by the hand, and together they disappeared quickly through the crowd into the night. The shocked bystanders, their holiday forgotten, surrounded the limp body of the clown. Somebody sent for the police, for surely this was murder! As the policeman bent over Petrushka's body, the old magician arrived. He looked scornfully at the silent, worried crowd, and the policeman. What a fuss about nothing! Petrushka was only a puppet, made of cloth and stuffed with sawdust. He picked up the frail body, and shook it hard. A trickle of sawdust fell on the ground. It was only another of his tricks, and the crowd had been taken in again!

It was quite dark. Snow was falling, and the fun was over. One by one, the people drifted away, intent on getting home. At last the magician was left, standing alone in the square, with the snow swirling around him. In his hand he held the tattered remains of the puppet. Suddenly he heard a noise. He turned, looking back at his booth.

There, on the roof, was Petrushka! He shook his fist defiantly at the magician who had tormented him. The old man was terrified by the unexpected apparition. He dropped the torn doll he was holding, and ran for his life. The triumphant figure of Petrushka fell forward over the roof, and the square was empty, left to the night and the falling snow.

The Tavern of the Rathshee

PATRICIA LYNCH

The fair mentioned in this story is very different from the one in 'Petrushka'! In Ireland there has always been a tradition of wandering folk – tinkers, ballad singers, musicians and storytellers – who go from town to town, and fair to fair, making a living by practising their particular craft. Patricia Lynch, an Irish writer, often used such characters in her stories, as well as magic and Irish folktales. The shee *in this story are the Irish fairy-folk, and a* rath *is a hill-fort.*

When he wasn't bringing turf, or helping his mother till the stony strip of land beside their cabin, or going to school, Colum Hennessy played the fiddle at every wedding, wake or fair he could reach. He liked the fairs best, for then he heard other fiddlers and he never came home without a new tune in his head.

'There'll be fiddlers and ballad singers from all over Munster at the Ballynarea Fair,' he told his mother. 'But it's that far I'll have to start out terrible early!'

'An' start back early, mind now,' his mother warned

him. 'An' just supposin' ye don't get a lift on the road, ye'll never make it.'

'Why wouldn't I set off the night before?' asked Colum. 'There'll be carts and drovers and all kinds on the road, and I can sleep and ride at the same time, and be at Ballynarea before the other fiddlers are half-way there.'

'Indeed an' ye won't!' cried Mrs Hennessy. 'Ye'll sleep in yer own good bed!'

Colum coaxed and coaxed until she gave in. On the day before the fair, the moment he had finished his tea, he jumped up, pulled on his Sunday boots, twisted the muffler his mother had knitted for his birthday round his neck, slung the fiddle in its canvas bag over his shoulder and was ready for the road.

'I'm a wee bit anxious,' said Mrs Hennessy. 'Mind an' keep close to the others goin' to the fair, an' don't be stravagin' along on yer lone.'

'Amn't I going to ride in a cart?' demanded Colum. ''Tisn't as if I'd be walkin' to Ballynarea.'

'I hope not. But ye never can tell what will happen the minit ye set fut outside yer home. Here's the market bag an' the list. If ye can't get all that's on it, what harrum? We'll manage. Remember now, kape to the highway an' don't be tryin' short cuts. But sure, ye're a good child an I'll not be tormentin' ye.'

From the doorway Colum looked back at the cosy room with the turf fire blazing on the hearth and the delph gleaming on the dresser. The lamp with its red shade shone in the window and, when he turned to go down the path, the sky was so stormy and the wind so wild, the boy almost wished he need not set off until morning.

Suppose there isn't anyone else on the road, he thought with a shiver.

But he was ashamed to confess that he felt afraid.

'You'll be proud when you see me comin' home from the fair with the bag crammed full an' me pockets burstin' with money,' he declared over his shoulder.

'I'll be watchin',' his mother promised. 'Make sure of yer lift back, before ye buy one box of matches, or the pound of tay.'

Colum ran down the path, dodging the rocks and beginning to be too excited to mind wind or darkness. When he looked back his mother was still gazing out over the half-door and waving her striped apron.

He waved the market bag and then remembered he had left the list on the table.

'I won't go back, I'll surely think of all we need,' he consoled himself.

He ran the whole way to the crossroads without stopping once. Then he was thankful to sit on the bank and wait for a cart that had room for a passenger.

There were drovers and their herds in plenty; donkey carts, loaded with big green cooking apples, hard, white cabbages, great yellow turnips and little golden ones, as well as the gleaming white kind, not to mind onions and carrots in bunches, went bundling by at a steady trot.

'If only there'd be a haycart on the road,' thought Colum. 'Or mebbe a yoke carrying calves, or just an empty cart with a farmer going in to buy. That would be best of all, if he'd a couple of old sacks to spread over me!'

One cart was loaded with young kids and Colum would have liked to journey with them, but there was barely room for the driver himself.

'We should have a goat,' grumbled Colum. 'Couldn't it sleep in the shed? And why wouldn't we have real milk in our tea, and not a bit of sweet stuff out of a tin? It ud be grand if I could bring a kid home with me!'

Boys were helping the drovers, and dogs trotted with their masters, their tongues hanging out, their tails wagging.

But Colum couldn't see a cart where there was room for a boy to stretch himself and sleep.

'I'll walk on,' he decided. 'Mebbe I'll catch up with one.'

He was a quick walker and a strong one, but he was glad to shelter behind a cart loaded with crates of hens, for the wind was blowing fiercer every moment.

'Why wouldn't ye give us a bit of a tune on the fiddle, young lad?' asked a tall, thin woman, who carried a basket of eggs on her head.

'I'm hurrying to get a lift,' Colum explained. 'When I'm sitting up on a cart, you'll hear me soon enough.'

'Let's hope ye get the lift, young lad,' she said, striding along as if the basket held feathers, not eggs.

It was all the boy could do to keep up with her and answer her questions. She asked where Colum lived and how was he: had his mother a good hand with fowl and apple cake? What book was he in at school and what would he do when he was a man?

''Tis a long way for a gossoon to be walkin',' said the egg woman when she couldn't think of any more questions. 'Ye should have waited till the mornin'. 'Tis then the big carts does be on the road. Ye'll be droppin' wid the tiredness before we reach Ballynarea, an' I'm afeard the rain will be spillin' on us before then.'

I'll never get in front of this cart, thought Colum. I'd best fall behind an' see if I have better luck that way.

He let a man driving sheep go by and then a boy and a woman with a small red cow. Following came a herd of bullocks, crowding on one another and filling the roadway. Colum stood back against the low, stone wall to let them pass and it was then he saw a great haycart piled high, lumbering along.

The other carts had lighted lanterns swinging at the side, but this came in darkness and in silence, for the horse's hoofs made no sound on the stony road and the wheels turned without creaking. The driver sat with his arms folded and his head sunk on his chest.

'Hi, mister!' shouted Colum. 'Will ye give me a lift?'

There was no answer.

An old man hobbled along, leaning on a stick.

'If ye're goin' the way he's goin', let ye hoist yerself up at the back,' he wheezed.

'I'm for the fair at Ballynarea!' cried Colum, and he reached for the rope trailing in the dirt.

It slipped through his fingers and, as he made a grab, he stumbled and fell. Scrambling to his feet, Colum's only thought was for his fiddle, but it was safe in the canvas case, though the market bag had fallen and lay trampled as though a dozen bullocks had marched over it.

He rubbed his knees and raced on, determined to overtake the haycart.

But where *was* the haycart?

Swinging round a bend in the road where the bogland rose to the mountainside, went the hen cart, the egg woman, and the cart laden with kids; the lanterns bobbing and fluttering like bog candles. When they went out of sight he was alone on the road, with the wind blowing his hair backwards and the moon glimmering beyond the streaming clouds.

Colum was terrified of the loneliness and ran with the wind against him until he caught up with the egg woman. He felt she was an old friend and didn't mind how many questions she asked.

'Where in the wide worruld did ye get to?' she wanted to know. 'When I missed ye, I was afeared ye cudn't kape up. But sure we're gettin' on for a quarter o' the journey.'

'Is Ballynarea that far?' cried Colum in dismay. 'Isn't there a place where we'd get a sit down an' a bite an' sup? Me mother gave me a threepenny, just in case. 'Tis a lucky one, with a hole in it.'

'Ye're welcome to an egg, though sure, raw eggs is cold comfort,' said the egg woman kindly. 'I'm as starvin' meself as if I'd been walkin' on hungry grass, but unless ye find the way to the Tavern of the Rathshee you'll go hungry till ye reach Ballynarea. Yer mother should a' give ye a cut o' soda bread to kape ye goin'.'

'I never heard tell of the Tavern of the Rathshee,' said Colum. 'Where is it?'

The woman looked around cautiously.

'Amn't I the foolish one? Doesn't everyone know 'tis unlucky to talk of THEM at the full o' the moon? 'Twas yer fiddle med me do it.'

'The *Shee*?' whispered Colum.

She nodded.

'Their rath is somewhere in the mountains. 'Tis there for them that long for the drink of forgetfulness. An' they're crazy about music. In coorse they have their own fiddlers, but if they see ere a one goin' the roads they'll coax him in to play for them. If ye plaze them, nothin's too good for ye, but if ye make a poor fist of the playin', they run ye.'

'I'd play for them, an' gladly!' declared Colum.

'Whist now. Whist!' exclaimed the woman. 'Why didn't I kape a still tongue in me head! 'Tis the wind has me moidhered. Bad cess to it!'

She walked on in silence and Colum forgot hunger and tiredness in thinking of the *Shee* and their rath and what happened to those that played for them.

He didn't notice the rain sweeping along on the wind until his face was dripping with it.

'I never remember rain tasting strong and sweet like the honey drink me mother made in the summer,' he muttered.

'Don't say another worrud,' the egg woman warned him. 'When rain or snow tastes sweet and strong it manes they've set eyes on ye an' they're determined to have ye. Hide yer fiddle among them hins an' ye may go safe. They'll not interfere with anything that has feathers on it!'

As she spoke the wind came with a rush. She clung to the cart with one hand and called Colum to keep close beside her.

There was such a tumult of wind and rain that he did not hear her. There was rain on his hair, on his eyelashes, and if he opened his mouth he tasted that rich, sweet savour. He stumbled along until he discovered that the rain had ceased, the wind had dropped, a smooth grass path was under his feet and, in front of him, was a low whitewashed cabin tucked snugly between two great rocks.

A smiling woman leaned over the half-door, and behind her rose the glow of a huge fire.

'Enter, young fiddling lad,' she said. 'Here is rest and food and the best of drink.'

Colum stepped inside and the door closed behind him. He did not notice for, instead of a cabin, he had entered a great hall, lit by hundreds of blazing torches. It was crowded at this end with people sitting at long tables, eating and drinking. Some were grandly dressed in silks and satins. Some wore armour that Colum had seen before only in picture-books, while others were as poorly dressed as himself. Strange animals wandered in and out among the tables and the boy longed to take home with him one that was like a milk-white pony, with a twisted horn sticking straight out from its forehead and big, brown eyes.

I heard tell of a unicorn and 'twas like that, thought

the boy, but I didn't know there were any in these parts.

Beyond the tables there was dancing, and never in all his life had Colum seen such dancers. They danced right up in the air, leaping over their partners and kept on dancing while they were in the air. But there was no music and, though the boy was hungry, he thought such fine dancers deserved the best music he could give them.

He took his fiddle from the case. He tightened the bow and twanged the strings. Instead of the reel he meant to play he found he was playing the song he'd heard a blackbird singing one evening when the elder tree at the back of his mother's cabin was in flower.

As he played he could see the white, scented blossoms nodding at him and the blackbird's yellow bill opening to let its song rise on the air.

At the same time, Colum was wishing he could be eating the roast chicken and green peas he could see on the table, with golden chip potatoes piled beside them. He was always hungry, even when there were only the little pig potatoes to eat. But chicken and green peas – he had never dreamed of such food.

There wasn't a sound from the people in the hall. The dancers didn't stop for one moment, but whirled and leaped noiselessly and all in time to Colum's playing. As he lifted the bow from the strings he knew he had never played better, yet they all sat silent, and the dancers stood motionless on tiptoe, waiting for him to play again.

Once, before dawn, when he was coming home from a wake at Goatsferry, Colum heard an old man playing a tune on a whistle made from a reed. It was a sad little tune and yet it made him happy. The sun had not yet risen and frost lay thick on the rocks, but he felt the music warming him through and through. The man was old and bent but, though Colum ran, he could not catch up with him. Yet he remembered the tune and he played it now to the people at the Tavern of the Rathshee.

Even the dancers did not move, but stayed on tiptoe gazing at Colum down the long hall.

The ones I know give a lad a lot of praise and he doin' his best to please. But, sure we all have our ways, thought the boy.

And he couldn't help longing for some of the plum pudding he saw on a plate, with thick cream sauce all over it.

'I'd like me mother to be seein' the lashin's some folk have, and she always telling me to ate me praties an' be content,' grumbled Colum to himself.

Once more he twanged the strings and tightened two of them. He knew the tune he'd play and it would be the last, for he was hungrier and thirstier than he thought it was possible to be.

One day he had been out gathering sticks and he sat down to rest beside a grassy mound. He was almost asleep when he heard a gay, quick tune that made him want to go dancing away down the road. He never saw the player, though he searched and searched. He forgot the sticks he had worked so hard to gather and ran home to play the tune while it was fresh in his mind, and his mother said it was the best tune she had ever heard, though she had to go out and fetch in the sticks herself.

As the first notes came from his fiddle the bow darted up and down at such a rate that Colum could scarcely hold it. The dancers leaped and twirled; the people sitting at the tables stamped; the little old men who ran about with plates and glasses hummed and whistled, and the cooks with their long beards tucked inside their aprons beat on the pots and pans with iron spoons. Colum's wrist was tired, his eyes blinked, he nearly yawned his head off, and suddenly everyone in that great hall shouted: 'Hail to the Fiddler of the Rathshee!'

'No!' cried Colum. 'I'm for the fair at Ballynarea!'

'Run!' whispered the friendly woman, tugging at his sleeve. 'Run, or you've seen your last fair!'

Even as he made for the door, he thought how like the egg woman she looked.

They all ran after him. Hands clutched at his clothes and caught him by the arms. But he broke through. He was at the half-door when he tripped and fell out into the pouring rain.

'Wake up, young lad. We're at the crossroads!'

Who was talking? Who was shaking him awake?

Colum rubbed his eyes. Then he sat up. He was lying at the back of a cart with a sack over him and a very small kid stretched across his knees. The market bag, crammed full, was at his back. Two loaded creels were at his feet and the fiddle, safe in its canvas case, was under the sack beside him.

The driver was lighting his pipe and he puffed contentedly.

'Ye're the man who drove the load of kids,' said Colum. 'But we're coming away from the fair! How will I ever get there at all?' he cried indignantly.

The rain had ceased, there wasn't a breath of wind and the moon was high in a clear sky so that the whole wet countryside, the mountains, the bog, even the road itself shone and glittered.

'Sure, ye're only half-awake,' the driver told him. 'Listen to me now. 'Tis from the fair I'm comin' meself. I was half-way through the gap when a wumman hailed me an' bundled yerself an' yer belongin's into me cart. "See the lad safe home," ses she. "Tell him the three tunes will make him famous throughout Ireland," ses she. "But I've packed a few bits for him to take home to his mother," ses she. Wasn't it lucky I got rid of all me kids, barrin' the sheeshy one, that not a soul would look at, an' ye can have that for a hansel.'

Colum rubbed his eyes again and looked at the ham and the tea, the sugar and the candles poking out of the market bag and wondered at what he couldn't see. A string of sausages was hanging out of one creel and a lump of red cheese sat on top of the other.

The kid butted Colum and stood up unsteadily.

'The dote!' exclaimed the boy. 'I'll call her Pegeen.'

'Which way now?' asked the driver.

'Up along,' replied Colum.

'What place do yerself an' the strange wumman hail

from?' asked the driver. 'I never heard tell of a dwellin' up there and though I tried to see where she went, I cudn't.'

'There's THE TAVERN OF THE RATHSHEE,' said Colum slowly, looking at the man sideways.

'THE TAVERN OF THE RATHSHEE!' cried the man. 'I knew there was somethin' quare about ye! Get off me cart an' yer bundles too! I'll not be surprised if the silver money that one gave me turns to dead leaves in me pocket. Off wid ye!'

He flung the creels and the market bag out on the mud of the road and the kid leaped after them.

Colum grabbed his fiddle and jumped. He could hear money rattling in his pocket.

'I'll pay for Pegeen!' he called. 'And I'm real thankful for the lift!'

''Tis a phouka ye should have to bring ye home an' may that same Pegeen heartscald ye!' the man shouted over his shoulder as the horse clattered off. 'Kape yer fairy money!'

'What will I do now?' grumbled Colum. 'I can't carry two creels and a market bag as well as me fiddle! If you were bigger, Pegeen, you could carry the lot!'

The kid kicked up its heels and capered round him.

Colum looked up, and there was the lamp shining in the windows of his home and the firelight streaming out over the half-door. His mother was hurrying down the rocky path, for she had been watching since nightfall.

'Did ye do well at the fair, child?' she called.

'I did better than the fair!' shouted Colum. 'Look at

Pegeen! Look at all I've brought! But wait till I tell you the whole story!'

The creels were so heavy they could carry only one at a time between them. When the loads were all inside, Colum settled the kid in the shed, while his mother made a big pot of tea and buttered the hot potato cake she had ready.

Then they sat beside the hearth on their creepies, with their elbows on their knees, while Colum told how he had played the three tunes at the Tavern of the Rathshee, and he wasn't ended until the wag-at-the-wall told them it was the morning of the next day and it Sunday.

The Fiddler in the Fairy Ring

JULIANA HORATIA EWING

In the last story, Colum knows what can happen to those who stay too long with the fairy folk. In this story the farmer's son and the fiddler both suffer as a result of their stupid behaviour. Juliana Horatia Ewing's grandfather was a naval chaplain, who had looked after Horatio Nelson as he lay dying at the battle of Trafalgar, and her second name was given in Nelson's honour. She wrote many stories for children during a busy life in which she lived in several different countries with her husband, who was a soldier.

Generations ago, there once lived a farmer's son, who had no great harm in him, and no great good either. He always meant well, but he had a poor spirit, and was too fond of idle company.

One day his father sent him to market with some sheep for sale, and when business was over for the day, the rest of the country folk made ready to go home, and more than one of them offered the lad a lift in his cart.

'Thank you kindly, all the same,' said he, 'but I am going back across the downs with Limping Tim.'

Then out spoke a steady old farmer and bade the lad

go home with the rest, and by the main road. For Limping Tim was an idle, graceless kind of fellow, who fiddled for his livelihood, but what else he did to earn the money he squandered, no one knew. And as to the sheep path over the downs, it stands to reason that the highway is better travelling after sunset, for the other is no such very short cut; and has a big fairy ring so near it, that a butter woman might brush it with the edge of her market cloak, as she turned the brow of the hill.

But the farmer's son would go his own way, and that was with Limping Tim, and across the downs.

So they started, and the fiddler had his fiddle in his hand, and a bundle of marketings under his arm, and he sang snatches of strange songs, the like of which the lad had never heard before. And the moon drew out their shadows over the short grass till they were as long as the great stones of Stonehenge.

At last they turned the hill, and the fairy ring looked dark under the moon, and the farmer's son blessed himself that they were passing it quietly, when Limping Tim suddenly pulled his cloak from his back, and handing it to his companion, cried, 'Hold this for a moment, will you? I'm wanted. They're calling for me.'

'I hear nothing,' said the farmer's son. But before he had got the words out of his mouth, the fiddler had completely disappeared. He shouted aloud, but in vain, and had begun to think of proceeding on his way, when the fiddler's voice cried, 'Catch!' and there came flying at him from the direction of the fairy ring, the bundle of marketings which the fiddler had been carrying.

'It's in my way,' he then heard the fiddler cry. 'Ah, this is dancing! Come in, my lad, come in!'

But the farmer's son was not totally without prudence, and he took good care to keep at a safe distance from the fairy ring.

'Come back, Tim! Come back!' he shouted, and, receiving no answer, he adjured his friend to break the bonds that withheld him, and return to the right way, as wisely as one man can counsel another.

After talking for some time to no purpose, he again heard his friend's voice, crying, 'Take care of it for me! The money dances out of my pocket.' And therewith the fiddler's purse was hurled to his feet, where it fell with a heavy chinking of gold within.

He picked it up, and renewed his warnings and entreaties, but in vain; and, after waiting for a long time, he made the best of his way home alone, hoping that the fiddler would follow, and come to reclaim his property.

The fiddler never came. And when at last there was a fuss about his disappearance, the farmer's son, who had but a poor spirit, began to be afraid to tell the truth of the matter. 'Who knows but they may accuse me of theft?' said he. So he hid the cloak, and the bundle, and the money-bag in the garden.

But when three months passed, and still the fiddler did not return, it was whispered that the farmer's son had been his last companion; and the place was searched, and they found the cloak, and the bundle, and the money-bag, and the lad was taken to prison.

Now, when it was too late, he plucked up a spirit, and told the truth; but no one believed him, and it was said that he had murdered the fiddler for the sake of his money and goods. And he was taken before the judge, found guilty, and sentenced to death.

Fortunately, his old mother was a wise woman. And when she heard that he was condemned, she said, 'Only follow my directions, and we may save you yet; for I guess how it is.'

So she went to the judge, and begged for her son three favours before his death.

'I will grant them,' said the judge, 'if you do not ask for his life.'

'The first,' said the old woman, 'is, that he may choose the place where the gallows shall be erected; the second, that he may fix the hour of his execution; and the third favour is, that you will not fail to be present.'

'I grant all three,' said the judge. But when he learned that the criminal had chosen a certain hill on the downs for the place of execution, and an hour before midnight for the time, he sent to beg the sheriff to bear him company on this important occasion.

The sheriff placed himself at the judge's disposal, but he commanded the attendance of the gaoler as some sort of protection; and the gaoler, for his part, implored his reverence the chaplain to be of the party, as the hill was not in good spiritual repute. So, when the time came, the four started together, and the hangman and the farmer's son went before them to the foot of the gallows.

Just as the rope was being prepared, the farmer's son called to the judge, and said, 'If your Honour will walk twenty paces down the hill, to where you will see a bit of paper, you will learn the fate of the fiddler.'

'That is, no doubt, a copy of the poor man's last confession,' thought the judge.

'Murder will out, Mr Sheriff,' said he; and in the interests of truth and justice he hastened to pick up the paper.

But the farmer's son had dropped it as he came along, by his mother's direction, in such a place that the judge could not pick it up without putting his foot on the edge of the fairy ring. No sooner had he done so than he perceived an innumerable company of little people dressed in green cloaks and hoods, who were dancing round in a circle as wide as the ring itself.

They were all about two feet high, and had aged faces, brown and withered, like the knots on gnarled trees in hedge bottoms, and they squinted horribly; but, in spite of their seeming age, they flew round and round like children.

'Mr Sheriff! Mr Sheriff!' cried the judge, 'come and see the dancing. And hear the music, too, which is so lively that it makes the soles of my feet tickle.'

'There is no music, my Lord Judge,' said the sheriff, running down the hill. 'It is the wind whistling over the grass that your lordship hears.'

But when the sheriff had put his foot by the judge's foot, he saw and heard the same, and he cried out,

'Quick, Gaoler, and come down! I should like you to be witness to this matter. And you may take my arm, Gaoler, for the music makes me feel unsteady.'

'There is no music, sir,' said the gaoler; 'but your worship doubtless hears the creaking of the gallows.'

But no sooner had the gaoler's feet touched the fairy

ring, than he saw and heard like the rest, and he called lustily to the chaplain to come and stop the unhallowed measure.

'It is a delusion of the Evil One,' said the parson; 'there is not a sound in the air but the distant croaking of some frogs.' But when he too touched the ring, he perceived his mistake.

At this moment the moon shone out, and in the middle of the ring they saw Limping Tim the fiddler, playing till great drops stood out on his forehead, and dancing as madly as he played.

'Ah, you rascal!' cried the judge. 'Is this where you've been all the time, and a better man than you as good as hanged for you? But you shall come home now.'

Saying which, he ran in, and seized the fiddler by the arm, but Limping Tim resisted so stoutly that the sheriff had to go to the judge's assistance, and even then the fairies so pinched and hindered them that the sheriff was obliged to call upon the gaoler to put his arms about his waist, who persuaded the chaplain to add his strength to the string. But as ill luck would have it, just as they were getting off, one of the fairies picked up Limping Tim's fiddle, which had fallen in the scuffle, and began to play. And as he began to play, everyone began to dance – the fiddler, and the judge, and the sheriff, and the gaoler, and even the chaplain.

'Hangman! Hangman!' screamed the judge, as he lifted first one leg and then the other to the tune, 'come down, and catch hold of his reverence the chaplain. The prisoner is pardoned, and he can lay hold too.'

The hangman knew the judge's voice, and ran towards it; but as they were now quite within the ring he could see nothing, either of him or his companions.

The farmer's son followed, and warning the hangman not to touch the ring, he directed him to stretch his hands forwards in hopes of catching hold of someone. In a few minutes the wind blew the chaplain's cassock against the hangman's fingers, and he caught the parson round the waist. The farmer's son then seized him in like fashion, and each holding firmly by the other, the fiddler, the judge, the sheriff, the gaoler, the parson, the hangman, and the farmer's son all got safely out of the charmed circle.

'Oh, you scoundrel!' cried the judge to the fiddler; 'I have a very good mind to hang you up on the gallows without further ado.'

But the fiddler only looked like one possessed, and upbraided the farmer's son for not having the patience to wait three minutes for him.

'Three minutes!' cried he; 'Why, you've been here three months and a day.'

This the fiddler would not believe, and as he seemed in every way beside himself, they led him home, still upbraiding his companion, and crying continually for his fiddle.

His neighbours watched him closely, but one day he escaped from their care and wandered away over the hills to seek his fiddle, and came back no more.

His dead body was found upon the downs, face downwards, with the fiddle in his arms. Some said he had really found the fiddle where he had left it, and had been lost in a mist, and died of exposure. But others held that he had perished differently, and laid his death at the door of the fairy dancers.

As to the farmer's son, it is said that thenceforward he went home from market by the highroad, and spoke the truth straight out, and was more careful of his company.

The Sleeping Beauty in the Wood

CHARLES PERRAULT
retold by Edith Nesbit

This story doesn't have a dance in it! However, one of the most popular and beautiful ballets ever devised, with music by Peter Tchaikovsky, is based on the story. In the ballet version, the princess is called Aurora, and the Good Fairy becomes the Lilac Fairy.

Whenever you give a christening party you must always remember to ask all the most disagreeable people you know. It is very dangerous to neglect this simple precaution. Nearly all the misfortunes which happen to princesses come from their relations having forgotten to invite some nasty old fairy or other to their christenings. This was what happened in the case of the Sleeping Beauty.

She was not called the Sleeping Beauty at her christening, of course; for though she was certainly a beauty even then, she did not sleep more than any other little baby. She was called Benevola, after the most powerful of the seven good fairies who were invited to her christening. And because one name is never enough for a princess, she had six other names, which were the names of the other six fairies.

It was a charming christening party. The queen had never had a baby of her own before, and she wished the christening party to be one of those parties that people remember and talk of for a long time afterwards. Well, she had her wish; for though this all happened hundreds of years ago, that party has never been forgotten – and here we are talking about it now!

The queen insisted that the party should not be given in the town palace, but in the beautiful country palace where the court usually spent the summer. It was a lovely place, with gardens and terraces, and peacocks, and fountains and goldfish; and all round it was a park, and round the park was a wood, and the palace itself was old and grey and beautiful, with big towers like beer mugs, and little turrets like pepper-pots, and a dovecot like a great round cheese with holes in it, and a lawn in the courtyard that was like a green velvet table cover.

And here the christening feast was given. Everything was pink and white. The walls were hung with white satin looped up with festoons of pink roses; the queen wore a white dress and a pink velvet mantle; the baby had white cambric robes tied up at the sleeves with pink ribbon (because it was a girl; if it had been a boy the ribbons would have had to be blue, and I don't know how the court decorators would have managed about the roses, for blue roses are very uncommon). There were strawberry and lemon ices – pink and white – and pink and white blancmange; and the christening cake was covered with white icing, with 'Benevola! Bless her!' on it in pink letters; and the very tablecloths were white, and the very toes of the baby the prettiest pink you ever saw.

After dinner the fairies all gave their christening presents to the little princess, beginning with the youngest. They gave her beauty and grace, and wit and loving-kindness, and the sense of humour, and the sense of honour. What princess could wish for more?

'And now, Benevola dear,' said the happy mother queen, turning to the eldest good fairy, 'I'm just dying to know what your present is. I know it'll be something perfectly lovely. *Oh!*'

The last word was nearly a scream; and everyone else screamed too, though, as a rule, screaming is not allowed at court. But on an occasion like this no one was shocked. It was, people agreed afterwards, enough to make anybody scream. For quite suddenly, with a clap of thunder and a nasty flash of forked lightning, the fairy Malevola dropped through the ceiling, and stood with her ugly flat feet firmly planted on the white and pink rose-leaves that were heaped round the baby's cradle.

'How do you do?' said the king, breaking the dreadful silence.

'So pleased you were able to come,' twittered the queen. 'Most kind of you to drop in like this.'

Malevola scowled and spoke. 'You didn't ask me to this christening party.'

The king murmured something about having lost her address.

'You never looked for my address; you didn't want my address. You didn't ask me to your party. No one ever does ask me to their parties.'

'And I don't wonder,' whispered the youngest lady-in-waiting. Malevola, indeed, did not look exactly the sort of person to be the life and soul of a party. She had a cruel, ugly, yellow face, shiny bat's wings, which she pretended were a fashionable cloak, and a bonnet trimmed with live snakes. Her scarf was tied together with a bunch of earthworms, and she wore a live toad for a brooch.

'However,' she went on, 'I'm not offended. I've brought your dear daughter a little present.'

'Now that's really charming of you,' said the poor queen, looking round for Benevola. But Benevola had disappeared.

'*Such* a nice present,' said the wicked fairy. 'Benevola you've called her, have you? Sweet little pet! Well, Benevola darling, you shall prick your hand with a spindle and die of the wound. *Won't* that be nice?'

And with that, and another clap of thunder, Malevola vanished.

The queen caught up the baby, and Benevola crept cautiously out from behind the white velvet window curtains.

'Is she gone?' she asked. 'Cheer up, dear queen. I'm glad I kept my gift to the last.'

'Then you can undo Malevola's wicked work,' cried the queen, smiling through her tears.

'No, not that; but I can change it. My little god-daughter must prick her hand with a spindle, but she shall not die of it. She shall only sleep for a hundred years.'

'That's just as bad for me,' said the queen, hugging her baby.

'Not quite, dear,' said Benevola kindly. 'You'll see.'

'In the meantime,' said the king, who had been very busy with his tablets, 'Heaven helps those who help themselves. I've made a new law. Shall I recite it?'

'Oh, do, your Majesty!' said everybody; and the youngest lady-in-waiting whispered, 'His Majesty does write such sweet, pretty laws.'

'The law is,' said the king, '"No spindles allowed in my kingdom, on pain of death".'

Everyone clapped their hands, and the queen dried her eyes and kissed the baby.

Princess Benevola grew up a perfect dear, and her parents loved her more and more, and when she asked if she mightn't keep her eighteenth birthday at the country palace they saw no reason why she shouldn't.

That business of Malevola had almost been forgotten. No spindles were ever seen in that country, and where there are no spindles it is impossible to prick yourself with them.

So the birthday party was given in the same hall that had been hung with white and pink for the christening party, and now the festoons of roses were red and white, and pink and yellow; 'For,' said Benevola, 'I love them all.'

On the day after the party the princess explored the castle, and she and her maids had a good game of hide-and-seek. When it was the princess's turn to hide she thought it would be amusing to hide in one of the little round turrets that were like pepper-pots. So she opened the door of one, and there sat an old woman doing something so interesting that the princess at once forgot all about the hide-and-seek.

'What are you doing, good dame?' the princess asked.

'Spinning flax, child,' said the old woman. And she was – the shining, polished spindle twirled round and round in her fingers.

'It's pretty work,' said the princess. 'Do you think I could do it?'

'You can try, and welcome,' said the old woman. 'Sit in my chair, and take the spindle in your hand.'

Benevola did as she was told; but as she sat down one pointed end of the spindle knocked against the arm of the chair, and the other pointed end ran into the palm of her hand. The blood started out on her white gown, and Benevola fell to the ground in a swoon.

'Ha, ha!' said the old woman, and turned into Malevola before the princess's eyes (only those eyes were shut). 'Ha, ha! Your father never thought how easily I could make a spindle when the time came.' And with that and the usual clap of thunder she vanished.

And so when the princess's ladies burst into the room in their game of hide-and-seek, all laughing and chattering like a cageful of bright-coloured parrots, they found the princess lying flat on the floor, as white as a snowdrop and as still as death.

The ladies ran screaming to tell the king and queen, and when they climbed the turret stairs and lifted their dear lifeless daughter between them the spindle fell out of the folds of her dress and rattled and spun on the bare floor.

So then they knew.

'Send for Benevola,' moaned the queen. 'Oh, send for Benevola – do!' And the king tried to drown his grief by giving orders about the bed his child was to lie on during her long sleep, as many another father has done before and since.

They laid the white princess on a bed of carved ebony hung with curtains of silver cloth, and over her body they laid a coverlet of cloth of gold that fell to the ground on both sides in folds that looked like folds carved in the solid metal. And they put a pink rose and a white rose and a yellow rose on her breast, and crossed her hands above them; and over all they laid a veil of white gauze that covered her from head to feet, and they shut the door and went away and left her.

And then Benevola came. The poor queen rushed down the throne steps and along the great hall to meet her, and —

'Oh, my girl!' she cried. 'Oh, my pretty little baby! She will sleep for a hundred years, and I shall be dead long, long years before she wakes up, and I shall never see her pretty eyes or her dear smile or hear her call me mother ever again.'

And with that she broke once more into wild

weeping. Benevola put her arms round the queen's neck and kissed her.

'You poor dear!' she said. 'Don't grieve so. Your daughter must sleep for a hundred years. But what of that? *So shall you.* Yes, and the king her father, and all the courtiers and waiting-maids, and knights and men-at-arms – and the very dogs and cats. And when she wakes you shall all waken too, and, in the light of the happiness you will know when you feel her loving arms round you again all this present sorrow will be to you as a dream is when one wakes to see the brave sun shining.'

'You are sure she *will* wake?' said the mother queen, clinging to her.

'When the hundred years are over a prince shall come and wake her,' said the fairy. 'He will love her very much, and he shall be her husband.'

'Then I shall lose her anyway,' sighed the queen.

'That's what mothers are born to,' said the fairy. 'Come, eat and drink a little, all of you, before you go to sleep.'

So the tables were set, and everyone ate and drank, though it was with a heavy heart. And as the dinner was drawing to an end the fairy suddenly spoke the spell, and everyone in the palace fell asleep in his place. The king and queen at the high table, the page filling the wine cup, the butler carrying fruit on a salver, the servants cleaning pots in the kitchen, the huntsman feeding his hounds, the hounds leaping round him, the cat basking on the terrace, the pigeons cuddled on the roof tiles – all were struck into sleep just as they were, so that the palace looked as though it were peopled with waxworks instead of living folk.

The fairy sighed and smiled, and sighed again. Then she laid a spell on the place so that no dust or decay should come near it in those hundred long years. And she laid a spell on the gardens, that no weeds should grow, and that all the flowers should stay just as they were, to the last leaf or bud. The wood, too, she laid a spell on, and at once the branches grew thick and many, the briars and creepers wound in and out among the branches, and in a moment there was a thicket round the garden as tough and unpassable as any old quickset hedge.

There was one more spell to lay, and Benevola laid it. It was on the people, so that they should not seek to find or to bring back their king and queen. She laid a spell to make them all republicans for a hundred years, when they should become loyal again the moment the king awoke – which was really quite a good idea, and met every possible difficulty.

So a year went by, and the seasons changed the face of the country from brown to green, and from green to yellow, and from yellow to russet, and from russet to white. But in the garden within the ring of the wood nothing changed at all. There it was always high midsummer, and the roses flamed in the sunshine, and the jasmine flowers shone like stars in the twilight. And the years went on and on, and people were born and grew up, and married and died, and still all was summer and sleep and silence in the palace in the wood.

And at long last the hundred years were all but accomplished. There remained but one day of all their many, many, many days.

And on that day a prince came riding through the town. He stopped in the marketplace, and said:

'Where is the country palace of your king?'

'We have no king,' a stout grazier answered him; 'we're a free and happy republic, we are.'

'But you had a king once,' said the prince. 'Where was his country palace?'

'I've heard Granfer tell it was out yonder,' said the grazier, 'beyond the wood that no man can pass.'

So the prince went on, and by asking his way of all the old people he met on the country road he came at last to the wood that no man could pass.

'It ain't no good, master,' said an old shepherd, who could just remember hearing that there *was* a palace inside there; 'you'll never get through. What's set you on finding out a place that's dead and gone, and clean forgot?'

'I dreamed,' said the prince, 'three happy nights I dreamed that within your king's country palace I should find the light of my eyes and the desire of my heart.'

'And what are they?' the shepherd asked.

'I do not know yet,' said the prince, 'but I shall know.'

'I'd turn back and get me home along, if I was you,' said the shepherd. 'Why, suppose it was lions inside there, or dragons? There'd be a pretty how-de-do!'

'I can't turn back,' said the prince; 'my dream is calling me, and I must follow. You take my horse and be good to him. If I come back safe to my own kingdom, I will pay you. If not, then you have a good horse for your pains.'

So saying, he dismounted, drew his sword, and went forward to the wood.

'*You'll* never get through,' said the old shepherd. 'A many's tried that. Why, the boys is always at it. They never get nothing but scratched faces and torn hands to show for it. What do *you* expect to get?'

'I don't know,' said the prince again; 'but I *shall* know.'

And he struck with his sword at the great twisted branches interwoven with briars and thick honeysuckle and thorny eglantine. And though they were so hard and thorny, at the touch of his sword they grew soft as dandelion stalks, so that he cut his way through them as easily as a man mows young grass with a scythe.

'Well, if ever I did!' said the old shepherd.

The prince went on deeper and deeper to find the heart of the wood, and when he found the heart it was a green garden, all bright and fair and orderly, with rolled grass plots and smooth paths, and roses of all the colours there are, and starry tangles of jasmine. And in the middle of the wood's heart was the palace of his dreams. The garden was so still that it seemed to him as though he might even yet be dreaming, so he plucked a red rose, and smelled it, and knew that it all was real, and no dream.

On he went, up the terraces and through the hall where, at the table, and at their service, king, queen and courtiers slept, looking like life-sized figures in

wax. At the end of the hall were golden curtains, and it was from behind them that his dream beckoned to him. He parted the curtains and went in. There on the carved ebony bed lay the princess, between the silver cloth curtains, covered with cloth of gold, and with the veil of white gauze laid over her from head to feet. He turned down the veil, and set his red rose beside the others that lay at her breast, fresh and dewy as when they had been plucked a hundred years ago.

'Waken,' he said softly, 'oh, waken! Light of my eyes! Desire of my heart!'

But the princess did not awake. Then he put his hand on the silver cloth pillow, and leaned over and kissed her softly, and she put up her arm sleepily round his neck, and kissed him back.

Then she woke, and jumped up, throwing back the golden coverlet.

'Oh, is it you?' she cried. 'What a long time you've been! I've been dreaming about you for a hundred years!'

Then they went out into the hall, hand in hand, to tell the king and queen that they were engaged to be married. And of course the king and queen were awake, and the courtiers. The page finished filling the cup, the butler set the fruit on the table; down at the kennels the huntsman went on feeding the hounds; the cat scratched herself and yawned; and the pigeons circled round the little turrets that were like pepper-pots.

'Mother dear,' said Princess Benevola, running up to the queen and whispering in her ear, 'this is my dear prince who came and woke me up – and I'm going to marry him, and we've never been introduced, and I don't even know his name!'

So they were married, and all the people in the country forgot their republican dream, and woke up as loyal as ever, and all the bells were set a-ringing, and all the children scattered roses of all the colours there are for the bride to walk on as she came out of church.

And when Malevola heard of it she lay down and died of sheer spite to think that anyone in the world was so happy as the prince, and his bride who had been for a hundred years the Sleeping Beauty in the wood!

Wait for It!

JANET McNEILL

*Zelma McCrum is the kind of person strange and colourful
things happen to. So when she says the world will end next
Friday, during the school concert, Mary believes her ...
This story is by a writer who is particularly good at seeing
how funny and fantastic the ordinary world is.*

Zelma's father, Mr McCrum, was the manager of
the cinema in the main street, so Zelma could go
in any time she wanted without paying. Perhaps that
was what made her the sort of person she was.
Everything for Zelma was a size bigger, a shade more
brilliant, more alarming, more fabulous, more breath-
taking than it was for anybody else. She even talked in
capital letters and exclamation marks. She hit top and
bottom notes smack on, but hadn't much interest in
the notes in between. She expected things in everyday
life to happen to her as they did to the heroes and
heroines on the wide, wide screen, and more often
than not she turned out to be right.

She really did have a long-lost uncle in Australia
who arrived in the village without any warning, with
money dripping off the tips of his fingers and sticking
out of his ears. When the very rare bird escaped from
its cage in the Wildlife Sanctuary it was Zelma's back

garden that it chose to roost in, and Zelma's mum
who got on the telly news, saying 'I simply couldn't
believe my eyes!' and pointing to the tree. (You could
see a corner of Zelma's gym blouse flapping on the
clothes-line if you were quick enough to spot it.) When
the Lady Mayoress from the city came to open the
new baths at school she happened to be talking to
Zelma when the man from the newspaper decided to
take the photograph, and there was Zelma next day,
slap in the middle of the front page, smiling every bit
as widely and graciously as the Lady Mayoress, though
not with such impressive teeth.

So one morning when Zelma arrived at school
with her face pink and shiny and her eyes as round
as gooseberries, people steered clear of her. They
knew that 'Come on, coax me, you'll never guess
what' kind of look. Of course they were really itching
to hear the latest excitement, whatever it was,
but they weren't going to please Zelma by letting
her see. It had begun to seem a little unfair to the
Year Nines that life for Zelma McCrum was such a
highly coloured affair, while for the rest of them it was
just a procession of flat brown days, one after another,
so that 'same again' was as much as anybody really
needed to write in his or her diary. All those glossy
white pages had looked and smelled so wonderful at
Christmas, but by the middle of March filling them in
had become a bit of a bore and hardly worth the
effort.

So Zelma prowled around before the bell went,
looking buttoned up and fateful, pining for the loan

of some eager ears, but nobody was willing to oblige. In the end she had to spill the hot news herself, just before the headteacher came into assembly.

'It's the end of the world on Friday week, did you know?' she said to Bill Timmins who was standing next to her.

Bill stopped chewing long enough to say, 'It can't be, there are five more episodes to go,' and Zelma told him not to be a clot, she wasn't talking about the serial on the telly. Bill asked what she was talking about, but there wasn't time for her to answer, because the headmaster had announced the hymn. ' "Courage, brother, do not stumble," ' Zelma sang, in such a smug doomladen voice that Bill lost his nerve and swallowed the rest of his sweet in the middle of the second verse. He'd been hoping that it would last him right through the first lesson.

There wasn't much of a chance to discuss the news or to ask Zelma where her information had come from until break, but a good deal of whispering went on between desks, so that by the time they had spilled out into the playground everybody in the class had heard that according to Zelma McCrum, the world was coming to an end on Friday week.

They were still careful not to let Zelma know she had made an impression, though this wasn't easy. Most people were inclined to be doubtful, a few were openly full of scorn. It was funny on Sunday afternoons when the preacher in the park talked about the end of the world. When Zelma talked about it, it wasn't so funny.

'It's been going to be the end of the world dozens of times and it never has,' Mary protested and Zelma said, 'No, not yet,' and looked mysterious. Someone asked what about the rainbow and God's promise to Noah, and someone else said that was to do with floods, not with the end of the world which was different. 'The world has to come to an end some time,' Stan conceded, and Marlene snapped that the man on the telly had said it wouldn't happen for several billions of light years, which seemed a lot more comfortable than Friday week. Stan said his dad wouldn't half be fed up, because the big match was on the Saturday after the all-important Friday, and Marlene remarked, with a slightly shaky giggle, that her mum's expensive perm – she'd had it done last week – was going to be a bit of a waste then, wasn't it? Everyone was trying to dodge the uncomfortable thought that it was just possible that what Zelma said was true, and how alarming and inconvenient it was going to be. They remembered unwillingly that Zelma had a way of being on the spot when important or exciting things happened – she'd been the only passenger in the school bus the time it went over the hedge and landed up in the middle of the field, and when the helicopter with the Royal Person inside it came down unexpectedly in the park Zelma had been a few yards off, practising her skipping. So on the face of it, it seemed not unlikely that the end of the world, when it happened, would feature Zelma McCrum.

But they needed further details. 'How do you know, anyway?' Stan demanded. He'd sent off a month's pocket-money yesterday for a model construction kit, delivery time three weeks, the advertisement had said. 'Who told you it was Friday week?'

'My mum.'

'But who told your mum?'

'She had a letter from our Aunt Ethel in Canada.'

They remembered Zelma's Aunt Ethel. She had paid a visit home last summer, a sharp-nosed, metallic-tongued, blue-haired lady who said what she thought and had a disturbing way of thinking right. It was Zelma's Aunt Ethel who had declared that Mary's elder sister's baby was twins, when nobody else had even considered the possibility; she had forecast that it would rain on Sports Day, and it came down in buckets; at the church sale she had guessed the weight of the cake to the last half ounce.

'How did your Aunt Ethel know?'

Zelma explained that her Aunt Ethel had been attending a series of lectures given by a very clever and important professor who understood all the signs and portents, and that according to him Friday week was undoubtedly the day.

'Bet you he's got it wrong,' Bill said stoutly, but the supporting murmur wasn't prompt enough to be convincing. Zelma plus her Aunt Ethel plus the professor in Canada might have got it right. Friday week. They gulped and took stock of the situation. Perhaps it would be better to agree and be ready, so that you could be pleased when it didn't happen rather than be caught indignant and open-mouthed when it did.

They didn't talk about it very much among themselves, but next day in assembly when they sang 'Ten Thousand Times Ten Thousand, in Sparkling Raiment Bright', most of them in their secret hearts were thinking that though Zelma might look smashing in her sparkling raiment the rest of them would look and feel a right soft lot, like they had when they were the Roman rabble in *Julius Caesar*. Anyway, eternity was going to be a long, long time. *Julius Caesar* had only been for three performances.

Thinking about next Friday week and what just might possibly be going to happen was like sucking a sweet which never became any smaller and didn't taste good. It was there all the time, waiting for each of them to finish what he or she was doing and remember it again. Mary's head ached with remembering and thinking. By Monday evening she was very tired of the whole idea. No amount of private mockery would chase it. She had hoped that the clergyman might have something helpful to say about it in church on Sunday, but he didn't mention it. She finished her homework early on Monday. She had been learning the 'Tomorrow and tomorrow and tomorrow' speech out of Shakespeare. This was Monday. Perhaps there were now only four tomorrows left. Geography and nature were her other lessons, though the map of Tasmania and the domestic habits of the spider weren't really important if what Zelma's Aunt Ethel's professor had said was right.

It was very comfortable and peaceful in Mary's home this evening. How happy they all were, Mum and Dad

and Grandpa and elder sister Susie who had brought the twins for a visit, and Mary's young brother, Danny. Bliss, Mary thought, would have to be good if it was going to be better than this. The end of the world seemed a pity.

Danny had finished his homework early too. He always talked to Mary about everything on their way to school and on their way home, but he hadn't said a word to her about Friday, though news of it must have leaked into his class. This evening he had brought his cage of pet mice in from the shed and set it down at the back of the sofa in the kitchen. He was handling the little animals one by one. Danny loved those mice. Mary knew that when he was cross or in any sort of trouble he went and talked to his mice and life became smoother. This evening she could see that he was holding them as if they had become even more special and important to him, though if Zelma's aunt was right they might not have the chance of winning any prizes for him at this year's pet show. He picked up the mother mouse who had produced the exciting family of babies a few weeks ago, and looked at her as if he was apologizing that she should have gone to so much trouble.

It occurred to Mary that perhaps they had all heard the news, Mum and Dad and Grandpa and elder sister Susie. They knew what next Friday was. Perhaps they weren't telling her in case she was frightened. The time she'd had her appendix out nobody had told her that the postcard from the hospital had come until the very morning that she was due to go in, though she'd wondered why everybody had been so particularly obliging and kind for a week. Now, because of her uncomfortable secret, Mary found that all kinds of small things became significant. Mum was ironing. Was it Mary's fancy, or was she slapping the iron down on next week's laundry as if it didn't really matter since it was already too late? Grandpa was fidgeting his way through the pages of a newspaper. Now he blew his nose and declared that things couldn't go on like they were for ever, and Mum, suddenly enraged by the price of milk, agreed that there would have to be an end to it all some time. Susie, sitting on the sofa hugging the pink and blue bundles, said weren't they just the sweetest ever, and she didn't want them to grow up.

'Time you were pruning the roses,' Mary's mum said to her dad. Every year, regular as the daffodils, Dad made a fine fuss over pruning the roses. 'This is the time you always do them,' Mum urged, 'not like you to leave it as late as this. I don't know what's got into you.' Dad went on stuffing tobacco into his pipe with his thumb and growled that next week would be time enough. You never knew, he said. You never knew what?

Mum finished the last of the handkerchiefs and switched off the iron. She told Danny to take his mice out to the shed, and he closed the door of their box slowly, allowing the soft noses of the animals to snuffle at his fingers through the wire after he had fastened the latch. Mary knew he never liked making prisoners of them.

'All ready for the big day, are you?' Mum asked Mary.

Mary gulped and remembered just in time that Friday, as well as being the end of the world, was the afternoon of the annual School Concert. She was sorry now that if the end of the world had to happen it couldn't have fallen on Thursday instead of on Friday.

She had been chosen this year to dance a solo dance in the flower-garden scene, and already the idea of being perched up there on the platform in front of everybody's mums and dads, and aunts, uncles and cousins, filled her with bleak private terror. Would she be able to remember her steps? One way and another Friday was going to be an eventful day.

When she had heard that IT was going to happen on Friday she had asked Zelma – in a joking kind of way which meant of course she didn't believe a word of it – whether her Aunt Ethel had given any idea what time IT was going to take place. The morning would have suited Mary so much better than the afternoon. But Zelma told her that Bill Timmins had worked it out, and comparing clocks in England with clocks in Canada, it was due to happen slap in the middle of the concert programme. Around ten or five minutes to four, Bill said, certainly before four o'clock. Mary's solo dance came half-way through the programme. This meant she might start a *pirouette* on the school platform and end up on a fleecy cloud. Of course it was funny if you said it like that. Should it not be solemn and full of awe? It hadn't been funny on the telly when the people of the Out Planet and their planet along with them had come into the range of the Supreme Captain's deadly ray gun, and had all shuddered and twisted, shrunk and withered into swirling wisps of dust. Mary hoped with all her heart that if she had to dance her performance would be complete and she would be back in the wings, crammed comfortably up against the rest of the flower fairies of the Year Nines when whatever it was that might happen would happen, if it did.

On the Thursday before the important Friday the hymn in assembly was 'For those in Peril on the Sea', which was disappointing. It wouldn't make so very much difference, would it, whether you were on the sea or on dry land? On Friday itself nobody noticed what the hymn was. Probably they sang it, but they were watching the school clock and ticking off the hours. The headmaster said he expected all girls and boys to arrive in good time this afternoon, as there was a lot to be got through, and Mary, who was standing next to Bill Timmins, heard him breathe, 'You're telling me!'

In spite of what the headmaster had said Mary was very nearly late for school in the afternoon. This was because Danny, just as they had started off down the path, said he'd forgotten something and slipped round to the back of the house. He was looking a bit peculiar when he joined her again, but Mary, jigging up and down on the gravel, trying to find out if her feet remembered the patterns of the dance and wondering whether it was worth their while to bother, didn't ask and didn't really want to know what it was that Danny had turned back for.

As they went through the gate, Mum tapped at her bedroom window and waved. She was putting on her best hat to come to the concert. 'Good luck!' she called. They waved back. Mary knew that Mum would be glad she'd decided to wear her best hat if the occasion turned out to be as special as Zelma's aunt had declared it would be.

All the way to school Danny didn't utter a word. He was in the choir at school. Mary told herself that he was thinking about the solo verse which he had to sing in the sea shanty. He'd been singing it round the house for weeks, Mary's ears were tired of the sound of it. 'You'll be all right, you know it backwards,' she told him, but he just kicked stones along the gutter and didn't answer. All the ordinary things, as they passed them on the road, seemed different today, in some way remarkable and dear and special. This evening's moon was already in the sky, silver and uncertain.

Nobody at school mentioned Zelma's aunt, but everyone knew how everyone else was feeling. 'All very quiet and sober this afternoon, aren't we?' joked the dancing mistress when she was counting the flower fairies in the girls' cloakroom and they were smoothing the creases out of each other's wings and lining up to have lipstick on their mouths. 'Stage fright, is that it? Well, we must just forget all about that and remember we've come here to enjoy ourselves, mustn't we? No time at all, and it will all be over!'

The concert got under way. The gym display was over. Now Mary could hear the school choir shuffling their way into positions on the stage. 'Not long to wait now,' the dancing mistress said, 'and everyone's going to get a big surprise, aren't they?'

Zelma McCrum was the queen of the flower fairies. The star on the top of her wand was crooked. 'Come here and let me straighten it for you, Zelma,' the dancing mistress said, 'it would never do for you to go on with a crooked star!'

The choir finished 'Lady Greensleeves' and had embarked on the sea shanty. Mary knew that Danny's verse came third. He got through it with only a hint of a wobble. Good for Danny. The choir sang 'I will arise and go now', and came down from the platform. Their feet were loud in the passage as they went past the girls' cloakroom. People in the hall were clapping. The clock on the cloakroom wall said twenty-five to four. It had moved almost to ten to four when the Infants' Class had finished their recitations and the dancing mistress gave the signal for the flower fairies to move forward, ready for their entrance. Through the window in the passage, Mary could see that the afternoon sky was darkening and that the moon had changed from silver to very pale gold.

Zelma led the way. The stage hands had already wheeled her flowery throne into position, ready for her. Someone gave her a leg up, and she struck her royal pose bravely, trying to avoid the prickles of the plastic petals. The art class had certainly done a good job with that throne. They had banked roses and carnations, lilies, delphiniums and orchids in such massed profusion that nothing of the wooden frame which the carpentry class had made was visible. Mary envied Zelma her throne. It seemed a good place to be in case IT happened.

Zelma's star was crooked again. 'Oh Zelma!' cried the dancing mistress, but she was too late, the music had begun, the curtain was lifting, the first of the flower fairies came from the wings to do homage to their queen.

Mary's solo dance was almost due, she would be the next fairy to make an entrance. 'Ready, Mary?' whispered the dancing mistress, prodding gently, and Mary took a step forward, making sure that her wings were rigid and that her weight was on the right foot.

From here she couldn't see the clock. She had a good view of the stage, with Marlene and Lil drifting around waving their sheaves of poppies. She could see the queen, remote and serene, perhaps a trace uneasy. Was Zelma remembering her Aunt Ethel, or had she after all landed on a spike? She could see the pale faces of the first four rows of parents and relations, their heads tilted comically back into their necks, their faces smiling. She could see the young man from the newspaper fidgeting about on the side aisle with his camera, waiting for a dramatic moment.

Surely Marlene and Lil were being a little too careless with their poppy sheaves. Perhaps their hands were shaky, probably they could see the clock. 'Not all over the place like that,' scolded the dancing mistress in a useless whisper, 'nice and even, nice and even, one-and-two-and- a BIG FIRM CURVE!' A few of the poppies came loose and fell out, and Mary heard the dancing mistress sigh and click her tongue crossly against her teeth.

And then – then Mary heard something else. The music had sunk to a faint whisper of melody, Marlene and Lil were kneeling in homage before their sovereign. But outside from the street the village clock struck four o'clock, firm and clear, the friendly voice that Mary had heard all her life, at home and at school, dividing up the days and the nights so that nothing lasted too long and everything that was wonderful and exciting really did happen in the end. It was four o'clock. If it happened, Bill had said it would certainly happen before four. Four o'clock! That meant that Zelma was wrong, that Zelma's Aunt Ethel was wrong, that the important professor in Canada was wrong! The world was going on.

'Now Mary!' the dancing mistress directed, prodding again.

Mary knew from the moment she took her first step on to the stage that there was nothing at all to fear, from herself or from her audience. She felt the footlights flood warmly over her, she felt the expectant attention of all those rows of people. They were waiting for her. She would make it worth their while. Her feet and her arms and her legs were her obedient servants, she created the pattern of the music as she danced. Any mistake was impossible. She wasn't dancing in homage to the queen of the plastic flower fairies, or because the dancing mistress had prodded her and told her to dance. She was giving thanks and praise, she was dancing hallelujahs and hosannas, she was laughing at herself and at Zelma McCrum and at Zelma's Aunt Ethel. She was celebrating all the unwritten tomorrows in her diary.

Perhaps it was the force of the applause that greeted

her performance, perhaps Zelma had reached the end of her endurance and had leaned too far forward, perhaps the carpentry class hadn't secured the framework for the flowery bower as well as they should have done. Perhaps the relief of all the other children who had also heard the clock striking set off some kind of communal vibration. Whatever it was, just as Mary completed her dance and sank in a low, slow curtsy, there was a sharp creaking noise from the throne, then a rumble and a crack. Dozens of lilies, festoons of orchids, whole banks of roses, carnations and delphiniums in abundance shuddered and sagged, came apart and scattered, and then the whole of the floral edifice collapsed round the fairy queen. One shoe and the star on her wand appeared above the wreckage. Out in the hall the pale rows of faces were laughing – forgive them, they were laughing!

Afterwards Mary walked home with Danny. Mum and Dad had gone ahead so that Grandpa wouldn't have to wait too long for his tea. 'You were all right,' Danny said sideways to Mary, and she said, 'You were all right yourself.'

The moon, now established high in the sky, burned firmly, and every star was steady and secure in its place. All the landmarks on the way home were waiting for them. The garden gate, as Mary swung it open, felt hard and solid to her fingertips.

Mum was in the hall. She had taken off her hat and was smoothing back her hair. 'You danced splendidly, Mary,' she said, 'everybody was saying they'd never seen you dance as well. Your dad and I were real proud! What a mercy you got your piece over before the throne fell down!'

Dad had come in from the back door. He had been out at the shed fetching coal. 'It was champion, Mary,' he said, but his face was worried. He turned to Danny. 'Danny, before you went out did you see to your mice?'

Danny nodded.

'Something wrong, Dad?' Mum asked.

'The door of their box hadn't been properly latched. You can look for yourself, lad.'

Danny headed out into the yard with Mary following him. The door of the cage swung unfastened. The cage was empty.

'Oh Danny!' Mary cried. 'Oh, Danny! They've gone, every one of them!'

To her surprise Danny snapped 'All right, you don't need to tell me!'

'You mean – you mean you knew?'

His finger fiddled with the catch on the door. He nodded.

Then Mary understood. 'That was why you went back when you said you'd forgotten something. You left the cage open yourself.'

Danny nodded again. He didn't look at her. 'In case Zelma was right,' he growled, 'in case it did happen. It didn't seem fair for them to be locked up at a time like that. Gosh, it wasn't half funny this afternoon when the throne fell down!' and he laughed and gave the empty box a shove with his toe.

Zelma McCrum? Oh yes, it was a splendid photograph that the young man from the newspaper had taken. It filled half a page. There was Zelma stepping delicately out from the floral debris, wings, crown and star all crooked, but smiling like true royalty and wiggling her fingertips at the camera.

'Young Zelma McCrum,' the newspaper said, 'unthroned but undismayed. "After all," the queen of the flower fairies told our reporter gaily, "anything can happen. It wasn't as if it was the end of the world!"'

Tom's Evening Out

ALEXANDRE DUMAS
retold by Troy Alexander

Alexandre Dumas wrote long, exciting stories, like The Three Musketeers *and* The Count of Monte Cristo. *He was also a playwright, a journalist, and a very good cook! He wrote stories for children, and was very fond of animals, writing an entire book of stories about his own pets. Here is another of his animal stories, this time about a friend's pet.*

In the year 1832, a well-known artist named Décamps lived in Paris. He was a close friend of many of the best and most famous writers, artists and scientists of his time, and he adored animals of all kinds. He loved painting them, and his studio was like a small zoo – a bear, a monkey, a tortoise and a frog lived there together in peace and harmony (more or less).

The bear was called Tom, the monkey's name was Jacko I, the frog was Mademoiselle Camargo and the tortoise was Gazelle.

This story is about Tom, the bear. Tom had only lived in Paris for six months, but he was one of the nicest bears you could hope to meet. He would run and open the door when the doorbell rang, he played soldiers, standing on guard for hours on end on his hind legs with a halberd in his paw, and he could dance a minuet most gracefully, holding a broomstick behind his head.

It was the night of Shrove Tuesday. Tom had spent all his time that day practising his skills – everyone who had come to the studio had enjoyed watching him – and he had gone to bed in the cupboard he used as a hutch, when there was a knock at the front door. Jacko immediately got so excited that Décamps guessed that the visitor must be Fan, the person who had appointed himself teacher to the two animals. He was quite right, for a moment later, the studio door opened, and Fan came in, dressed as a clown. Jacko hurled himself joyfully into Fan's arms.

'Very good, very good,' said Fan, putting the monkey down on the table and giving him a stick. 'You're a charming creature. *Shoulder arms – present arms – make ready – fire!* Well done! I'll have a proper uniform made for you, and you can come and be a soldier, instead of me. But it's not you I've come for tonight. It's your friend Tom I want. Where is he?'

'In his cupboard, I expect,' said Décamps.

'Tom! Here, Tom!' called Fan.

Tom gave a low growl, just to show he knew they were talking about him, but was in no hurry to come out.

'Well!' exclaimed Fan. 'Is this how you obey my orders? Tom, my dear chap, don't push me to extremes!'

Tom stretched one big paw out of the cupboard, without showing any more of himself, and started to yawn pathetically, like a child who has just woken up from his first sleep.

'Where's the broomstick?' asked Fan threateningly, as he rattled through the collection of bows, arrows and spears that stood behind the door.

'Ready!' cried Décamps, pointing at Tom who, hearing these familiar sounds, had got up without further ado, and was walking towards his teacher looking quite innocent and blameless.

'That's right,' said Fan, 'now be a good bear, particularly since I've come all this way on purpose to collect you.'

Tom nodded his head up and down.

'Right – now shake hands with your friends – well done!'

'Are you proposing to take him out with you?' asked Décamps.

'Yes, indeed!' replied Fan. 'And I'm going to give him a good time, too.'

'And where are you going?'

'To the Masked Ball at the Mardi Gras carnival, no less! Now then, Tom, old man, come along. I've got a cab I've hired waiting outside.'

As though he appreciated the force of this argument, Tom went downstairs four steps at a time, followed by his friend. The cab driver opened the door, and Tom, guided by Fan, got in as though he had always ridden in cabs.

'My eye! That's a queer sort of fancy dress,' said the cabby. 'Anyone would think he was a real bear. Where to, gentlemen?'

'The Odéon Theatre,' said Fan.

'Grrrrh,' commented Tom.

'All right,' said the cabby. 'Keep your hair on. It's a good way from here, but we'll get there eventually.'

Half an hour later, the cab stopped at the theatre door. Fan got down first, paid the driver, helped Tom out, bought two tickets, and went inside without attracting any special attention.

By the time they had walked round the crush-bar twice, people were beginning to follow Fan. Some lovers of natural history had noticed how perfectly his companion imitated the walk and movements of the animal whose skin he was wearing. They came closer and closer, hoping to find out if he was equally good at imitating a bear's voice, and then started to pull at his fur and ears.

'Grrrrh,' said Tom.

An admiring murmur ran through the crowd. The sound was completely lifelike!

Fan led Tom to the buffet, and offered him some little cakes. He liked these very much, and started to eat them so greedily that the people around him began to laugh. Then Fan poured out a tumbler of water, which Tom took carefully in his paws – as he was used to doing whenever Décamps allowed him to have his dinner at the table – and with one swallow he gulped the water down. The crowd was very enthusiastic. In fact, they were so pleased and interested that when Fan eventually tried to leave the buffet, he found they were penned in by such a huge crowd he was afraid that Tom might be frightened, and try and clear a space with his claws and teeth. He therefore led the bear to a corner, placed him with his back to a wall, and told him to wait there until he got further instructions.

As has already been mentioned, this sort of thing was quite normal for Tom, and suited his basic laziness. A harlequin offered him a hat, and he settled down comfortably, with one big paw on his wooden gun.

'Do you know who you've lent your hat to?' said Fan to the harlequin.

'No,' replied the harlequin.

'You mean to say you can't guess?'

'No, not at all.'

'Well, take a good look at him. See the graceful way he moves, look at the way he holds his head slightly on one side, like Alexander the Great, listen to his brilliant imitation of a bear's voice – can you really not guess who it is?'

'Absolutely not – I haven't a clue.'

'It's Odry!' whispered Fan mysteriously. 'You know the famous comedian Odry – he's dressed in his costume from *The Bear and the Pasha*!'

'Oh, but he acts a white bear in that play, you know.'

'Exactly! That's why he's chosen a brown bear's skin as a disguise.'

'Brilliant! That's fantastic,' cried the harlequin.

'Grrrrh,' said Tom.

'Well, now you mention it, I do recognize his voice. I'm surprised I hadn't spotted it before. You must ask him to disguise it better.'

'Yes,' said Fan, moving towards the ballroom. 'But it wouldn't do to annoy him. However, in a little while I'll try and persuade him to dance a minuet.'

'Oh, could you really?'

'He promised he would. Just pass it on to your friends, and try and stop them from teasing him.'

'All right.'

Fan made his way through the crowd, while the delighted harlequin went from one masked guest to another, passing on the message, which people accepted happily.

Just then the sounds of a lively dance tune were heard, and there was a general rush into the ballroom. The harlequin paused for a moment to whisper in Tom's ear, 'I know you, in spite of your fine costume.'

'Grrrrh,' replied Tom.

'Growl if you like, but you will dance a minuet, won't you, old man?'

Tom nodded his head up and down, as he did when

anyone asked him a question, and the harlequin, pleased with this silent consent, ran off to find a columbine and join in the dance.

Tom stayed behind in the crush-bar with the waiters, keeping quite still as he'd been instructed, but looking longingly at the table where there were large numbers of plates piled with delicious cakes. The waiters noticed his steady gaze, and wanting to encourage a customer, offered him a plate. Tom stretched out his paw, and carefully took a cake – then a second one, then a third. The waiters didn't seem to get tired of offering them, or Tom of taking them, and so when the dance finished and the dancers came back to the crush-bar, Tom had finished dozens of little cakes.

Harlequin had found a columbine and a shepherdess, and he introduced them to Tom as partners for the minuet. He whispered a few words to Tom as though he were an old friend, and Tom, who was feeling very happy after eating so many cakes, replied with his most gracious growl. The harlequin, turning towards the throng, announced that his lordship was pleased to comply with everyone's request. To loud applause, the shepherdess took one of Tom's paws and the columbine took the other. Tom walked between his two partners like an accomplished escort, looking at them in turn in a surprised way. He soon found himself with his partners on the dance floor – the theatre pit, which was used as a ballroom. Some of the spectators watched from the boxes, others from the galleries, but most of them formed a circle round the dancers. The orchestra struck up.

Tom's Evening Out

The minuet was Tom's greatest triumph, and Fan's masterpiece. It was a success from the beginning, and by the time Tom reached the end of the dance the applause was thunderous.

Tom was swept off triumphantly into a box, where the shepherdess took the wreath of roses off her head and crowned Tom with it. The watchers' applause was so huge the whole theatre rang.

Tom leaned over the front of the box gracefully just as the sounds of the orchestra striking up a new dance were heard. Everyone went off to find partners, except a few people who stayed behind hoping to get free tickets for the theatre from Tom, but to all their hints he only said, 'Grrrrh'.

After a while this became rather boring, and gradually the people round Tom drifted away. They said to themselves that although he was brilliant dancer, his conversation was rather dull. An hour later, Tom was on his own – so brief is public popularity!

The ball was nearly over. The dance floor was emptying, and there was no one in the boxes. The pale light of morning was glimmering into the hall when a cleaner, doing her rounds, heard snoring coming from one of the boxes that overlooked the stage. She opened the door, and there was Tom, who was tired out after his exciting night, and had gone to sleep on the floor. The cleaner stepped into the box, and told him it was six o'clock in the morning, and time to go home.

'Grrrrh,' said Tom.

'Yes, indeed,' said the cleaner, 'I heard you – I know you're asleep, my good man, but you'll sleep even better in your own bed. Come on, your wife must be getting worried about you! Goodness – I don't think he's heard a word I said! He's really deeply asleep!' And she shook Tom by the shoulder.

'Grrrrh!'

'All right, all right! It's time to stop pretending. We all know who you are. Look, they're putting out the lights. Shall I get you a cab?'

'Grrrrrrrrrrh.'

'Come on – the Odéon Theatre isn't a hotel! Come on – go home! Now stop that at once! Really, Monsieur Odry – that's quite enough! I'll call the guard – the officer on duty hasn't gone home yet. Now, now! You won't behave? Are you trying to hit me? A woman – and I used to work in your company, Monsieur Odry. Stop it this minute! Here, help – guards – inspector – help!'

'What's the matter?' shouted the fireman on duty.

'Help!' screamed the cleaner, 'help!'

'What's the matter?' asked the sergeant whose men had been on guard at the ball.

'Oh, it's old mother what's her name, shrieking for help in one of the boxes!'

'Coming!' called the sergeant.

'This way, this way,' called the cleaner.

'All right, my dear, here I am. Where are you?'

'Down here – come on, there are no steps – straight on this way – he's in the corner. Oh, the beast – he's as strong as an ox!'

'Grrrrh,' said Tom.

'Did you hear that? What sort of language is that?'

'Come on, chum,' said the sergeant, who had at last worked out where Tom was in the dim light. 'We all know what it is to be young – I like a joke as much as anyone – but rules are rules, and it's time to go home. So up you get – come on, hop it!'

'Grrrrh . . . '

'OK – it's a great imitation. But let's try something else for a change. Come on, old man, get moving. Oh! You won't! You're going to be difficult, are you? Come on, lads, get a grip on him and turn him out.'

'He won't walk, Sergeant.'

'Well, what are the butt ends of your muskets for? Come on, a tap or two won't hurt.'

'Grrrrrrrr – Grrrrrrrrh – Grrrrrrrrh — '

'Go on, give it to him.'

'I say, Sergeant,' said one of the men, 'strikes me he's a *real* bear. I caught hold of him by the collar just now, and the skin seems to be growing on the flesh.'

'Oh, if he's a real bear, then treat him very carefully. His owner might sue for damages. Go and get a lantern from that fireman.'

'Grrrrh.'

'Here's the lantern,' said someone. 'Now, throw some light on the prisoner.'

The soldier did as he was ordered.

'That's definitely a real snout,' declared the sergeant.

'Help!' shrieked the cleaner, running off. 'A real live bear!'

'Yes, indeed, a real live bear. Let's see if he has a name and address on him, and take him home. I expect he's strayed, and being a friendly bear came into the masked ball.'

'Grrrrh.'

'There you are! He agrees.'

'Hey!' called out one of the guards.

'What's the matter?'

'He has a little bag hanging round his neck.'

'Open the bag.'

'A card!'

'Read the card.'

The soldier took the card out and read: 'My name is Tom. I live at 109 Faubourg St Denis. I have five francs in my purse, two for a cab, and three for whoever takes me home.'

'That's right, there are five francs in the bag,' exclaimed the sergeant. 'Now then, two volunteers for escort duty.'

'Here!' cried every soldier.

'Don't all speak at once! The two seniors can have the job – off with you, lads!'

Two of the municipal guards came up to Tom, and slipped a rope round his neck, with an extra loop round his snout, just in case. Tom didn't resist – he didn't want to be tapped with the butt end of a musket again. When they were fifty yards away from the theatre one of the soldiers said, 'I say! It's a fine morning. Suppose we don't take a cab. The walk will do him good.'

'Right,' said the other. 'Then we should have two and a half francs each, instead of only one and a half.'

'OK.'

Half an hour later they stood at the door of 109.

After knocking hard, a very sleepy concièrge looked out.

'Look out here, Mother Wideawake,' said one of the soldiers. 'Here's one of your lodgers. Do you recognize him?'

'Why, indeed I do. It's Monsieur Décamps' bear!'

That same day, Odry the comedian was mystified to receive a bill for cakes, totalling seven and a half francs.

The Hookywalker Dancers

MARGARET MAHY

After a story about a bear dancing a minuet, another about dancing animals . . . even more unexpected ones! This tale is wild and funny and imaginative – just the kind of story that New Zealander Margaret Mahy is famous for writing.

In the heart of the great city of Hookywalker was the School of Dramatic Art. It was full of all sorts of actors and singers and wonderful clowns, but the most famous of them all was the great dancer, Brighton.

Brighton could leap like an antelope and spin like a top. He was as slender as a needle. In fact, when he danced you almost expected little stitches to follow him across the stage. Every day he did his exercises at the *barre* to music played on his tape-recorder.

'One and a *plié* and a stretch, two-three, and *port de bras* and back to first!' he counted. He exercised so gracefully that, outside the School of Dramatic Art, pedlars rented ladders so that lovers of the dance could climb up and look through the window at Brighton practising.

Of course, life being what it is, many other dancers were often jealous of him. I'm afraid that most of them ate too much and were rather fat, whereas Brighton had an elegant figure. They pulled his chair away from under him when he sat down, or tried to trip him up in the middle of his dancing, but Brighton was so graceful he simply made falling down look like an exciting new part of the dance, and the people standing on ladders clapped and cheered and banged happily on the windows.

Although he was such a graceful dancer, Brighton was not conceited. He led a simple life. For instance, he didn't own a car, travelling everywhere on roller-skates, his tape-recorder clasped to his ear. Not only this, he did voluntary work for the Society for Bringing Happiness to Dumb Beasts. At the weekends he would put on special performances for pets and farm animals. Savage dogs became quiet as lambs after watching Brighton dance, and nervous sheep grew wool thicker than ever before. Farmers from outlying districts would ring up the School of Dramatic Art and ask if they could hire Brighton to dance to their cows, and many a parrot, temporarily off its seed, was brought back to full appetite by seeing Brighton dance the famous solo called *The Noble Savage in the Lonely Wood*.

Brighton had a way of kicking his legs up that suggested deep sorrow, and his *demi-pliés* regularly brought tears to the eyes of the parrots, after which they tucked into their seed quite ravenously.

One day, the director of the School for Dramatic Art called Brighton to his office.

'Brighton,' he said, 'I have an urgent request here from a farmer who needs help with a flock of very nervous sheep. He is in despair!'

'Glad to help!' said Brighton in his graceful fashion. 'What seems to be the trouble?'

'Wolves – that's what the trouble is!' cried the director. 'He lives on the other side of the big forest, and a pack of twenty wolves comes out of the forest early every evening and tries to devour some of his prize merinos. It's disturbing the sheep very badly. They get nervous twitches, and their wool is falling out from shock.'

'I'll set off at once,' Brighton offered. 'I can see it's an urgent case.'

'It's a long way,' the director said, doubtfully. 'It's right on the other side of the forest.'

'That's all right,' said Brighton. 'I have my trusty roller-skates, and the road is tarred all the way. I'll take my tape-recorder to keep me company, and I'll get there in next to no time.'

'That's very fast,' the director said in a respectful voice. 'Oh, Brighton, I wish all my dancers were like you! Times are hard for the School of Dramatic Art. A lot of people are staying at home and watching car crashes on television. They don't want art – they want danger, they want battle, murder and sudden death – and it's becoming much harder to run the school at a profit. If all our dancers were as graceful as you there would be no problem at all, but as you know a lot of them are just a whisker on the fat side. They don't do their exercises the way they should.'

Little did he realize that the other dancers were actually listening at the keyhole, and when they heard this critical remark they all began to sizzle with jealousy. You could hear them sizzling with it. 'I'll show him who's fat and who isn't,' muttered a very spiteful dancer called Antoine. 'Where are Brighton's skates?'

Brighton's skates were, in fact, in the cloakroom under the peg on which he hung his beret and his great billowing cape. It was but the work of a moment to loosen one or two vital grommets. The skates looked all right, but they were no longer as safe as skates ought to be.

'There,' said Antoine, laughing nastily. 'They'll hold together for a little bit, but once he gets into the forest they'll collapse, and we'll see how he gets on then, all alone with the wind and the wolves – and without wheels.'

The halls of the School of Dramatic Art rang with the jealous laughter of the other dancers as they slunk off in all directions. A minute later Brighton came in, suspecting nothing, put on his beret and his great billowing cape, strapped on his skates, and set off holding his tape-recorder to his ear.

Now, during the day, the wolves spent a long time snoozing and licking their paws clean in a clearing on top of the hill. From there they had a good view of the Hookywalker road. They could look out in all directions and even see as far as Hookywalker when the air was clear. It happened that their present king was a great thinker, and something was worrying him deeply.

'I know we're unpopular,' sighed the King of the Wolves, 'but what can I do about it? It's the nature of things that wolves steal a few sheep here and there. It's part of the great pattern of nature.' Though this seemed reasonable he was frowning and brooding as he spoke. 'Sometimes – I don't know – I feel there must be more to life than just ravening around grabbing the odd sheep and howling at the moon.'

'Look!' cried the wolf who was on look-out duty. 'Someone is coming down the great road from the city.'

'How fast he's going!' said another wolf. 'And whatever is it he is holding to his ear?'

'Perhaps he has earache,' suggested a female wolf in compassionate tones. None of the wolves had ever seen a tape-recorder before.

'Now then, no feeling sorry for him,' said the King of the Wolves. 'You all know the drill. We get down to the edge of the road, and at the first chance we tear him to pieces. That's all part of the great pattern of nature I was mentioning a moment ago.'

'That'll take his mind off his earache,' said one of the wolves with a fierce, sarcastic snarl.

As the sun set majestically in the west, Brighton, his cloak billowing round him like a private storm cloud, reached the great forest. It was like entering another world, for a mysterious twilight reigned under the wide branches, a twilight without moon or stars. Tall, sombre pines looked down as if they feared the worst. But Brighton skated on, humming to himself. He was listening to the music of *The Noble Savage* and was waiting for one of the parts he liked best. Indeed, so busy was he humming and counting the beats that he did not notice a sudden wobble in his wheels. However, a moment after the wobble, his skates gave a terrible screech and he was pitched into the pine needles by the side of the road.

'Horrakapotchkin!' cried Brighton. 'My poor skates!' (It was typical of this dancer that his first thought was for others.) However, his second thought was of the forest and the wolves that might be lurking there. It occurred to him that they might be tired of merino sheep, and would fancy a change of diet.

'Quick thought! Quick feet!' he said, quoting an old dancing proverb. He rushed around collecting a pile of firewood and pine-cones, and then lit a good-sized fire there on the roadside. It was just as well he did, because when he looked up he saw the forest was alight with fiery red eyes. The wolves had arrived. They stole out of the forest and sat down on the edge of the firelight, staring at him very hard, all licking their lips in a meaningful way.

Brighton did not panic. Quietly, he rewound his tape-recorder to the very beginning, and then stood up coolly and began to do his exercises. A lesser dancer might have started off dancing straight away, but Brighton knew the greatest challenge of his life was ahead of him. He preferred to take things slowly and warm up properly in case he needed to do a few tricky steps before the night was out.

The wolves looked at each other uneasily. The king hesitated. There was something so tuneful about the music and so graceful about Brighton's dancing that he would have liked to watch it for a bit longer, but he knew he was part of nature's great plan, and must help his pack to tear Brighton to pieces. So he gave the order. 'Charge!'

As one wolf the wolves ran towards Brighton, snarling and growling, but to their astonishment Brighton did not run away. No! He actually ran towards them and then, leaped up in the air – up, up and right over them – his cloak streaming out behind him. It had the words HOOKYWALKER SCHOOL OF DRAMATIC ART painted on it. The wolves were going so fast that they could not stop themselves until they were well down the road. Brighton, meanwhile, landed with a heroic gesture, wheeled around, and then went on with his exercises, watching the wolves narrowly.

Once again, the wolves charged, and once again Brighton leaped. This time he jumped even higher, and the wolves couldn't help gasping in admiration, much as they hated missing out on any prey.

'Right!' cried the King of the Wolves. 'Let's run round him in ever-decreasing circles.' (This was an old wolf trick.) 'He'll soon be too giddy to jump.' However, being a wolf and not used to classical ballet, the king didn't realize that a good dancer can spin on his toes without getting in the least bit giddy. Brighton spun until he was a mere blur and actually rose several inches in the air with the power of his rotation. It was the wolves who became giddy first; they stumbled over one another, ending up in a heap, with their red eyes all crossed. Finally, they struggled up with their tongues hanging out but they had to wait for their eyes to get uncrossed again.

Seeing they were disabled for the moment by the

wonder of his dancing, Brighton now gave up mere
jumps and spins and began demonstrating his
astonishing technique. Used as he was to dancing for
animals, there was still a real challenge about touching
the hearts of wolves. Besides, he knew he couldn't go
on twirling and leaping high in the air all night. His
very life depended on the quality of his dancing. He
began with the first solo from *The Noble Savage*. Never

in all his life, even at the School of Dramatic Art, had he been more graceful. First, he danced the loneliness of the Noble Savage, and the wolves (though they always travelled in a pack, and were never ever lonely) were so stirred that several of them pointed their noses into the air and howled in exact time to the music. It was most remarkable. Brighton now turned towards the wolves and began to express through dance his pleasure at seeing them. He made it very convincing. Some of the wolves began to wag their tails.

'He's really got something!' said the King of the Wolves. 'This is high-class stuff.' Of course, he said it in wolf language, but Brighton was good at reading the signs and became more poetic than ever before.

'Let me see,' said the King of the Wolves, fascinated. 'With a bit of practice I could manage an act like this myself. I always knew there was more to life than mere ravening. Come on! Let's give it a go!' The wolves began to point their paws and copy whatever movements Brighton made.

Seeing what they were about, Brighton began to encourage them by doing a very simple step and shouting instructions.

'You put your left paw in, you put your left paw out . . . '

Of course, the wolves could not understand the words, but Brighton was very clever at mime and they caught on to the idea of things, dancing with great enthusiasm. Naturally, they were not as graceful as Brighton, but then they had not practised for years as he had. Brighton could not help but be proud of them as they began a slow progress down the road back to the city, away from the forest and the sheep on the other side. The moon rose higher in the sky, and still Brighton danced, and the entranced wolves followed him pointing their paws. It was very late at night when they entered the city once more. People going home from the cinema stared and shouted, and pointed (fingers not toes). A lot of them joined in, either dancing or making music on musical instruments – banjos, trombones, combs – or anything that happened to be lying around.

In the School of Dramatic Art, wicked Antoine was just about to dance the very part Brighton usually danced when the sound of the procession made him hesitate. The audience, full of curiosity, left the theatre. Outside was Brighton, swaying with weariness but still dancing, followed by twenty wolves, all dancing most beautifully by now, all in time and all very pleased with themselves, though, it must be admitted, all very hungry.

'Oh,' cried the director of the School of Dramatic Art, rushing out to kiss Brighton on both cheeks. 'What talent! What style! This will save the School of Dramatic Art from extinction.'

'Send out for a supply of sausages,' panted Brighton, 'and write into the wolves' contracts that they will have not only sausages of the best quality, but that their names will appear in lights on top of the theatre. After all, if they are dancing here every night, they won't be able to chase and worry sheep, will they?'

After this, there was peace for a long time, both in

the city and out on the farms (where the sheep grew very fat and woolly). The School of Dramatic Art did wonderfully well. People came from miles around to see Brighton and his dancing wolves, and, of course – just as he had predicted – after dancing until late at night, the wolves were too weary to go out ravening sheep. Everyone was delighted (except for the jealous dancers who just sulked and sizzled). Antoine, in particular, had such bad attacks of jealousy that it ruined his digestion and made his stomach rumble loudly, which forced him to abandon ballet altogether. However, Brighton, the wolves, the farmers, the director, and many other people, lived happily ever after in Hookywalker, that great city which people sometimes see looming out of the mist on the fringe of many fairy stories.

The Nutcracker

E. T. A. HOFFMANN
translated and retold by Anthea Bell

The original story of the nutcracker was a mysterious, rather scary tale for adults, written by the German author E. T. A. Hoffmann. Alexandre Dumas (whose story about Tom the bear is in this collection) rewrote Hoffmann's story for children, and it's this version that was used to create the famous ballet The Nutcracker, *with music by Peter Tchaikovsky. Another of Hoffmann's stories was turned into the ballet* Coppélia.

It was after dark on Christmas Eve when little Marie and her brother Fritz had their Christmas presents – for presents are given on Christmas Eve in Germany, where Marie and Fritz lived in the last century. They had some wonderful presents, too: dolls, toy soldiers, picture books, and a beautiful toy castle their godfather, old Mr Drosselmeier, had made them. However, the present Marie liked best of all was a nutcracker in the shape of a dear little man with a funny, kindly face, and dressed in fine clothes. She was very sad when her brother Fritz, playing roughly with Nutcracker, broke his jaw. Marie tied poor Nutcracker's head up in her handkerchief, and nursed him for the rest of the evening, sitting on in the living-room with all the toys after the rest of the family had gone to bed.

Just as Marie put Nutcracker away in the toy cupboard, the clock struck twelve. And on the stroke of midnight, some very strange things began to happen. Mice came out from behind the skirting and up through the cracks in the floorboards: a whole army of mice led by the terrible great Mouse King, who had seven heads. Then all the dolls and soldiers and the other toys came to life.

Nutcracker himself drew his little sword, waved it in the air, and shouted, 'My loyal subjects, will you stand by me in battle?'

'Yes, sir, we'll follow you to death or glory!' replied the toys.

Under Nutcracker's command, the toys fought a great battle with the mice. At last, however, Nutcracker was driven right back to the glass-fronted toy cupboard, with only a few of his soldiers. The Mouse King himself scurried up, all seven throats squealing triumphantly. Nutcracker was in great danger, and Marie, watching, couldn't bear it any longer.

'Oh, poor Nutcracker!' she sobbed.

Hardly knowing what she was doing, she took off her left shoe and threw it into the middle of the mice, aiming at their king. Then everything swam in front of her eyes, she felt a pain in her left arm, and she fell to the floor in a faint.

When Marie woke she was lying in her bed, with the doctor and her mother beside her. 'Oh, Mother, have the nasty mice gone away? Is Nutcracker all right?' she whispered.

'Now, Marie, you mustn't talk nonsense!' said Mother. 'What a fright you gave us! You must have stayed up so late playing that you felt sleepy, and when something startled you, you put your arm through the glass in the toy cupboard door and cut yourself quite badly. I found you on the floor there, with all the toys lying around you. Nutcracker was beside you, and your left shoe was on the floor a little way off.' And when Marie tried to tell her mother and the doctor about the great battle they wouldn't believe her, but said she had a temperature and must stay in bed for a few days.

Poor Marie was very bored, but one evening Godfather Drosselmeier came to see her and Fritz. To her delight, he brought her Nutcracker back, with his jaw mended. 'But he's not the most handsome of fellows, you must admit,' said Godfather Drosselmeier. 'If you like, I'll tell you how the Nutcracker family came to be so ugly! Have you ever heard the story of Princess Pirlipat, Mistress Mousie the witch, and the Watchmaker? It's called the "Tale of the Hard Nut".'

Some months before the birth of Princess Pirlipat (Godfather Drosselmeier told the children) her father the king invited some other kings and princes to a great banquet of sausages. The queen herself made the sausages in a big golden pot, and the moment came when fat bacon for the mixture was to be cut up and fried in silver pans. As the bacon began to sizzle, the queen heard a tiny voice whispering, 'Give me some

of that bacon, sister! I'm a queen too, and I'd like to join the feast!'

The speaker was Mistress Mousie, who claimed to be Queen of Mousolia, and held court under the kitchen stove. 'Come along, Mistress Mousie,' said the kind queen, 'and you may have some of my bacon.' But Mistress Mousie's seven great, rough sons came out too, fell upon the bacon, and ate nearly all of it. When the sausages were served, the king was in dismay.

'Not enough bacon!' he gasped, vowing to be revenged on Mistress Mousie for stealing it. And he called in his Court Watchmaker, whose name (said Godfather Drosselmeier) happened to be Drosselmeier just like mine, and who made some clever little mousetraps to catch Mistress Mousie's seven sons. One day, while the queen was cooking her husband's supper, Mistress Mousie reappeared.

'My sons are dead!' said she. 'So take care the Mouse Queen doesn't bite your own little princess in two!'

When Princess Pirlipat was born, there had never been a prettier baby. Her little face was soft and pink and white, her eyes were bright blue, and she had shining, curly golden hair. Everyone was delighted except for the queen, who worried over Mistress Mousie's threat. She had Pirlipat's cradle very closely guarded. Two nurses had to sit beside the cradle, and by night there were six more nurses in the room, each holding a cat on her lap, stroking it all the time to keep it awake and purring, for the Court Astronomer had said this was the only way to keep Mistress Mousie away.

One night, however, one of the nurses woke from a deep sleep. All the other nurses and the cats were asleep too – and a huge, ugly mouse was standing on its hind legs with its dreadful head on the princess's face. The nurse leaped up, with a cry of horror, the others woke too, and Mistress Mousie scuttled away. Little Pirlipat began wailing miserably. When the nurses looked at her, they were horrified. Her angelic, pink and white face had changed to a fat, shapeless head on a tiny shrivelled body.

The king and queen were dreadfully upset. The king blamed it all on the Court Watchmaker for catching Mistress Mousie's sons in his mousetraps, and decreed that he must find out how to restore the princess to her old shape, or he would be beheaded.

With the help of the Court Astronomer, the Court Watchmaker discovered that the spell on the princess would be broken if she ate the sweet kernel of the crackatuck nut. It must be bitten open by a man who had never shaved, and never worn boots, and he must give her the nut with his eyes shut and take seven steps backward without stumbling before he opened them again.

So the Watchmaker set out in search of the crackatuck nut. He had been on his travels for fifteen years when he went to see his cousin, a dollmaker, and told him his story. To his surprise and delight, the dollmaker had the crackatuck nut itself in his possession, and the dollmaker's son, young Drosselmeier, who had never shaved or worn a pair of boots, was just the man to open it.

But there were other young men too who wanted to try cracking the nut, since the king had promised his daughter's hand in marriage to anyone who could do it. Nobody could crack its shell, however, until young Drosselmeier tried – and then the princess ate the kernel, and became beautiful again. But Mistress Mousie appeared once more, tripped young Drosselmeier up as he took the last of his seven steps backwards with his eyes shut, and turned him as ugly and wooden-looking as the princess had been before. He was just like a nutcracker! 'Oh, take that ugly nutcracker away!' cried Princess Pirlipat. And he was thrown out, but the Court Astronomer consulted the stars and saw that young Drosselmeier could still break the spell if he defeated the seven-headed Mouse King – Mistress Mousie's son born after the other seven were dead – and found a lady to love him in spite of his ugliness.

So that is the Tale of the Hard Nut (said Godfather Drosselmeier).

When Marie could play in the living-room again, and saw Nutcracker in the toy cupboard, it suddenly struck her that the tale her godfather had told must be Nutcracker's own story. Of course! He was really her godfather's nephew, who had been bewitched by Mistress Mousie – for she felt quite sure that the Court Watchmaker was Godfather Drosselmeier himself. And she told herself that Princess Pirlipat was a nasty, ungrateful girl.

Not long after this, one moonlit night, Marie was awakened by a strange sound in her bedroom: a pattering and a squeaking and a whistling. Then she saw the Mouse King coming through a hole in the wall. He scurried around the room, his eyes and his crowns all sparkling, and then he jumped up on Marie's bedside table, squealing, 'Teehee! You must give me your sugar plums and marzipan, little girl, or I'll eat your Nutcracker up!'

Next evening, Marie put her sugar plums and marzipan down at the foot of the toy cupboard – and they were gone in the morning! But soon the Mouse King was back, demanding Marie's collection of little sugar dolls, and another night he said he must have her books and her nice new dress. Marie was in despair. 'Oh, Nutcracker, how can I help you now?' she said, picking her Nutcracker up. 'Even if I do give the Mouse King my books and my dress, he'll still want more!'

But to her amazement, Nutcracker grew warm in her hand. 'If only you can get me a sword, I'll do the rest!' he told her, before he turned to stiff, cold wood again.

'I can give Nutcracker a sword!' said Fritz, when Marie had told him the whole story. And they took a silver sword off one of his toy soldiers, and buckled it on Nutcracker.

Marie could not sleep that night for terror, and about midnight she thought she heard a great many strange noises in the living-room, and a loud squeak. Then there came a soft knocking at her door, and a little voice saying, 'Don't worry, dear Marie! Good news!'

Putting on her shawl, Marie opened the door, and there stood Nutcracker, with his bloodstained sword in one hand.

'Dear lady,' he told her, 'you alone gave me strength and courage to kill the wicked Mouse King!' And he gave Marie all the Mouse King's seven crowns, as tokens of his victory. 'Now,' he went on, 'there are many wonderful things I can show you if you'll just come with me!'

Nutcracker led Marie to the big old wardrobe, where she saw a pretty little cedarwood staircase coming down through the sleeve of Father's travelling coat. They climbed the stairs, and when they reached the top, dazzling light and delicious fragrance met them. They were in Prince Nutcracker's own country, and Marie admired all the beautiful sights as they went over Sugar-candy Meadow, into a wonderful little wood called Christmas Wood where gold and silver fruit hung from the branches, and then on beside Orange Brook, Lemonade River, and past Almond Milk Lake. Next they came to Gingerbread Village on the Honey River, and Barleysugar Town, but still they went on to the prince's capital city, in a boat shaped like a shell that carried them down a rose-red river.

They landed in a pretty thicket called Sugarplum Grove. 'And there ahead of us is the capital, Candy City!' Nutcracker told Marie. In the middle of the city stood Marzipan Castle, a fine sight with its hundred towers shining with lights. Four beautiful ladies, who must surely be princesses, came out and embraced Nutcracker, who introduced them to Marie as his sisters, telling them how she had saved his life. 'If she hadn't thrown her shoe at just the right moment, or got me that soldier's sword, I'd be dead now!' he said.

The ladies flung their arms around Marie, and they all went into a hall with walls made of sparkling crystal. The princesses set to work to prepare a delicious meal, using plates and dishes of delicate china, and silver and gold pots and pans. Watching them pressing fruit, pounding spices and grating sugar, Marie wished she could help. The prettiest of Nutcracker's sisters seemed to guess her thoughts, for she handed her a little golden pestle and mortar, saying, 'My dear, would you crush a little candy for me?'

So Marie happily pounded away, while Nutcracker told his sisters about the battle . . . but somehow, veils of silvery mist were rising, there was a singing and a whirring and a humming in the air, and Marie herself rose on swelling waves, higher and higher, up and up . . .

Bump! Marie fell from a great height. When she opened her eyes, she was in her own little bed, and there stood Mother. 'Oh, Mother!' cried Marie. 'Where do you think Nutcracker, who is really Godfather Drosselmeier's nephew, took me last night?' And she told her mother all about her adventures, insisting that they had not been just a dream . . . for after all, she had the Mouse King's seven crowns to show.

When no one would believe her, however, Marie stopped talking about that wonderful fairy kingdom. But she couldn't forget it, and one day, when Godfather Drosselmeier was repairing a clock in the house, she sat by the toy cupboard looking at Nutcracker. 'Oh, if you were really alive,' she burst out, 'I know I wouldn't act like Princess Pirlipat and despise you after you gave up your handsome face and figure for me!'

Then there was such a bang, and a jolt, that she fell off her chair in a faint. When she woke up, Mother was bending over her, saying, 'Look, here's your godfather's nephew come to visit us!' And there stood a young man, rather small but very handsome and finely dressed. When he was alone with Marie, he thanked her for all she had done in breaking the spell that had turned him into a nutcracker.

So soon Marie was engaged to be married to Godfather Drosselmeier's nephew, and after a year and a day he sent a golden carriage drawn by silver horses for her. And so far as I know, Marie and her nutcracker prince rule the Kingdom of Sweets to this day.

The Constant Tin Soldier

HANS CHRISTIAN ANDERSEN

All ended happily in the story of 'The Nutcracker' – but here's a story about toys that doesn't end happily. Yet the tin soldier's love for the dancer is greater than disaster . . . Hans Christian Andersen was one of the greatest story-tellers in the world. He was Danish, the son of a shoe-maker who died when Hans was eleven. He had to leave school and work in factories before getting small jobs in theatres. It was years before his talents as a story-teller were recognized, but then his work became popular and he travelled all over Europe, making friends with writers like Charles Dickens.

There were once five-and-twenty tin soldiers, all brothers, for they had all been made out of one old tin spoon. They carried muskets in their arms, and held themselves very upright, and their uniforms were red and blue – very gay indeed. The first word that they heard in this world, when the lid was taken off the box wherein they lay, was 'tin soldiers!'

It was a little boy who made this exclamation, clapping his hands at the same time. They had been given to him because it was his birthday, and he now set them out on the table. The soldiers resembled each other to a hair; one only was rather different from the rest; he had but one leg, for he had been made last, when there was not quite enough tin left; however, he stood as firmly upon his one leg as the others did upon their two. And this identical tin soldier it is whose fortunes seem to us worthy of record.

On the table where the tin soldiers were set out were several other playthings, but the most charming of them all was a pretty pasteboard castle. Through its little windows one could look into the rooms. In front of the castle stood some tiny trees, clustering round a little mirror intended to represent a lake, and waxen swans swam in the lake, and were reflected on its surface. All this was very pretty; but prettiest of all was a little damsel standing in the open doorway of the castle. She, too, was cut out of pasteboard; but she had on a frock of the clearest muslin, a little sky-blue riband was flung across her shoulders like a scarf, and in the midst of this scarf was set a bright gold spangle. The little lady stretched out both her arms, for she was a dancer, and raised one of her legs so high in the air that the tin soldier could not find it, and fancied that she had, like him, only one leg.

'That would be just the wife for me,' thought he; 'but then, she is of rather too high rank, she lives in a castle. I have only a box; besides, there are all our five-and-twenty men in it, it is no place for her! However, there will be no harm in my making acquaintance with her.' And so he stationed himself behind a snuff-box that stood on the table; from this place he had a full view of the delicate little lady, who still remained standing on one leg, yet without losing her balance.

When evening came, all the other tin soldiers were put away into the box, and the people of the house went to bed. The playthings now began to play in their turn; they pretended to visit, to fight battles, and give balls. The tin soldiers rattled in the box, for they wanted to play too, but the lid would not come off. The nutcrackers cut capers, and the slate-pencil played at commerce on the slate; there was such a racket that the canary bird waked up, and began to talk too; but he always talked in verse. The only two who did not move from their places were the tin soldier and the little dancer; she constantly remained in her graceful position, standing on the point of her foot, with outstretched arms; and as for him, he stood just as firmly on his one leg, never for one moment turning his eyes away from her.

Twelve o'clock struck – *Crash*! open sprang the lid of the snuff-box; but there was no snuff inside it; no, out jumped a little black conjuror; in fact, it was a Jack-in-the-box.

'Tin soldier!' said the conjuror, 'will you keep your eyes to yourself?'

But the tin soldier pretended not to hear.

'Well, only wait till tomorrow!' quoth the conjuror.

When the morrow had come, and the children were out of bed, the tin soldier was placed on the window-ledge, and, whether the conjuror or the wind occasioned it, all at once the window flew open, and out fell the tin soldier, head foremost, from the third storey to the ground. A dreadful fall was that! His one leg turned over and over in the air, and at last he rested, poised on his soldier's cap, with his bayonet between the paving-stones.

The maid-servant and the little boy immediately came down to look for him; but although they very nearly trod on him, they could not see him. If the tin soldier had but called out, 'Here I am!' they might easily have found him; but he thought it would not be becoming for him to cry out, as he was in uniform.

It now began to rain; every drop fell heavier than the last; there was a regular shower. When it was over, two boys came by.

'Look,' said one, 'here is a tin soldier! he shall have a sail for once in his life.'

So they made a boat out of an old newspaper, put the tin soldier into it, and away he sailed down the gutter, both the boys running along by the side and clapping their hands. The paper boat rocked to and fro, and every now and then veered round so quickly that the tin soldier became quite giddy; still he moved not a muscle, looked straight before him, and held his bayonet tightly clasped.

All at once the boat sailed under a long gutter-board; he found it as dark here as at home in his own box.

'Where shall I get to next?' thought he. 'Yes, to be sure, it is all that conjuror's doing! Ah, if the little maiden were but sailing with me in the boat, I would not care for its being twice as dark!' Just then a great water-rat, that lived under the gutter-board, darted out.

'Have you a passport?' asked the rat.

But the tin soldier was silent, and held his weapon with a still firmer grasp. The boat sailed on, and the rat followed. Oh! how furiously he showed his teeth, and cried out to sticks and straws, 'Stop him, stop him! He has not paid the toll! He has not shown his passport!' But the stream grew stronger and stronger. The tin soldier could already catch a glimpse of the bright daylight before the boat came from under the tunnel, but at the same time he heard a roaring noise, at which the boldest heart might well have trembled. Only fancy! where the tunnel ended, the water of the gutter fell perpendicularly into a great canal; this was as dangerous for the tin soldier as sailing down a mighty waterfall would be for us.

He was now so close that he could no longer stand upright; the boat darted forwards, the poor tin soldier held himself as stiff and immovable as possible, no one could accuse him of having even blinked. The boat spun round and round, three, nay, four times, and was filled with water to the brim; it must sink. The tin soldier stood up to his neck in water, deeper and deeper sank the boat, softer and softer grew the paper; the water went over the soldier's head, he thought of the pretty little dancer, whom he should never see again, and these words rang in his ears:

> *Wild adventure, mortal danger*
> *Be thy portion, valiant stranger!*

The paper now tore asunder, the tin soldier fell through the rent; but in the same moment he was swallowed up by a large fish.

Oh, how dark it was! Worse even than under the gutter-board, and so narrow too! But the tin soldier's resolution was as constant as ever; there he lay, at full length, shouldering his arms.

The fish turned and twisted about, and made the strangest movements! At last he became quite still; a flash of lightning, as it were, darted through him. The daylight shone brightly, and someone exclaimed, 'A tin soldier!'

The fish had been caught, taken to the market, sold, and brought home into the kitchen, where the servant-girl was cutting him up with a large knife. She seized the tin soldier by the middle with two of her fingers, and took him into the parlour, where everyone was eager to see the wonderful man who had travelled in the maw of a fish; however, our little warrior was by no means proud. They set him on the table, and there – no, how could anything so extraordinary happen in this world! the tin soldier was in the very same room in which he had been before; he saw the same children, the same playthings stood on the table, among them the beautiful castle with the pretty little dancing maiden, who was still standing upon one leg, whilst she held the other high in the air; she, too, was constant. It quite affected the tin soldier; he could have found it in his heart to weep tin-tears, but such weakness would have been unbecoming in a soldier. He looked at her, and she looked at him, but neither spoke a word.

And now one of the little boys took the soldier and threw him without ceremony into the stove. He did not give any reason for so doing, but, no doubt, the conjuror in the snuff-box must have had a hand in it.

The tin soldier now stood in a blaze of red light; he felt extremely hot; whether this heat was the result of the actual fire, or of the flames of love within him, he knew not. He had entirely lost his colour; whether this change had happened during his travels, or were the effect of strong emotion, I know not. He looked upon the little damsel, she looked upon him, and he felt that he was melting; but, constant as ever, he still stood shouldering his arms. A door opened, the wind seized the dancer, and, like a sylph, she flew straightaway into the stove, to the tin soldier; they both flamed up into a blaze – and were gone! The soldier was melted to a hard lump, and when the maid took the ashes out the next day, she found his remains in the shape of a little tin-heart: of the dancer there remained only the gold spangle, and that was burnt black as a coal.

The Barrel-Organ

ELEANOR FARJEON

*A thoughtful, very short story, in which a lost traveller is
reminded of a happy moment in his childhood, and becomes
aware of the world all around him. Were the barrel-organ
and the organ-grinder magic?*

There was once a traveller who had a long way to
go. He couldn't manage to get there by nightfall,
so he walked all night.

His way lay through woods and over hills, where
there were no towns and no villages, and not even
houses all by themselves. And as it was dark night he
couldn't see his way, and after a while he lost it in the
middle of a wood.

It was a night as still as it was dark, and he could
hear as little as he could see. So for want of company
he began to talk to himself.

'What shall I do *now*?' said the traveller. 'Shall I go
on, or shall I stop still? If I go on I may go the wrong
way, and by morning be further off than ever. Yet if I
stop still I shall certainly be no nearer than I am now,
and may have seven miles to walk to breakfast. What
shall I do now? Supposing I stop still, shall I lie down
or shall I stand up? If I lie down I may lie on a prickle.
Yet if I stand up I shall certainly get a cramp in my

legs. *What* shall I do?'

When he had got this far in his talk, which was not very far after all, the traveller heard the sound of music in the wood. No sooner was there something else to listen to, than he stopped talking to himself. It was surprising music to hear in that place. It was not somebody singing or whistling, or playing the flute or a fiddle – sounds which anybody might expect to hear in such a place at such a time. No, the music the traveller heard in that dark wood on that dark night was a tune on a barrel-organ.

The sound of the tune made the traveller happy. He no longer felt he was lost, the tune made him feel as though he was quite near now, and his home was just round the corner. He walked towards it, and as he walked he seemed to feel the grass flutter under his feet and the leaves dance against his cheeks. When he came close to the tune he called out, 'Where are you?' He was sure there must be somebody there, for even a barrel-organ in a wood can't turn its handle by itself. And he was right, for when he called out, 'Where are you?' a cheerful voice answered, 'Here I am, sir!'

The traveller put out his hand and touched the barrel-organ.

'Wait a bit, sir,' said the cheerful voice, 'I'll just finish this tune first. You can dance to it if you want to.' The tune went on very loud and jolly, and the traveller danced very quick and gay, and they both finished with a flourish.

'Well, well!' said the traveller. 'I haven't danced to a barrel-organ since I was ten years old in a back street.'

'I expect not, sir,' said the organ-grinder.

'Here's a penny for you,' said the traveller.

'Thank you,' said the organ-grinder. 'It's a long time since I've taken a penny.'

'Which way are you going?' asked the traveller.

'No way in particular,' said the organ-grinder. 'It's all one to me. I can grind my organ here as well as there.'

'But surely,' said the traveller, 'you need houses with windows in them, or how can people throw the pennies out?'

'I've enough for my needs without that,' said the organ-grinder.

'But surely,' said the traveller again, 'you need the back streets with the children in them, or who's to dance when you play?'

'Why, there you've hit it,' said the organ-grinder. 'Once upon a time I played to the houses with windows every day till I'd got my twelvepence, and then for the rest of the day I played in the back streets. And every day I spent sixpence and saved sixpence. But one day it happened I caught cold and had to lie up, and when I came out I found another organ in one of my back streets, and a gramophone in a second, and a harp and cornet in a third. So I saw it was time to retire, and now I grind my organ wherever I please. The tune's the same, here or there.'

'But who's to dance?' asked the traveller again.

'There's no want of dancers in a wood,' said the organ-grinder, and turned his handle.

As soon as the tune started, the traveller felt the

grass and leaves flutter as before, and in a moment the
air was full of moths and fireflies, and the sky was full
of stars, come out to dance like children in a back
street. And it seemed to the traveller, by the light of
the dancing stars, that flowers came up in the wood
where a moment before there had been none, pushing

272

their way in haste through the moss to sway to the tune on their stalks, and that two or three little streams began to run where a moment before they had been still. And the traveller thought there were other things dancing that he couldn't see, as well as flowers and streams and stars and moths and flies and leaves in the night. The wood was quite full of dancing from top to toe, and it was no longer dark, for the moon had hopped out of a cloud, and was gliding all over the sky.

Long before this the traveller was dancing too; he danced as he used to when he was ten years old, till the tune of the organ was faint to hear. For he had danced his way through the wood and was out in the road, with the lights of the city at the other end, and his way before him.

Cinderella

CHARLES PERRAULT
retold by Edith Nesbit

This is the world's most popular fairy-story, perhaps the most famous story about a dance ever written! Not surprisingly, two world-famous musicians, Rossini and Prokofiev, have written music for ballets based on the tale. This is a very satisfying retelling, full of fun.

There was once a gentleman of a fine fortune and studious habits who had a dear wife and one little daughter. And all three were so fond of each other that there were not three happier people in the world. The little daughter grew up very beautiful, very good, and quite clever enough to be the light of her parents' eyes. And when she was fifteen Bad Fortune, which seemed to have forgotten this happy little family, suddenly remembered them. The mother caught a fever and died in three days. The father was heartbroken. He would not leave the house even to walk in the pleasant gardens that lay round it. He would not even open one of his once-loved books, and it was difficult to get him to eat enough to keep the life in him. He would sit, all day long, looking at the chair where his wife had been used to sit with her book or her sewing. His daughter tried in vain to rouse him, and at last she began to be afraid that if he went on like this he would lose his reason.

So she persuaded him to give away his house and furniture to his poor neighbours, and to go a long journey to a distant country, where there would be nothing to remind him of the dear treasure he had lost.

Arrived in the new country, he did indeed seem less wretched. He became once more absorbed in his studies, but he ate and drank what was set before him, and did not refuse to go out for walks, or sometimes to a neighbour's house to supper. But he was a changed and broken man to the day of his death.

He had a kind and gentle nature, and he imagined that all women were as good as his dear dead wife, so that when a neighbour told him that a certain widow lady was dying of love for him the simple gentleman said, 'If this be so I will marry her – only she must be told that my heart is buried in my wife's grave.'

'She will bear with that,' said the matchmaking neighbour, 'and her two girls will be nice company for your daughter.'

So the widow married the gentleman, and that was the beginning of trouble. Because it was not he that she loved, but his fortune – and as for his daughter, she and her girls hated the poor child from the first, though they pretended to be very fond of her until everything was settled as they wished.

Directly after the wedding he said to his new wife:

'My dear, we are now married, which is what you

wanted. All that I have is yours, and you are the mistress of my house. Be kind to my poor child, and please arrange everything without bothering me. My books are my constant companions, and you may entertain your friends as much as you like as long as you leave me in peace.'

In this way he handed over his daughter to her stepmother and stepsisters.

Now as soon as these saw that the master of the house never noticed anything that went on in it, and that his daughter was much too fond of her father to worry him with complaints, they decided to put that child in her proper place. They began by forbidding her to appear at table when there was company. Then they said she might as well make herself useful and dust her own and her sisters' rooms. Then she was told to sweep as well as dust. After that the washing of the dishes was put upon her. And soon she was doing the work of a house-maid, a parlour-maid, a kitchen-maid, two general servants, and a boy in buttons, without a penny of wages or a kind word from month's end to month's end. All her jewels and pretty clothes were taken away – the jewels her father had bought for her, and the clothes sewn and embroidered for her by the loving hands of her dead mother. She used to sit on the kitchen hearth and cry when the servants had gone to bed, to think of the happy times when her mother was alive and her father had not grown stupid and helpless with sorrow. And as she sat crying one day Marigolda, the eldest sister, came rustling into the kitchen in her pink flounced silk, and saw her among the ashes, and laughed and said:

'Don't put the fire out with all those water fountains, you nasty, dirty little Cinderella!'

And after that she was never called anything else. And she was called all day long. It was, 'Cinderella, you haven't made my bed,' 'Cinderella, black my boots this minute,' 'Cinderella, peel the potatoes,' 'Cinderella, clean the kitchen grate,' and a thousand other 'Cinderellas', each with some work tacked on to it, from morning till night.

Cinderella did her best. But it is difficult to be in half a dozen places at once – which was the least that her steprelations expected of her. She would not complain to her father. She was determined to bear everything rather than make him unhappy.

She had only the commonest clothes to wear, and even they were ragged, because she had no time to mend them. She ate the least pleasant bits left over from yesterday's dinner, and her bed was a wooden box full of straw in a corner of the kitchen, which she shared with the kitchen cat and the fat old turnspit dog, who were her only friends.

'Oh, well,' sighed poor Cinderella, 'I must just go on bearing it, and if I am good something nice will happen to me some day.'

And sure enough something did.

The king of that country had his palace quite near the house where Cinderella lived so uncomfortably. And the king's son happening to be twenty-one, the king decided to give birthday parties every night until he should have invited all the gentlepeople who lived near. Father and mother and Dressalinda and Marigolda were invited, but the gentleman who arranged the invitations had never heard of Cinderella, who had not a single friend in that strange country to speak a word for her when the cards were being sent out.

Dressalinda and Marigolda were immensely excited when the invitation came, brought by a herald blowing a trumpet and walking very stately, with a train of beefeaters bearing hundreds of large gilded envelopes with crowns on the flaps, in silver waste-paper baskets. And when the girls tore open the envelope and saw the gilded card with the royal arms on it, and their own names, they were wild with delight, because everybody knew that this series of birthday parties was given so that the young prince might see as many girls as possible, and that out of them all he might choose a bride. He was such a very nice young man, to say nothing of his being the prince and the heir to all the kingdom, that no one imagined that any girl could say anything but 'Yes' if he should say, 'Will you marry me?'

And no girl could have said it unless she had happened to be in love with some other nice young man.

And now nothing was talked of but the royal ball. Cinderella had to do her dirty kitchen work jut as usual, and besides that she had to wash and iron every petticoat and chemisette, every scrap of lace or muslin that her stepsisters had – to mend and iron all their fine dresses, because they had decided to try on every single thing they had, so as to see what suited them best. I should have thought they might have got new dresses and have done with it. But they didn't. Perhaps it was because no money could have bought them the delicate gold and coloured embroidery, the fairy-like lace that Cinderella's mother had wrought and woven for her dear little daughter.

The great day came at last, and father, stepmother, and stepsisters went off in the family coach. The last words Cinderella heard were:

'Now, you lazy little cat, be sure to tidy up our rooms before you dare to go to bed.'

So she sighed as the wheels of the coach rumbled away, and set herself to do as she was told, and tidy up the litter of laces, ribbons, hairpins, curl-papers, slippers, dressing-gowns, artificial flowers, fans, brooches, necklaces, handkerchiefs, bracelets, veils, tiaras, and all the rest of it. And when that was done she sat down in the quiet kitchen among the grey ashes, and cried and cried and cried.

'Oh, I wish,' she sobbed out at last, 'oh, I *do* wish I could go to the ball!'

'Do you, love? Then you shall!' said a voice quite close to her – such a kind voice too; and it was more than a year since she had heard a voice that was kind.

She started up, and found herself face to face with a fairy. She knew at once that it was a fairy, though the face was gentle enough to have been an angel's, because the wings were fairy-shape, and not angel-shape.

'Oh!' she cried, 'who are you?'

'I'm a very old friend of your mother's,' said the fairy, 'and now I'm going to be your friend. If you want to go to the king's ball, to the king's ball you shall go, or my name's not Benevola!'

'But I can't go in this dress,' said Cinderella, looking down at her dreadful old clothes.

'Wash away your tears, my love,' said the fairy, 'and then we'll see.'

So Cinderella had a good wash in the wooden bowl on the kitchen sink, and came back looking as fresh as a rose after rain.

'Now,' said the fairy, 'go at once to the end of the kitchen garden and bring me the biggest pumpkin you can find.'

Cinderella took the stable lantern and went out. She came back with a great orange pumpkin, so big that she could hardly carry it.

'I'll run back for the lantern,' she said.

'Do,' said the fairy, 'and at the same time get me the old rat who is asleep inside the bucket that stands by the well.'

Cinderella went. She did not much like picking up the rat, but she did it, and he was quite kind and gentle, and did not try to bite or to run away.

'Now see if there are any mice in the trap in the old summer-house,' said Benevola. There were six, and Cinderella brought them, running about briskly in the trap.

'Now six lizards from the lettuce bed,' said the fairy; and these were caught and brought in in a handkerchief.

Then Benevola, standing there in her beautiful fairy clothes, waved her silver wand over Cinderella and her rags, and instantly her rags changed to a gown that was like white mist and diamond dew and silver moonshine, and on her head was a little crown of stars that shone among her dark hair.

Cinderella looked at herself in the polished lid of the brass preserving pan, and cried, 'Can that be me? Oh, how pretty I am!' It was not one of the moments when grammar seems important.

'You are,' said Benevola. 'You're every inch a princess, my dear, like your dear mother before you. Let's see: have you got everything? – fan, gloves, handkerchief?'

Yes, Cinderella had them all.

'But my shoes,' she said shyly, looking down at her poor old black slippers.

'Bless me! I nearly forgot the shoes,' said the fairy. 'Here they are – dear little magic glass ones. No one at the ball will dance like my goddaughter!' And she plunged her arm into her big pocket and pulled out a dear little pair of glass slippers. Real glass they were, and shone like the drops on a crystal chandelier. And yet they were soft as any kid glove.

'Put them on, my darling, and enjoy yourself in them,' she said; 'but remember you mustn't stay later than half-past eleven, or twenty to twelve at the very most, because the magic won't last after midnight. You'll remember, won't you?'

Cinderella promised to remember. Then Benevola set the pumpkin, the rat, the mice, and the lizards in the road opposite the front door, waved that wonderful wand of hers, and instantly the pumpkin was a golden coach more splendid than the king's, the mice were six white horses, the lizards six footmen in green and gold liveries, and the old rat was the stoutest and most respectable coachman who ever wore a three-cornered hat, and gold lace on his coat.

Cinderella kissed her godmother and thanked her again and again. Then she jumped into the coach and snuggled in among soft satin cushions. Benevola gave the order, 'To the palace,' and the white horses bounded forward.

In the palace everyone was enjoying itself very much indeed. All the ladies looked their very prettiest, and all the gentlemen thought so, and all the ladies knew that the gentlemen thought so. And when this is the case a party is usually a success.

One of the court gentlemen, who had gone out to stand on the palace steps for a breath of fresh air, caught a glimpse of Cinderella, and rushed off to the prince.

'I say, your Highness,' he whispered, 'the loveliest princess in all the world has just driven up in a golden coach drawn by six white horses. Oughtn't someone to go and welcome her?'

'*I* will,' said Prince Charming eagerly; 'there's no sense in disturbing the king and queen.'

And so it happened that Cinderella, in her dress of dew and mist and moonlight, was received at the very door of the palace by Prince Charming himself, in his court suit of cloth of gold sewn with topazes. As he handed her up the marble steps of the grand staircase every one murmured, 'What a handsome pair!'

But the prince was saying to himself, 'Oh, you dear

little princess! Oh, you pretty little princess! I'll never marry any one but you – never, never, never!' While aloud, to her, he was saying the dullest, politest things about the weather, and the music, and the state of the roads that led to the palace.

Cinderella looked so lovely that no one could take their eyes off her, and even her unkind sisters, who did not recognize her in the least, owned that she was the most beautiful lady they had ever seen.

The prince danced with her, and took her in to supper, and as the evening went on he began to talk of other things than the weather. He told her that her eyes were stars, and her mouth a flower, and things like that – quite silly things, because, of course, no one's eyes are like stars or their mouths like flowers – quite silly, but still she liked to hear them. And at last he said in that blunt, downright manner which is permitted to princes, 'There is no one like you in the world. Will you marry me?'

She was just going to say, 'Yes, please,' for, indeed, she thought there was no one like *him* in the world, when the palace clock struck the half after eleven. She turned in a flash and ran down the corridor – and the magic glass slippers that had made her dancing the wonder of all the court now made her running as swift as the wind's going, so that she had reached her coach and jumped in before the prince, pursuing her, had turned the first corner in the grand staircase.

She got home just as the clock struck twelve, and at the last stroke coach and horses, coachman and footmen, turned into what they had been before, and she herself was once more the shabby, dusty little Cinderella who had sat and cried into the ashes.

When her sisters came home she had to listen to their tales of the ball, and of the strange princess who was so beautiful that she took everybody's breath away, and as she listened, yawning, she could hardly believe that she herself had really been that lovely lady.

She dreamed all night of the prince. And next day the herald came round with the king's compliments, and would everyone who had been at the ball last night kindly come round to the palace again that evening?

And everything happened as before. The others drove off early, the fairy godmother came and waved her wand, and the prince, anxiously watching at the head of the grand staircase, saw his princess threading her way through the crowd like a moonbeam through dark water.

That night everyone saw that it was going to be a match. The king and queen were as pleased with Cinderella's pretty manners as Prince Charming was with her pretty face and the dear self that looked out of her eyes.

'Tell me your name, loveliest and dearest,' he said. 'Give me your hand and tell me the name of my bride.'

And Cinderella, pale with happiness, and with eyes that really did look rather starry, gave him her hand and said:

'Dear Prince, my name is —' And then, boom, boom,

boom! – the great clock in the palace tower began to strike midnight.

'Let me go – let me go!' cried Cinderella, and tore her hands from the prince's, and ran, the magic slippers helping her all they could. But they could not help enough. Before she could get out of the palace grounds her beautiful dress had turned to rags, and as she reached the gate the only traces left of her grand coach and six and her fine servants were six scampering mice, six furtive lizards, a fat old running rat, and a big yellow pumpkin bowling along the road as hard as it could go, all by itself.

The night had changed its mind and turned out wet, and she had to run all the way home in the mud; and it was very difficult, because she had dropped one of her glass slippers in her haste to get away, and:

> *'You know how hard it is to run*
> *With one shoe off and one shoe on.'*

When the prince, wild with anxiety and disappointment, rushed out to ask the sentries about the magnificent princess who had driven away, they told him that no one had passed out except a ragged beggar girl, running like a mad thing. So he went back to the palace with despair in his heart, and his dancing shoes wet through.

He did not sleep a wink all night, and next morning he sent for the herald, who was a very good fellow, and rather clever in his way.

'My dear herald,' said the prince, sitting on the edge of his bed in his blue satin dressing-gown sewn with

seed-pearls, and waggling the toes of his gold-embroidered slippers, 'you saw that strange princess last night . . .? Well . . .'

'Bless you, your Highness,' said the herald, who was about the same age as the prince, 'I know all about it. Lost lady. Love of a life. No expense spared. Return and all will be forgotten and forgiven. You want to find her?'

'I should think I did!'

'Well, it's quite simple. What's that sparklety thing sticking out of the breast pocket of your dressing-gown?'

'Yes', said the Prince oddly, and drew out Cinderella's slipper.

'Well, then!' said the herald, and unfolded his idea, which pleased Prince Charming so much that within an hour the herald had set out, with the glass slipper borne before him on a blue cushion with a fringe of peacock's feathers, and the trumpets blowing like grampuses, and the pennons flying like pretty pigeons all about him, to find the lady whose foot that slipper would fit. For in those days shoes were not sold ready-made in shops, but were made specially to fit the people who were to wear them. And besides, the glass slipper was magic, and so had too much sense to have fitted anyone but its owner, even if the country had been full of shops selling Rats' Ready-made Really Reliable Boots.

The herald called at every house, great and small, and every girl in every house had to try on the slipper. At last, when it was evening, and he was getting very tired of the whole business, and was beginning to wish that shoes had never been invented at all, he came to the house where Cinderella lived.

Blow, blow! went the trumpets; flutter, flutter, went the pennons; and the herald's voice, rather faint and husky, cried:

'Oyez, oyez, oyez! Prince Charming offers his hand and heart to the lady who can wear this little glass slipper. Who'll try? Who'll try? Who'll try? Will ye try? Will ye try? Will ye try, try, try?' So that he sounded like a butcher in the Old Kent Road of a Saturday night, only they say 'buy' instead of 'try'.

Dressalinda and Marigolda pushed and hustled Cinderella to make her open the door quickly. She was quite as anxious as they were to open it, for reasons of her own – reasons which you know as well as she did.

So the door was thrown open, and in came the herald, and the trumpeters and men-at-arms grouped themselves picturesquely about the doorsteps, to the envy and admiration of the neighbours.

Dressalinda sat down in the big carved chair in the hall, and stuck out a large stout foot.

'No good,' said the herald. 'I'm sorry, miss. It's a fine foot – as fine as ever I saw – but it's not just the cut for the glass slipper.'

And even Dressalinda had to own that it wasn't.

Then Marigolda tried. And though she had had time to slip upstairs and put on her best fine silk stockings then little glass slipper would not begin to go on to her long flat foot.

'It's the heel, miss,' said the herald. 'I'm sorry, but it's not my fault, nor yours either. We can't help our heels, nor yet other people's. So now for the other girl.'

'What other girl?' 'There *is* no other girl,' said the two sisters together.

But the herald said, 'What about the one who opened the door?'

'Oh, that was only Cinderella,' 'Just a kitchen wench,' said Marigolda and Dressalinda, tossing their heads.

'There's many a pretty foot under a ragged skirt,' said the herald; and he went to the top of the kitchen stairs, and called 'Cinderella! Cinderella!' – not because he thought it at all possible that the slipper would fit a kitchen wench, but because he had undertaken to try it on *all* girls. Also, he disliked the elder sisters as much as anyone possibly could on so short an acquaintance. When you knew them better, of course, it was different.

So poor Cinderella came, all ragged and dusty, but with her bright beauty shining through the dust and the rags like the moon through clouds. And the herald knew that she was the lost princess, even before she slipped on the little glass shoe, pulled the other one from her pocket, slipped that on too, and stood up in the pair of them.

'Found!' cried the herald. 'Oh, joy! the long-lost princess! You are to come with me at once to the palace.'

'I can't come like this,' said Cinderella, looking at her rags. 'I can't, and I won't!'

But the fairy godmother appeared most opportunely from the cupboard under the stairs where the boots and galoshes were kept, and with one wave of her wand clothed Cinderella from head to foot in cloth-of-splendour.

Then Cinderella looked at her unkind sisters, and said timidly, 'Goodbye.'

And the sisters looked at her, and frowned, and

'Goodbye' said they.

Then the fairy smiled, and, pointing her wand at them, said, 'Speak the truth.' And there in the presence of Cinderella and the fairy and the herald and each other and the hat-and-umbrella-stand they had to speak it.

'I have been very unkind and hateful to Cinderella,' said Dressalinda, 'and I am very sorry. I have been sorry since the night before last, but I was ashamed to say so. I am sorry because on that night I lost my heart to a good gentleman, who lost his to me, and I hate the thought of all the wickedness that makes me unworthy of him.'

'That's right,' said the herald kindly. ' "A fault that's owned, is half atoned." And what does the other lady say?'

'I say the same as my sister,' said Marigolda, 'and I hope Cinderella will forgive us.'

'Of course I do,' said Cinderella heartily. So that was settled.

They all went to court – the fairy godmother made the pumpkin coach again in a moment – and Prince Charming met Cinderella at the steps of the palace, and kissed her before the whole crowd there assembled, and everyone cheered, and a chorus of invisible fairies sang:

> *'Take her, O prince, faithful and true;*
> *That little foot was just made for the shoe.*
> *We are so glad! Every one knew*
> *That little princess was just made for you.*

'Shout for the pair, Army and Fleet!
Lonely policeman, hurrah on our beat!
May life be long, joy be complete,
Rose-strewn the path of those dear little feet!'

The two noble gentlemen rushed forward, as soon as politeness to the prince allowed, to greet their dear ladies, who had been the wicked sisters, and who now were so sorry and ashamed, because love had taught them to wish to be good.

They were all married the next day, and when Marigolda and Dressalinda confessed to their father how horrid they had been to Cinderella, he said, 'Dear, dear! and I never noticed! How remiss of me!' and went back to his books.

But the cruel stepmother, who had brought up her children so badly, and who was not sorry at all, was sent to a Home for the Incurably Unkind. She is treated kindly, but she is not allowed the chance of being unkind to anyone else.

And Cinderella and Charming and the sisters and their husbands all lived exactly as long as was good for them, and loved each other more and more every day of their lives. And no one can ask for a better fate than that!

The Cutlers' Ball

BERLIE DOHERTY

From the magic and splendour of Cinderella *to a more normal sort of ball! Most people enjoy going to dances, and for Dorothy (the Granny of the title) it was very exciting indeed to be able to go to the Cutlers' Ball on her seventeenth birthday. This extract comes from the prize-winning novel* Granny Was a Buffer Girl.

Today was a special day for Dorothy. It was Saturday, February 26th, 1931. Dorothy was seventeen today. It was also the day of the cutlers' ball, when her firm was to hold its annual dance at the Cutlers' Hall in town. This year everyone who worked for the firm had been invited.

'It'll be a right birthday treat for you, Dolly!' Louie had said. Her big awkward husband, Gilbert, had gladly given her leave to go without him, and she was grateful for that. She was going to find it hard enough to coax Dorothy to go, and to enjoy herself when she got there, without dragging Gilbert along too.

Dorothy had been cold with excitement all day. It was the first time she'd been to a dance of any sort. It was the first time she'd celebrated a birthday.

'Come on, Dolly, let's get you fettled!' Louie called up to her, and Dorothy ran downstairs to wash the muck of work off her hands and her face, and out of her long thick hair. She and Louie scrubbed each other down, and then Louie sat her in the hearth while she crimped her hair for her. They chattered away, full of it all, holding the curling tongs in the heat of the coals till they glowed, and then wrapping Dorothy's hair quickly round them.

'Hold it still,' Louie ordered. 'Don't wriggle or the lines will come out all wobbly.'

'You'll ruin that girl's hair,' Mrs Beatty warned. She was pressing their frocks. She held the iron near her face to feel its heat. Her spittle fizzed on it. 'It'll drop out before she's twenty-one, you'll see.'

'I don't care if it does drop out before she's twenty-one.' Louie's laugh was the sort that cracked inside your earhole. She could break bones in half with her voice. 'So long as it's all right for tonight, that's all.'

Mrs Beatty draped the hot dresses over the chair-back and settled down for a rest. She nagged on comfortably. 'When I was a girl it didn't do for young ladies to show their hair at all, never mind cook it.' But when old Mrs Beatty had been Dorothy's age the year had been 1876, and the world of young ladies then was a foreign land to them. 'I've seen more changes in my lifetime than you're ever likely to see in yours, or would want to see, neither. Things have got wicked.' She purred into her cocoa and nodded off, missing the fun of seeing Dorothy put on her lisle stockings and the blue satin dress with red posies that she'd helped her to make.

The little ones crowded round for a good look at

their sisters before they set off, and their clamour woke Mrs Beatty up again briefly. She had come to keep an eye on them while their widowed father was on night-shift at the steelworks, and to take advantage of a fire that she herself couldn't afford.

'You look bonny enough,' she murmured, and was asleep again before the girls had time to put on their powder. They slipped out into the street and ran arm in arm across the cobbles to where their friends were waiting for them at the tram stop.

The Cutlers' Hall was in Church Street, near the middle of town. Lights blazed from all its windows. Even from the street outside, with all its bustle of trams and traffic, you could hear the strains of the orchestra, and the babble of voices and laughter. Dorothy, shy, held on to her sister's arm as they went up the steps to the entrance hall. She gazed round at the black and green walls that gleamed like marble, the crystal chandeliers, the glowing polish of the woodwork; at the height of the pillars and the decorated ceiling, and at the broad sweep of the grand staircase that she was going to have to climb up if she was ever going to get near the ballroom. A woman in a pale green taffeta dress rustled down from the top flight on the arm of a young man and stood poised on the landing. She turned to smile at another group who were coming down to her, and the huge mirror behind her held her poised like one of the paintings round the walls. Her hair was permed in rows like the deep waves of the sea, in the newest fashion, and real jewels flashed at her throat.

'That's boss's wife,' Louie whispered. 'And that's boss's son, Mr Edward. In't he a peach!' She laughed loudly, in the shrieking way she had, and the party on the stairs turned their heads slightly towards them, and away again, and Dorothy blushed – not at her sister's coarseness, but because Mr Edward, son of the owner of one of the most famous cutlery firms in the world, had caught her eye and was staring coolly at her.

And she felt his eyes on her all evening, especially when she found herself laughing for joy at the dancing and singing to herself the tunes that she had only heard before in the singing at work. The little orchestra now filled them out with harmonies: 'Danny Boy', 'I'll Take You Home Again Kathleen', 'Roses are Blooming in Picardy' . . .

'I say,' whispered a voice in her ear. 'Did you know you're the prettiest girl here?'

'Am I?' She daren't turn her face to look at Mr Edward, even though his breath was warm on her cheek.

'You've eyes the colour of bluebells.'

She smiled at a plate of cakes on the buffet table.

'I'd like to ask you for the next dance,' he went on. 'And I shan't take no for an answer.'

She looked round for her friends, but they'd all gone off somewhere; smoking, or blotting their glowing cheeks with powder. Mr Edward put his hand on her shoulder and steered her out to the centre of the floor and she stood rigid with mortification while they waited for the music to start. She knew how to dance

all right. Louie had seen to that, giving her lessons in the kitchen under the dripping clothes-rack while old Mrs Beatty hummed the tunes and tapped out the rhythm with her steel-tipped stick, and all her little brothers and sisters sat in their night-gowns on the kitchen bench to watch. She knew every dance there was to know, and was as light and lively on her feet as her mother had been. And Mr Edward could dance too. Now she knew that everyone's eyes were on her, and she didn't care. She wanted all the girls to notice her triumph. At the end of the dance his arms still held her and what's more his eyes held her too; and even though the music had stopped and all the other dancers were moving back to their seats she wanted that moment to hold her there for ever.

But, 'Edward! Edward!' his mother hissed at him, in a voice that was a shade too harsh for the smooth face under the permanent waves, and Mr Edward's firm grasp wilted.

'Wait for me after the ball,' he whispered. 'Will you?' Not looking at her but at his mother. 'Say you will.' And, 'I'll drive you home.'

'I'll drive you home!' Never had a motor car been in Dorothy's street! At the end of the dance, when she was queuing with her sister for her coat and easing her feet out of her shoes, she told Louie that even though the last tram had gone she wouldn't be walking home with her.

'Mr Edward's taking me in his car,' she whispered.

'Don't be mad!' said Louie. 'Him, bring you home! Down Attercliffe, with me dad waiting to strap him for his cheek. Forget it, Dorothy. He's having you on.'

So arm in arm the sisters and their friends scuttled down from the scented ballroom and limped their blistered way home through the dark streets to Attercliffe.

But Dorothy couldn't forget Mr Edward that easily. That night she dreamed about him, and all next day too, when she was busy with the cooking and the housework, and she held a picture of herself with him, a still, coloured image like a painting, but with music in the background, and it showed him with his face bent down towards her at the end of the dance, and her with her face held up to his. When

Albert Bradley from over the road lingered, as he always did, till Dorothy's father had gone to work, and knocked on her door for his morning kiss before racing down the street to clock on at the steelworks, he met with a fullness of lips that he'd never come across before.

'Why, Dolly, tha's coming on!' he said, stepping back for air, and Dorothy opened her eyes, shocked to think that Albert's blotched and bristly face should have put her in mind of Mr Edward.

'Get away with you, Albert Bradley,' she said, and he did, haring up the street to beat Dorothy's dad to the works gates, and grinning all day long at Dorothy's new magic.

Louie's strange husband, Gilbert, left for work at the same time, and she came round to Dorothy's house to help her to get the little ones up. Then they got ready for work together. They had to protect themselves from the gritty dust of the buffing wheel. They took newspapers from the pile that the neighbours brought round for them at the end of every week and tied sheets of them round each other – chest, arms, stomach, legs, till there was no clothing left to be seen except for the newly washed and daisy-white calico head-squares that they tied round their crimped hair. They collected their sandwiches, and left Mrs Beatty her penny for taking the little ones to school and back; and set off, rustling, for their tram, gathering their friends on the way. The girls chattered and shrieked and gossiped as the tram swayed down to town, and Dorothy gazed out at the houses with sunlight as pale as sand on their windows and thought of the rich gleam of chandeliers, and felt the warmth of Mr Edward's breath on her cheeks.

Much later that morning Mr Edward arrived at work. He'd had a bad weekend, dreaming about Dorothy. He was quite determined to find her again. All the people who had been to the ball had been employed by his father, so he knew that she would be in the building somewhere. He wouldn't let her slip away from him again, in her shyness.

In between inspecting the neat rows of boxed cutlery and candlesticks and meat plates that were lined up for export, he roamed from office to office and from floor to floor, anxious to get a glimpse of her; and Dorothy, standing all day long over her buffing wheel while clouds of black dust settled over her newspaper arms and body and her calico headsquare, kept casting glances over her shoulder, sensing with every nerve that he was somewhere in the building and that he was looking for her. But it never occurred to him to look among the buffer girls, even though the sickly sweet metal-and-hot-dust smell of their work lay heavy in every room, and the whirr of their machinery wound interminably through the day, and the lusty singing of the girls at their work chimed in every corner. If he had climbed up to the top floor of his father's building he would have seen the long buffing shop hot and bright with sunlight pouring through the roof windows, and the forty girls standing in their row putting the gleam on all those articles he inspected. They would be holding their faces away from the sand-dust that the wheel sprayed back at them, and from time to time they'd dash with their mugs to the tap in the corner and swill their mouths out, or they'd stretch back their shoulders to ease the ache, or flex the muscles of their feet.

'I'll take you home again, Kathleen' they'd be singing, or 'My old man, said follow the van, and don't dilly dally on the way . . .'. All day long they'd be singing, and from time to time the little one with eyes like bluebells in her blacked face would look over her shoulder for someone.

But at last it was clocking-off time. The machine stopped. The girls put out their pieces of holloware to be counted, and those with husbands' meals to cook and shopping to do on Attercliffe Common urged the ones who wanted to chat and dawdle to hurry up. They crowded out of the building together; newspaper arms and legs, faces, hands, calico headsquares, all as black as soot.

Dorothy clattered out behind the others, listening to their jokes and laughter and wrapped up still in her warm thoughts of the dance; and saw Mr Edward by the steps, dapper as a new sixpence and holding a posy of violets.

'For me!' she breathed.

His eyes flashed up and up the steps as the workers streamed out. Dorothy broke away from her sister to run to him, but Louie pulled her back.

'Don't,' she warned. 'He's never waiting for you.'

'He *is*,' said Dorothy, breaking free.

'Not *you*!' Louie's voice wailed.

Dorothy ran right up to Mr Edward, her newspapers flapping away from her arms. He had moved away as the top floor workers came down, and was about to give up his vigil.

'Mr Edward!'

He half turned, knowing the voice, and went back towards the steps. He had to push past the grimy blue-eyed girl on the pavement, and he brushed her dust off his coat in annoyance. The buffer girls yelled at Dorothy to hurry or they'd miss the tram; and, as she ran past him again, he realized that the girl he was looking for had vanished like the music and the lights and all the scents and laughter of the dance. He dropped the violets in the gutter and strode back to his car, and Louie, coming to hook Dorothy's arm in her own, bent down and picked them up for her kitchen table.

At the steelworks at the end of Dorothy's street Albert was about to finish his shift. He stood in the flare of heat as the great river of golden steel gushed down the channel into its mould. He would work here for the rest of his life, he knew that. And every night he would go back home to Dorothy. He thought of her morning kiss, and knew that he'd have to act fast before things got beyond his control. The furnace winked a white eye at him as the huge door was swung open and slammed shut again. He must go. Men shouted at him on their way past. His skin scorched with the heat, and still he couldn't move. He watched a massive rod of steel blaze white; red sparks from it spattered to the high, dark vault. He would ask her tonight.

He raced down to her house as soon as he'd clocked off. Dry as he was with the heat of the works, he didn't stop at the pub to slake his thirst as the other workers did. He reached Dorothy's door just as Mrs Beatty was coming out, and he hovered in the passage to let the old woman pass.

'You're early tonight, aren't you, Albert, for your kiss?'

'I've got special business tonight, Mrs Beatty.'

'Have you? What kind of business?'

'I'm going to pop her a question.'

Mrs Beatty chewed thoughtfully on the last bit of bread in her gums, and spat out the crusty bit that was annoying her. 'She's not in the mood for questions, Albert. I should come back tomorrow.'

'She's not poorly, is she?'

'She is.' Mrs Beatty pushed past him, sorry enough for the lad, but her back was hurting her. 'Not the sort of poorly you mean, though.'

'What sort of poorly?'

'Heart sort.' The old woman pushed open her door and went in for the night.

Dorothy heard Albert knocking but she lay in her bed with the candle out and not much of the day's grime washed off her face, except by tears.

'It's Albert, come for his kiss,' one of her sisters crept into the room to whisper to her. Dorothy bit her lip.

'Have I to tell him he can't have one tonight?'

'Yes. Tell him that.'

'Have I to tell him he can have one in the morning?'

'Tell him I'll see.'

The little sister passed on the message and then came up to creep into bed with her. Albert went home, ashamed.

'Dolly,' her sister whispered to her, much later, 'why are you crying?'

Dorothy sighed, and turned her head so that she could see out of her window to where the moonlight gleamed on the slate roof of Albert's house, and all down the terrace of slate roofs, and beyond that another street of slate roofs, and beyond that again another.

'I don't know, really,' she said. 'It's just that I'll never get away.' Never be posh, she thought. Never know where romance might lead me to.

'We don't want you to,' her sister said.

Dorothy watched, quiet, as the sky came to its full blackness and drained away again.

As soon as her father went out the next morning, Albert was at the door.

'Hello, Albert,' she said. 'It's you.'

He noticed how heavy her eyes were and decided to get on with it quick. 'Will you marry me, Dot?' he asked. Louie and Mrs Beatty were behind the door, listening. He knew that.

Dorothy sighed. 'All right.'

Albert tapped the step with his boot. Men hurried past on their way to work.

'Do you want a kiss this morning?'

'All right. But don't be late for work, will you, Albert Bradley? We want all the money we can get now, if we're to be wed.'

And she pushed her hair back and turned her face up to his, ready.

'Dear Florence'

JANE GARDAM

Jessica Vye's father had given up being a schoolmaster in a public school, and become a clergyman. This has meant great changes for all his family. Set during World War II, A Long Way From Verona, from which this extract is taken, tells of some of Jessica's adventures. When she is invited to a children's house party and dance in the country by the patronizing and snobbish wife of the Rural Dean, Jessica – who wants to be a writer – has to go, but she relieves her feelings by writing to her best friend about it.

High Thwaite Rectory
North Riding of Yorkshire
England, Home and Beauty

Dear Florence,

Don't know why I'm writing to you as I'll probably see you tomorrow or Monday, but I'm stuck at this awful place and nothing to do, so it passes the time till the bus goes this afternoon. For an awful moment when I looked out of the window this morning I thought we were snowed up, but it's only up here in the village. The buses are still running and it's just a question of walking to the lane end and I pray and I pray and I pray that they'll let me. Thank heaven we're not on the phone or I know she'd ring up (the mother) and ask if I could stay on and if I have to stay here a minute longer than they said at first I'll die.

It's the House Party I'm at – do you remember? Snowballing. There *was* snow of course and everything picture postcard. They're all terribly jolly. They all go to some boarding school, the girls. Thank our stars we don't. They're frightful. They call the new girls at the school 'the new bugs' and they play CRICKET in great big pads – I've seen them in the hall cupboard. They have long hair they toss about and they clean out their hairbrushes every Friday night at seven o'clock!!! They write one letter home every Sunday afternoon from 3.30 to four o'clock, and the staff READ it before it's posted. Think of that! You can't say if you're miserable or how filthy old Dobbs is being. Just like writing an essay. I'd go mad. I said so and they all looked at me and said they'd hate to go to a day school, because boarding school makes you Stand On Your Own Feet.

They're so conceited and they've done nothing. The school's apparent(ant?)ly in the wilds and they've never been in an air raid. There's no cinema and they've never been in a public library. They never go out of the school except to church on Sundays like Jane Eyre or something out of Girl's Own P.

Funny thing, but at this party last night there were a lot of aunts and friends of their mother's about called things like Auntie Boo and Lady Pap-Fisher (honestly) and they thought I was one of *them* and Auntie Boo who was in Red Crawss (you have to call it Crawss) uniform with a mouth like a safety pin and hardly ever spoke suddenly said, 'Good thing these girls are away from here, Barby. Raids getting no joke. Tees-side,' and Lady Pap-Musher said, 'But Boo-Boo (yes) you couldn't send them to a local school *anyway*. I mean they're so *crowded* and nobody *does*.' I could see the mother looking at me and pretending to be embarrassed but really rather enjoying it (she's the ghastliest and she hates me) and so I suddenly said, 'How can they be so crowded if nobody does?' and there was the most terrible, horrible silence all round the room.

That was at the supper table – huge great dining-room. It was all very grand. Mrs Fanshawe, the mother, was in a *long dress*! The food was marvellous – they've got their own chickens and I suppose you can get butter and stuff in the country. We had turkey and trifle and ICE CREAM. I'd forgotten what ice cream tasted like – she made it herself. They've got a fridge. It was chocolate. I wish I could have got you some. I'd love Rowley to have some he's never tasted it. Well, anyway, after I'd made this great *gaffe* about local schools there was suddenly a trembly, trembly voice from down the other end of the table, laughing very quietly all by itself. 'What was that, Archie?' Mrs F-S called, and it was the father, who's the rector, sitting down the other end just laughing away as if he was all alone or at the pictures or something. He's incredibly old with a long face very pale with freckles like national wheatmeal bread – there's a son, Giles, with the same face exactly, both very learned-looking with specs.

'Who is that child?' he said, the rector. 'Hush!' said

Mrs F-S, 'I believe Archie spoke,' and everyone was quiet. 'Who is that child – the child with the wild eyes,' he said (me!) and she said, 'That is Jessica Vye, my dear,' and *he* said, 'F. J. Vye's daughter. I might have guessed,' and went on with this trembly, trembly laugh.

Well, (I hope you're enjoying this) then the dance began. They've got a vast great room with a carpet rolled up and the sofas pushed back and a piano in the corner. Auntie Boo played it till it nearly burst – great marches and things. We had a Paul Jones to get us going but it was nearly all girls. Mrs F-S and the Nannie sort of person and Lady Pap had to be boys, and one or two of the big girls. The rector disappeared and so the only real boys were this speckly son and a couple of nondescript friends and the verger's grandson who arrived after supper and a soppy boy Lady Thing had brought. Half the time I seemed to get opposite Mrs F-S but we pretended I hadn't and grabbed just anyone. She's one of those people who can read your thoughts. We seem to be very uneasy in each other's company.

Well we did valetas and gay gordons and military two-steps and hokey-cokeys and pally-glides and Lambeth Walk. The verger's grandson suddenly shouted out, 'Let's 'ave knees oop Mother Brown,' but they pretended they hadn't heard.

Well all of a sudden I got awfully fed up with it all and so I got near the door and slunk off. Actually it's a lovely house. I wish I could be absolutely alone in it, just walking and walking through all the rooms in the moonlight. I walked down a corridor and up the back

stairs, and then I came down the main staircase again – it's curving and it has lovely curly iron banisters with roses and things. It would be marvellous for plays. And then I strolled about until I got to the library where we'd been when we first arrived and there was a coal fire in there and the shutters back and the snow shining in and over the fire in a chair with a high back there was a boy. I nearly had a fit. I thought he was a ghost because (don't tell *anyone* this) he was absolutely, exactly like Rupert Brooke. He was leaning forwards looking into the fire with his chin in his hand and his hands were very long and his wrists were very long, too, sticking out of his jacket that was too small for him and he had that marvellous face and his hair was terribly long and thick – all round at the back like you never see now, and you could tell it was the most marvellous blond – you could even see in the dark, what with the fire and the snow outside. He was better than Leslie Howard and about 16 I think.

Well, I just stood inside the door and in the end he said without even looking round, 'Who're you?' I said Jessica Vye and he said nothing, just went on staring at the fire, fiddling about, bashing at a log with a poker. Then all of a sudden he said, 'Jessica VYE!' and got up – he's terribly tall – and stood staring and staring at me. I was in that foul ANTEDILUVIAN viyella I had last year, with the waist nearly under my arms and the top of my legs all fat, but he just stared and stared. I thought it must be Romeo and Juliet or something (except that I haven't read it) and I must say I just stared and stared back. Then he said, 'Can I come and see him?' Just like that! I thought, crikey! and I said yes, I supposed he could and he said, 'When?' I said, 'Well any time I suppose. Why d'you want to see my father?' and he said, 'Because he is a Great Man.'

Just then there was a noise and a door opened and people were calling things out and the piano started

God Save the King like mad. 'The party's over,' this boy said. 'You'd better go back,' and he sat down again. So I went away and we waved off the guests who weren't staying the night, through the snow, and we all went to bed. Magdalene – the sister – and her friend talked for hours through the wall and giggled, and the two I was sharing the day nursery with sniggered on a bit, but I just shut my eyes and pretended to be asleep. Actually he is the most heavenly, marvellous person I've ever seen in my life and I didn't mean what I said at the beginning of this letter that I'm having an awful time, because I've never been so happy in my whole life.

Love Jessica

I finished and blotted the last page of this letter very carefully – it was in an exercise book that I'd got with me. I was writing at one of those little desks with drawers all down one side and a square of old green leather on top, which faced the garden where I saw all at once that snowballing was going on. I watched how everyone was running about, dark, sharp people on the soft snow against the rounded bushes and the uphill lawns. Mrs F-S was there, very rosy, and even the rector in a long sloppy coat over his cassock and two fawn mufflers. The little girls were leaping about the see-saw. Their breath was going up in blue puffs. The brown church tower went up behind them. It was happy and beautiful. I saw my mother, suddenly, in our cluttery kitchen, all in a flummox, pulling on a coat, over her apron, calling 'Freddie, look after Rowley for a minute. I've got to fly. I've forgotten . . .' And her awful hands. Sophie landed Giles a snowball on his glasses. 'Bravo,' cried the rector clapping his hands in the air while Mrs Fanshawe laughed her tranquil laugh.

And I hated them.

I read the letter through from beginning to end and then I turned back to where it said that I left the party – 'Well I got suddenly fed up' or something of the sort (I've had to write it from memory but I have a good one) and I carefully tore off just above it: and then I tore everything that came after it into the smallest possible pieces. I found an envelope – one of the thick, clean ones the invitation had come in – which was in a little wooden rack thing on the desk, and I put all the pieces into it and put it up my knicker leg.

Then I took another envelope and addressed it to Florence Bone and put the half-letter in just adding love from Jessica along the furry bottom edge, and as I stuck it up I felt somebody standing behind me in the door and I turned round. 'You coming for a walk?' he asked – the marvellous boy.

The Weeping Lass at the Dancing Place

SORCHE NIC LEODHAS

In Scotland (and Ireland) it was the custom to have a cleared patch of ground outside towns and villages, where after work and at holiday-time the young people of the community could meet and dance. This scary story is a traditional one, retold by an American who was very proud of her Scottish ancestry. As a child she loved to hear all the Scottish folk-tales told by her father and by relatives who visited her family in America.

Outside many a Scottish village, where the crossroads meet, there will be a level bit of ground lying in one of the triangles made by the intersection of the roads. In the old days folk would be calling such a spot the dancing place, because it was the custom of the young lads and lasses of the neighbourhood to gather there, to dance away the hours of a moonlit night. Generations of lively young feet trod down and packed the soil in these places, until the surface was as hard and smooth as stone. No fine laird and his lady could ever have found a grander floor to dance upon than a dancing place.

It was once in the summer twilight, a long, long time

ago, that a company of young folk gathered at such a dancing place to foot it gaily, by the light of the moon.

They came from all directions; those from the village on foot, and those who lived farther away on crofts or farmsteads, riding upon their shaggy wee Highland ponies or upon their workaday mares. Some of the lads came riding with their lasses perched on their saddles behind them, and some of them came walking with their sweethearts on their arms. Their gay voices rose sweetly on the fresh breeze of the summer evening, and the sound of talk and laughter filled the air as the young folk met.

Those who came alone soon found partners, except for one lass who came stealing along from the village, at the end of the merry line. She did not join the others but sat herself down in the shadows cast by a hedge along the road.

The voices of the dancers provided the music for their dancing. Having neither pipe nor fiddle to mark the measures, they moved to the tunes of the songs they sang, and if the breath of some of them failed in the exertion of the dance, there were always enough of the singers to keep the song going until the laggards could take up the tune again.

The lass who sat under the hedge made no move to join in the fun. Word had been brought to her in the early springtime, some months before, that her lover had been drowned in the sea during the herring fishing, and she had made a vow never to sing or dance again all her whole life long.

From the day they told her of her true love's death she had spent all her time lamenting and weeping. Even in her sleep she dreamed of her loss, and the tears ran down her cheeks while she slept.

It was the grief of her life that she could not sit and mourn beside the grave of her dead lover, but the seaside village to which he had gone for the fishing was at a distance from his own home. When his body was washed ashore, the villages had carried it to their own graveyard and buried it there.

Now the lass sat by herself in the shadow of the hedge, near the dancing place where she and her love had once been happy together, and watched and listened and wept.

While the dancers were merrymaking a man came cantering along the road on a great black horse. He pulled up his steed at sight of the merry throng, and swinging himself from its back, he hurried to join their sport. The dancers, intent upon their own amusement, paid him little heed, but opened their ranks to let him in. He, for his part, threw himself into the dance with a will. No voice laughed louder or sang more gaily, no foot moved more fleetly than that of the stranger in their midst.

So the night wore on, and many a reel and strathspey and jig was footed by the young folk, and many a gay lilt was sung. But all good things must come to an end. As the hour grew late, the dancers, tiring, began to steal away for home. One or two at a time they went at first, then in larger numbers, until the last stragglers in a body hurried away. No one was left then at the dancing place but the stranger who had ridden there upon his black horse and the lass who sat weeping under the hedge.

He strode up to the lass and stood looking down upon her.

'You were once a bonnie, bonnie lass,' said he. 'And you'd be bonnie again if your face were not so raddled with weeping and your eyes not so swollen red.'

She buried her face in her hands and wept harder. 'Why would I not be weeping?' said she. 'The tears I'm shedding are for my true love who is dead.'

'Greeting and grieving will not bring the dead back to life again,' the stranger said roughly. 'So much mourning serves no purpose but to make it so the dead cannot rest easy in their graves. Come, lass, dry your tears and hush your lament, and tread a measure with me!'

She looked up at him but could not see his face because of the tears in her eyes. She shook her head. 'I will not dance,' said she.

But he reached down and took her wrist in his hand, and pulling her to her feet, he drew her towards the dancing place. She held back and struggled with all her might, but he was stronger than she and he would not let her go. Against her will she found her feet were moving in the figures of the dance, while he whistled softly to mark the time of their steps.

'I will not!' she protested and tried to free herself.

'Aye, but you will!' said he, and she could not stop, because he whirled her so madly and held her so fast.

Then, she looked up at the face that bent above her.

318

A shaft of the cold moonlight lay white upon it, and she cried out. The face she saw was that of the lover whom she had mourned so long! Her heart leaped for joy and she called him by name. 'They told me you were dead!' she cried.

'Is that what they told you?' he asked.

'They said you were dead and long buried,' said she.

'Did they say so?' he asked, and whirled her faster and faster in the dance.

'You will never leave me again?' she begged him.

'I must be on my way from here, lass,' he told her. 'Long before the break of dawn.'

'Then I shall go too,' the lass cried out. 'Take me with you wherever you go!'

'My dwelling place is small and low,' he told her. 'I doubt you'd like it o'ermuch. The walls are damp and it is dark, and there is little more than room enough for me.'

'With me to help we'll soon earn a better,' the lass insisted stoutly. 'I'll help with my hands and share your toil each day.'

'You'd do better to find yourself a new love,' he said.

'You shall not go without me,' said she.

'Come then, if you must!' he said.

Then he took her up behind him on his great black horse, and off they galloped up the road the way he had come.

'Hold fast!' he bade her. 'The time is short. We have a long way to go and I must be home before the break of day.'

The black horse spurned the stones of the road with

his hooves until sparks flew out at either side. The wind came tearing after them, but never caught up with them as they sped by.

'Hold fast!' the lass's lover called to her over his shoulder, and at his command, she caught his belt in both her hands and held it tight.

Then a chill came over her. She felt so cold that she thought she could not bear it. She wondered that a summer night should freeze one to the bone like one of winter, but laid it to the speed at which they rode.

Her lover's garments whipped back against her. She wondered, as they touched her, why they felt so damp when no rain had fallen all along the way.

'Why is your cloak so wet?' she asked, but he made no reply at all.

The black horse raced faster and faster, through clachan and village, and over hill and down.

'Will we not soon be there?' the lass cried out in despair.

But her love whipped his steed on through the night without an answering word.

Then, of a sudden, her shawl flew up into her face. She had to take one hand from his belt to pull the shawl down and wrap it about herself. When she reached to take hold of the belt again she grasped, instead, a handful of his linen shirt. The cloth was icy cold and heavy with moisture. 'Why are your clothes so dripping wet!' she exclaimed. 'Och, a body'd think you'd been riding through a storm, but no rain at all has fallen. See then, my own clothes are dry.'

Just at that moment they came to the gate of a kirkyard where the kirk stood tall and dark with its graves on either side.

Her lover slowed his black horse down, and turned it in at the gate, bringing it to a stop among the graves at one side of the kirk.

'This is my dwelling place,' he told her, as he alighted from his horse. 'You gave me no rest in my grave. The sound of your voice lamenting kept me awake night and day. And if my clothes are wet, 'tis little wonder, for the tears you have shed have gathered and run down into the place where I lay. Now you shall cease your weeping and lie beside me in my grave, and I shall have peace at last.'

The lass looked down at the face that was turned up to her own. She saw, with horror, that it was not a face at all, but a bony skull, and under the clothes that clung so wetly there was no warm living flesh, but only whitened bones. Then she knew that her lover

The Weeping Lass

was dead indeed, and it was his ghost that had brought her here.

'Come!' he said, and reached up to pull her down from the back of the horse.

But she cried, 'Nay!' and slipped to the ground on the other side. She gathered up her skirts and ran away from him, faster than she'd ever run in all her life before.

He came after her, his bony hands outstretched to catch her. She felt his fingers take hold of the border of her shawl. But she cast off the shawl and ran on. She ran out from among the graves and down the path in front of the kirk, and through the gate of the kirkyard into the road. She was growing too short of breath to keep on running. She glanced over her shoulder to see how close he followed at her back. But just at the moment she looked, the dawn broke in the eastern sky, and on every side the cocks began to crow to greet the morn.

Like a puff of mist dissolving, ghost and horse disappeared, and the lass saw naught behind her but the kirk and the kirkyard with its graves, peaceful in the first grey morning light.

The shock of relief at finding her pursuer gone was too great for the lass to bear. She lost her senses and fell to the road, and there she lay.

A milkmaid on her way to milk her cows found the lass lying there in the middle of the road, and ran to the village close by to fetch help. Men came and carried her to a house where kind hands took her in and cared for her, until she came to herself again.

322

They were curious to know what had happened to her, and when she told her story they were amazed. They might have thought that she had dreamed it all, or even that she was daft, if it had not been for the shawl.

She had told them of casting her shawl away, when the spectre grasped it in his hand. And it was true she wore no shawl when she was found. It was two or three days later that one of the villagers went to the kirkyard to tidy the graves, and saw upon one of them what looked to be a bit of tartan cloth with fringe at the edge. He went to pick it up, wondering how it had come to lie there, but found that it was buried deep in the mound of the grave. Pull as he might, he could not get it out. Then he remembered the strange lassie's shawl, and hurried to tell his neighbours what he had found. They all ran to the kirkyard, and brought the lass with them.

' 'Tis my shawl,' she told them. 'I've had it many a year. I would not like to lose it.'

But it was so firmly fixed in the soil that the strongest man in the village could not pull the shawl out. In the end they had to fetch shovels and dig it out. They dug all the way down to the coffin but still they could not pull the shawl away. It was not until the minister said that they might open the coffin lid to release the end of the shawl, that they found out what held it so fast.

There, inside the coffin, was the corner of the shawl, held tight in the bony fingers of the man who was buried there. It was the grave of the lass's lover whose drowned body had been washed ashore and buried by the villagers.

When the lass recovered from the fright of that terrible journey she went back to her own village again. But she wept no longer for her dead lover, since she had no wish to disturb him, lest he come and carry her off again.

The Gifts of the Magician

ANDREW LANG

At first this story may not seem to be about dancing at all. But read on . . . In Sorche nic Leodhas's story 'The Weeping Lass at the Dancing Place', the dance is normal, but what happens afterwards is very frightening. But dancing itself can be scary. Here it's used to stave off disaster and teach a lesson! This story comes from Finland. It's one of the many folk tales that Andrew Lang collected, and which he put into a famous series of books called after different colours.

Once upon a time there was an old man who lived in a little hut in the middle of a forest. His wife was dead, and he had only one son, whom he loved dearly. Near their hut was a group of birch trees, in which some black-game had made their nests, and the youth had often begged his father's permission to shoot the birds. But the old man always strictly forbade him to do anything of the kind.

One day, however, when the father had gone to a little distance to collect some sticks for the fire, the boy fetched his bow and shot at a bird that was just flying toward its nest. But he had not taken proper aim, and the bird was only wounded and fluttered along the ground.

The boy ran to catch it, but though he ran very fast and the bird seemed to flutter along very slowly, he never could quite come up with it; it was always just a little in advance. But so absorbed was he in the chase that he did not notice for some time that he was now deep in the forest, in a place where he had never been before. Then he felt it would be foolish to go any farther, and he turned to find his way home.

He thought it would be easy enough to follow the path along which he had come but somehow it was always branching off in unexpected directions. He looked about for a house where he might stop and ask his way, but there was not a sign of one anywhere. He was afraid to stand still, for it was cold and there were many stories of wolves being seen in that part of the forest.

Night fell, and he was beginning to start at every sound, when suddenly a magician came running toward him, with a pack of wolves snapping at his heels. Then all the boy's courage returned to him. He took his bow and, aiming an arrow at the largest wolf, shot him through the heart. A few more arrows soon put the rest to flight. The magician was full of gratitude to his deliverer and promised him a reward for his help if the youth would return with him to his house.

'Indeed there is nothing that would be more welcome to me than a night's lodging,' answered the boy. 'I have been wandering all day in the forest and do not know how to get home again.'

'Come with me, you must be hungry as well as tired,' said the magician, and led the way to his house, where the guest flung himself on a bed and went fast asleep. But his host returned to the forest to get some food, for the larder was empty.

While he was absent the housekeeper went to the boy's room and tried to wake him. She stamped on the floor, shook him and called to him, telling him that he was in great danger, and must take flight at once. But nothing would rouse him, and if the boy did open his eyes he shut them again directly.

Soon afterward, the magician came back from the forest and told the housekeeper to bring them something to eat. The meal was quickly ready and the magician called to the boy to come down and eat it, but he could not be wakened, and they had to sit down to supper without him.

By-and-by the magician went out into the wood again for some more hunting, and on his return he tried afresh to waken the youth. But finding it quite impossible, he went back for the third time to the forest.

While he was absent the boy woke up and dressed himself. Then he came downstairs and began to talk to the housekeeper. The girl had heard how he had saved her master's life, so she said nothing more about his running away. Instead she told him that if the magician offered him the choice of a reward, he was to ask for the horse which stood in the third stall of the stable.

By-and-by the old man came back and they all sat down to dinner. When they had finished the magician said, 'Now, my son, tell me what you will have as the reward of your courage?'

'Give me the horse that stands in the third stall of your stable,' answered the youth. 'For I have a long way to go before I get home, and my feet will not carry me so far.'

'Ah, my son,' replied the magician, 'it is the best horse in my stable that you want! Will not anything else please you as well?'

But the youth declared that it was the horse, and the horse only, that he desired, and in the end the old man gave way. And besides the horse, the magician gave him a zither, a fiddle and a flute, saying:

'If you are in danger touch the zither; and if no one comes to your aid then play on the fiddle; but if that brings no help, blow on the flute.'

The youth thanked the magician and, fastening his treasures about him, mounted the horse and rode off. He had already gone some miles when, to his great surprise, the horse spoke, and said:

'It is no use your returning home just now, your father will only beat you. Let us visit a few towns first; something lucky will be sure to happen to us.'

This advice pleased the boy, for he felt himself almost a man by this time and thought it was high time he saw the world. When they entered the capital of the country everyone stopped to admire the beauty of the horse. Even the king heard of it and came to see the splendid creature with his own eyes. Indeed, he wanted directly to buy it and told the youth he would give any price he liked. The young man hesitated for a moment, but before he could speak, the horse contrived to whisper to him:

'Do not sell me, but ask the king to take me to his stable and feed me there; then his other horses will become just as beautiful as I.'

The king was delighted, when he was told what the horse had said, and took the animal at once to the stables and placed it in his own particular stall. Sure enough, the horse had scarcely eaten a mouthful of corn out of the manger, when the rest of the horses seemed to have undergone a transformation. Some of them were old favourites, which the king had ridden in many wars, and they bore the signs of age and of service. But now they arched their heads and pawed the ground with their slender legs as they had been wont to do in days long gone by.

The king's heart beat with delight, but the old groom who had had the care of them stood crossly by, and eyed the owner of this wonderful creature with hate and envy. Not a day passed without his bringing some story against the youth to his master, but the king understood all about the matter and paid no attention. At last the groom declared that the young man had boasted that he could find the king's war horse which had strayed into the forest several years before and had not been heard of since.

Now the king had never ceased to mourn for his horse, so this time he listened to the tale which the groom had invented, and sent for the youth. 'Find me my horse in three days,' said he, 'or it will be the worse for you.'

The youth was thunderstruck at this command, but he only bowed and went off at once to the stable.

'Do not worry yourself,' answered his own horse. 'Ask the king to give you a hundred oxen and to let them be killed and cut into small pieces. Then we will start on our journey and ride till we reach a certain river. There a horse will come up to you, but take no notice of him. Soon another will appear, which also you must leave alone, but when the third horse shows itself, throw my bridle over it.'

Everything happened just as the horse had said, and the third horse was safely bridled. Then the boy's horse spoke again:

'The magician's raven will try to eat us as we ride away, but throw it some of the oxen's flesh, and then I will gallop like the wind, and carry you safe out of his clutches.'

So the young man did as he was told and brought the horse back to the king.

The old stableman was very jealous, when he heard of it, and wondered what he could do to injure the youth in the eyes of his royal master. At last he hit upon a plan and told the king that the young man had boasted that he could bring home the king's wife who had vanished many months before, without leaving a trace behind her.

Then the king bade the young man come into his presence, and desired him to fetch the queen home again as he had boasted he could do. And if he failed, his head would pay the penalty.

The poor youth's heart stood still as he listened.

Find the queen? But how was he to do that, when nobody in the palace had been able to do so! Slowly he walked to the stable. Laying his head on his horse's shoulder, he said, 'The king has ordered me to bring his wife home again; how can I do that when she disappeared so long ago and no one can tell me anything about her?'

'Cheer up!' answered the horse. 'We will manage to find her. You have only to ride me back to the same river that we went to yesterday and I will plunge into it and take my proper shape again. For I am the king's wife who was turned into a horse by the magician from whom you saved me.'

Joyfully the young man sprang into the saddle and rode away to the banks of the river. Then he threw himself off and waited while the horse plunged in. The moment it dipped its head into the water its dark skin vanished and the most beautiful woman in the world was floating on the water. She came smiling toward the youth. She held out her hand and he took it and led her back to the palace. Great was the king's surprise and happiness when he beheld his lost wife standing before him, and in gratitude to her rescuer he loaded him with gifts.

You would have thought that after this the poor youth would have been left in peace; but no, his enemy the stableman hated him as much as ever, and laid a new plot for his undoing. This time he presented himself before the king and told him that the youth was so puffed up with what he had done that he had declared he would seize the king's throne for himself.

At this news the king waxed so furious that he ordered a gallows to be erected at once and the young man to be hanged without a trial. He was not even allowed to speak in his own defence, but on the very steps of the gallows he sent a message to the king and begged, as a last favour, that he might play a tune on his zither.

Leave was given him, and taking the instrument from under his cloak he touched the strings. Scarcely had the first notes sounded than the hangman and his helper began to dance and the louder grew the music the higher they capered, till at last they cried for mercy. But the youth paid no heed and the tunes rang out more merrily than before, and by the time the sun set the men both sank on the ground exhausted and declared that the hanging must be put off till to-morrow.

The story of the zither soon spread through the town, and on the following morning the king and his whole court and a large crowd of people were gathered at the foot of the gallows to see the youth hanged. Once more he asked a favour – permission to play on his fiddle, and this the king was graciously pleased to grant. But with the first notes, the leg of every man in the crowd was lifted high, and they danced to the sound of the music the whole day till darkness fell, and there was no light to hang the musician by.

The third day came, and the youth asked leave to play on his flute. 'No, no,' said the king, 'you made me dance all day yesterday; if I do it again it will certainly be my death. You shall play no more tunes. Quick! The rope round his neck.'

At these words the young man looked so sorrowful that the courtiers said the king, 'He is very young to die. Let him play a tune if it will make him happy.'

So, very unwillingly, the king gave him leave, but first he had himself bound to a big fir tree, for fear that he should be made to dance.

When he was made fast, the young man began to blow softly on his flute, and bound though he was, the king's body moved to the sound, up and down the fir tree till his clothes were in tatters, and the skin nearly rubbed off his back. But the youth had no pity and went on blowing, till suddenly the old magician appeared and asked, 'What danger are you in, my son, that you have sent for me?'

'They want to hang me,' answered the young man. 'The gallows is all ready and the hangman is only waiting for me to stop playing.'

'Oh, I will put that right,' said the magician; and taking the gallows, he tore it up and flung it into the air, and no one knows where it came down. 'Who has ordered you to be hanged?' asked he.

The young man pointed to the king, who was still bound to the fir, and without wasting words the magician took hold of the tree also, and with a mighty heave both fir and man went spinning through the air and vanished in the clouds after the gallows.

Then the youth was declared to be free and the people elected him their king; and the stable helper drowned himself from envy, for, after all, if it had not been for him the young man would have remained poor all the days of his life.

Toomai of the Elephants

RUDYARD KIPLING

Rudyard Kipling was born in India, and when he grew up he worked there as a journalist for several years. He was fascinated by the country, with its enormous variety of scenery and people, and used it as the basis for many stories and poems. One of the most famous of the books he wrote for children is The Jungle Book, *which has many stories set in India. This is one of them.*

I will remember what I was. I am sick of rope and chain.
I will remember my old strength and all my forest affairs.
I will not sell my back to man for a bundle of sugar-cane,
I will go out to my own kind, and the wood-folk in their
    lairs.

I will go out until the day, until the morning break,
Out to the winds' untainted kiss, the waters' clean caress:
I will forget my ankle-ring and snap my picket-stake.
I will revisit my lost loves, and playmates masterless!

Kala Nag, which means Black Snake, had served the Indian government in every way that an elephant could serve it for forty-seven years, and as he was fully twenty years old when he was caught, that makes him nearly seventy – a ripe age for an elephant.

He remembered pushing, with a big leather pad on his forehead, at a gun stuck in deep mud, and that was before the Afghan War of 1842, and he had not then come to his full strength. His mother, Radha Pyari – Radha the darling – who had been caught in the same drive with Kala Nag, told him, before his little milk-tusks had dropped out, that elephants who were afraid always got hurt; and Kala Nag knew that that advice was good, for the first time that he saw a shell burst he backed, screaming, into a stand of piled rifles, and the bayonets pricked him in all his softest places. So before he was twenty-five he gave up being afraid, and so he was the best-loved and the best-looked-after elephant in the service of the government of India. He had carried tents, twelve hundred pounds' weight of tents, on the march in Upper India; he had been hoisted into a ship at the end of a steam-crane and taken for days across the water, and made to carry a mortar on his back in a strange and rocky country very far from India, and had seen the Emperor Theodore lying dead in Magdala, and had come back again in the steamer, entitled, so the soldiers said, to the Abyssinian War medal. He had seen his fellow elephants die of cold and epilepsy and starvation and sunstroke up at a place called Ali Musjid, ten years later; and afterwards he had been sent down thousands of miles south to haul and pile big baulks of teak in the timber-yards at Moulmein. There he had half killed an insubordinate young elephant who was shirking his fair share of the work.

After that he was taken off timber-hauling, and

employed, with a few score other elephants who were trained to the business, in helping to catch wild elephants among the Garo hills. Elephants are very strictly preserved by the Indian Government. There is one whole department which does nothing else but hunt them, and catch them, and break them in, and send them up and down the country as they are needed for work.

Kala Nag stood ten fair feet at the shoulders, and his tusks had been cut off short at five feet, and bound round the ends, to prevent them splitting, with bands of copper; but he could do more with those stumps than any untrained elephant could do with the real sharpened ones.

When, after weeks and weeks of cautious driving of scattered elephants across the hills, the forty or fifty wild monsters were driven into the last stockade, and the big drop-gate, made of tree trunks lashed together, jarred down behind them, Kala Nag, at the word of command, would go into that flaring, trumpeting pandemonium (generally at night, when the flicker of the torches made it difficult to judge distances), and, picking out the biggest and wildest tusker of the mob, would hammer him and hustle him into quiet while the men on the backs of the elephants roped and tied the smaller ones.

There was nothing in the way of fighting that Kala Nag, the old wise Black Snake, did not know, for he had stood up more than once in his time to the charge of the wounded tiger, and, curling up his soft trunk to be out of harm's way, had knocked the springing brute sideways in mid-air with a quick sickle-cut of his head, that he had invented all by himself; had knocked him over, and kneeled upon him with his huge knees till the life went out with a gasp and a howl, and there was only a fluffy striped thing on the ground for Kala Nag to pull by the tail.

'Yes,' said Big Toomai, his driver, the son of Black Toomai who had taken him to Abyssinia, and grandson of Toomai of the Elephants who had seen him caught, 'there is nothing that the Black Snake fears except me. He has seen three generations of us feed him and groom him, and he will live to see four.'

'He is afraid of *me* also,' said Little Toomai, standing up to his full height of four feet, with only one rag upon him. He was ten years old, the eldest son of Big Toomai, and, according to custom, he would take his father's place on Kala Nag's neck when he grew up, and would handle the heavy iron ankus, the elephant-goad that had been worn smooth by his father, and his grandfather, and his great-grandfather. He knew what he was talking of; for he had been born under Kala Nag's shadow, had played with the end of his trunk before he could walk, had taken him down to water as soon as he could walk, and Kala Nag would no more have dreamed of disobeying his shrill little orders than he would have dreamed of killing him on that day when Big Toomai carried the little brown baby under Kala Nag's tusks, and told him to salute his master that was to be.

'Yes,' said Little Toomai, 'he is afraid of *me*,' and he took long strides up to Kala Nag, called him a fat old pig, and made him lift up his feet one after the other.

'Wah!' said Little Toomai, 'thou art a big elephant,' and he wagged his fluffy head, quoting his father. 'The government may pay for elephants, but they belong to us mahouts. When thou art old, Kala Nag, there will come some rich rajah, and he will buy thee from the government, on account of thy size and thy manners, and then thou wilt have nothing to do but to carry gold earrings in thy ears, and a gold howdah on thy back, and a red cloth covered with gold on thy sides, and walk at the head of the processions of the king. Then I shall sit on thy neck, O Kala Nag, with a silver ankus, and men will run before us with golden sticks, crying, "Room for the king's elephant!" That will be good, Kala Nag, but not so good as this hunting in the jungles.'

'Umph!' said Big Toomai. 'Thou art a boy, and as wild as a buffalo-calf. This running up and down among the hills is not the best government service. I am getting old, and I do not love wild elephants. Give me brick elephant-lines, one stall to each elephant, and big stumps to tie them to safely, and flat, broad roads to exercise upon, instead of this come-and-go camping. Aha, the Cawnpore barracks were good. There was a bazaar close by, and only three hours' work a day.'

Little Toomai remembered the Cawnpore elephant-lines and said nothing. He very much preferred the camp life, and hated those broad, flat roads, with the daily grubbing for grass in the forage-reserve, and the long hours when there was nothing to do except to watch Kala Nag fidgeting in his pickets.

What Little Toomai liked was the scramble up bridle-paths that only an elephant could take; the dip into the valley below; the glimpses of the wild elephants browsing miles away; the rush of the frightened pig and peacock under Kala Nag's feet; the blinding warm rains, when all the hills and valleys smoked; the beautiful misty mornings when nobody knew where they would camp that night; the steady, cautious drive of the wild elephants, and the mad rush and blaze and hullabaloo of the last night's drive, when the elephants poured into the stockade like boulders in a landslide, found that they could not get out, and flung themselves at the heavy posts only to be driven back by yells and flaring torches and volleys of blank cartridge.

Even a little boy could be of use there, and Toomai was as useful as three boys. He would get his torch and wave it, and yell with the best. But the really good time came when the driving out began, and the Keddah – that is, the stockade – looked like a picture of the end of the world, and men had to make signs to one another, because they could not hear themselves speak. Then Little Toomai would climb up to the top of one of the quivering stockade-posts, his sun-bleached brown hair flying loose all over his shoulders, and he looking like a goblin in the torchlight; and as soon as there was a lull you could hear his high-pitched yells of encouragement to Kala Nag, above the trumpeting and crashing, and snapping of ropes, and groans of the tethered elephants. '*Maîl, maîl, Kala Nag!* [Go on, go on, Black Snake!] *Dant do!* [Give him the tusk!] *Somalo! Somalo!* [Careful, careful!] *Maro! Mar!* [Hit him, hit him!] Mind the post! *Arré! Arré! Hai! Yai! Kya-a-ah!'* he would shout, and the big fight between Kala Nag and the wild elephant would sway to and fro across the Keddah, and the old elephant-catchers would wipe the sweat out of their eyes, and find time to nod to Little Toomai wriggling with joy on the top of the posts.

He did more than wriggle. One night he slid down from the post and slipped in between the elephants, and threw up the loose end of a rope, which had dropped, to a driver who was trying to get a purchase on the leg of a kicking young calf (calves always give more trouble than full-grown animals). Kala Nag saw him, caught him in his trunk, and handed him up to Big Toomai, who slapped him then and there, and put him back on the post.

Next morning he gave him a scolding, and said: 'Are not good brick elephant-lines and a little tent-carrying enough, that thou must needs go elephant-catching on thy own account, little worthless? Now those foolish hunters, whose pay is less than my pay, have spoken to Petersen Sahib of the matter.' Little Toomai was frightened. He did not know much of white men, but Petersen Sahib was the greatest white man in the world to him. He was the head of all the Keddah operations – the man who caught all the elephants for the Government of India, and who knew more about the ways of elephants than any living man.

'What – what will happen?' said Little Toomai.

'Happen! The worst that can happen. Petersen Sahib is a madman. Else why should he go hunting these wild devils? He may even require thee to be an elephant-catcher, to sleep anywhere in these fever-filled jungles, and at last to be trampled to death in the Keddah. It is well that this nonsense ends safely. Next week the catching is over, and we of the plains are sent back to our stations. Then we will march on smooth roads, and forget all this hunting. But, son, I am angry that thou shouldst meddle in the business that belongs to these dirty Assamese jungle folk. Kala Nag will obey none but me, so I must go with him into the Keddah; but he is only a fighting elephant, and he does not help to rope them. So I sit at my ease, as befits a mahout – not a mere hunter – a mahout, I say, and a man who gets a pension at the end of his service. Is the family of Toomai of the Elephants to be trodden underfoot in the dirt of a Keddah? Bad one! Wicked one! Worthless son! Go and wash Kala Nag and attend to his ears, and see that there are no thorns in his feet; or else Petersen Sahib will surely catch thee and make thee a wild hunter – a follower of elephants' foot-tracks, a jungle-bear. Bah! Shame! Go!'

Little Toomai went off without saying a word, but he told Kala Nag all his grievances while he was examining his feet. 'No matter,' said Little Toomai, turning up the fringe of Kala Nag's huge right ear. 'They have said my name to Petersen Sahib, and perhaps – and perhaps – and perhaps – who knows? Hai! That is a big thorn that I have pulled out!'

The next few days were spent in getting the elephants together, in walking the newly caught wild elephants up and down between a couple of tame ones, to prevent them from giving too much trouble on the downward march to the plains, and in taking stock of the blankets and ropes and things that had been worn out or lost in the forest.

Petersen Sahib came in on his clever she-elephant, Pudmini. He had been paying off other camps among the hills, for the season was coming to an end, and there was a native clerk sitting at a table under a tree to pay the drivers their wages. As each man was paid he went back to his elephant, and joined the line that stood ready to start. The catchers, and hunters, and beaters, the men of the regular Keddah, who stayed in the jungle year in and year out, sat on the backs of the elephants that belonged to Petersen Sahib's permanent force, or leaned against the trees with their guns across their arms, and made fun of the drivers who were going away, and laughed when the newly caught elephants broke the line and ran about.

Big Toomai went up to the clerk with Little Toomai behind him, and Machua Appa, the head-tracker, said in an undertone to a friend of his, 'There goes one piece of good elephant-stuff at least. 'Tis a pity to send that young jungle-cock to moult in the plains.'

Now Petersen Sahib had ears all over him, as a man must have who listens to the most silent of all living things – the wild elephant. He turned where he was lying all along on Pudmini's back, and said, 'What is that? I did not know of a man among the plains drivers who had wit enough to rope even a dead elephant.'

'This is not a man, but a boy. He went into the Keddah at the last drive, and threw Barmao there the rope when we were trying to get that young calf with the blotch on his shoulder away from his mother.'

Machua Appa pointed at Little Toomai, and Petersen Sahib looked, and Little Toomai bowed to the earth.

'He throw a rope? He is smaller than a picket-pin. Little one, what is thy name?' said Petersen Sahib.

Little Toomai was too frightened to speak, but Kala Nag was behind him, and Toomai made a sign with his hand, and the elephant caught him up in his trunk and held him level with Pudmini's forehead, in front of the great Petersen Sahib. Then Little Toomai covered his face with his hands, for he was only a child, and except where elephants were concerned, he was just as bashful as a child could be.

'Oho!' said Petersen Sahib, smiling underneath his moustache, 'and why didst thou teach thy elephant *that* trick? Was it to help thee steal green corn from the roofs of the houses when the ears are put out to dry?'

'Not green corn, Protector of the Poor – melons,' said Little Toomai, and all the men sitting about broke into a roar of laughter. Most of them had taught their elephants that trick when they were boys. Little Toomai was hanging eight feet up in the air, and he wished very much that he were eight feet under ground.

'He is Toomai, my son, Sahib,' said Big Toomai,

scowling. 'He is a very bad boy, and he will end in a gaol, Sahib.'

'Of that I have my doubts,' said Petersen Sahib. 'A boy who can face a full Keddah at his age does not end in gaol. See, little one, here are four annas to spend in sweetmeats because thou hast a little head under that great thatch of hair. In time thou mayest become a hunter too.' Big Toomai scowled more than ever. 'Remember, though, that Keddahs are not good for children to play in,' Petersen Sahib went on.

'Must I never go there, Sahib?' asked Little Toomai, with a big gasp.

'Yes.' Petersen Sahib smiled again. 'When thou hast seen the elephants dance. That is the proper time. Come to me when thou hast seen the elephants dance, and then I will let thee go into all the Keddahs.'

There was another roar of laughter, for that is an old joke among elephant-catchers, and it means just never. There are great cleared flat places hidden away in the forests that are called elephants' ballrooms, but even these are only found by accident, and no man has ever seen the elephants dance. When a driver boasts of his skill and bravery the other drivers say, 'And when didst *thou* see the elephants dance?'

Kala Nag put Little Toomai down, and he bowed to the earth again and went away with his father, and gave the silver four-anna piece to his mother, who was nursing his baby brother, and they all were put up on Kala Nag's back, and the line of grunting, squealing elephants rolled down the hill path to the plains. It was a very lively march on account of the new

345

elephants, who gave trouble at every ford, and who needed coaxing or beating every other minute.

Big Toomai prodded Kala Nag spitefully, for he was very angry, but Little Toomai was too happy to speak. Petersen Sahib had noticed him, and given him money, so he felt as a private soldier would feel if he had been called out of the ranks and praised by his commander-in-chief.

'What did Petersen Sahib mean by the elephant-dance?' he said, at last, softly to his mother.

Big Toomai heard him and grunted. 'That thou shouldst never be one of these hill-buffaloes of trackers. *That* was what he meant. Oh, you in front, what is blocking the way?'

An Assamese driver, two or three elephants ahead, turned round angrily, crying: 'Bring up Kala Nag, and knock this youngster of mine into good behaviour. Why should Petersen Sahib have chosen *me* to go down with you donkeys of the rice-fields? Lay your beast alongside, Toomai, and let him prod with his tusks. By all the gods of the hills, these new elephants are possessed, or else they can smell their companions in the jungle.'

Kala Nag hit the new elephant in the ribs and knocked the wind out of him, as Big Toomai said, 'We have swept the hills of wild elephants at the last catch. It is only your carelessness in driving. Must I keep order along the whole line?'

'Hear him!' said the other driver. '*We* have swept the hills! Ho! ho! You are very wise, you plains people. Anyone but a mud-head who never saw the jungle would know that *they* know that the drives are ended for the season. Therefore all the wild elephants tonight will – but why should I waste wisdom on a river-turtle?'

'What will they do?' Little Toomai called out.

'*Ohé*, little one. Art thou there? Well, I will tell thee, for thou hast a cool head. They will dance, and it behoves thy father, who has swept *all* the hills of *all* the elephants, to double-chain his pickets tonight.'

'What talk is this?' said Big Toomai. 'For forty years, father and son, we have tended elephants, and we have never heard such moonshine about dances.'

'Yes; but a plainsman who lives in a hut knows only the four walls of his hut. Well, leave thy elephants unshackled tonight and see what comes; as for their dancing, I have seen the place where – *Bapree-Bap!* how many windings has the Dihang River? Here is another ford, and we must swim the calves. Stop still, you behind there.'

And in this way, talking and wrangling and splashing through the rivers, they made their first march to a sort of receiving camp for the new elephants; but they lost their tempers long before they got there.

Then the elephants were chained by their hind legs to their big stumps of pickets, and extra ropes were fitted to the new elephants, and the fodder was piled before them, and the hilldrivers went back to Petersen Sahib through the afternoon light, telling the plains drivers to be extra careful that night, and laughing when the plains drivers asked the reason.

Little Toomai attended to Kala Nag's supper, and as

evening fell wandered through the camp, unspeakably happy, in search of a tom-tom. When an Indian child's heart is full, he does not run about and make a noise in an irregular fashion. He sits down to a sort of revel all by himself. And Little Toomai had been spoken to by Petersen Sahib! If he had not found what he wanted, I believe he would have burst. But the sweetmeat-seller in the camp lent him a little tom-tom – a drum beaten with the flat of the hand – and he sat down, cross-legged, before Kala Nag as the stars began to come out, the tom-tom in his lap, and he thumped and he thumped and he thumped, and the more he thought of the great honour that had been done to him, the more he thumped, all alone among the elephant-fodder. There was no tune and no words, but the thumping made him happy.

The new elephants strained at their ropes, and squealed and trumpeted from time to time, and he could hear his mother in the camp hut putting his small brother to sleep with an old, old song about the great god Shiv, who once told all the animals what they should eat. It is a very soothing lullaby, and the first verse says:

> Shiv, who poured the harvest and made the winds to
>   blow,
> Sitting at the doorways of a day of long ago,
> Gave to each his portion, food and toil and fate,
> From the king upon the *guddee* to the beggar at the gate.
> All things made he – Shiva the Preserver.
> Mahadeo! Mahadeo! He made all –
> Thorn for the camel, fodder for the kine,
> And mother's heart for sleepy head, O little son of mine!

Little Toomai came in with a joyous *tunk-a-tunk* at the end of each verse, till he felt sleepy and stretched himself on the fodder at Kala Nag's side.

At last the elephants began to lie down one after another, as is their custom, till only Kala Nag at the right of the line was left standing up; and he rocked slowly from side to side, his ears put forward to listen to the night wind as it blew very slowly across the hills. The air was full of all the night noises that, taken together, make one big silence – the click of one bamboo stem against the other, the rustle of something alive in the undergrowth, the scratch and squawk of a half-waked bird (birds are awake in the night much more often than we imagine), and the fall of water ever so far away. Little Toomai slept for some time, and when he waked it was brilliant moonlight, and Kala Nag was still standing up with his ears cocked. Little Toomai turned, rustling in the fodder, and watched the curve of his big back against half the stars in heaven; and while he watched he heard, so far away that it sounded no more than a pinhole of noise pricked through the stillness, the 'hoot-toot' of a wild elephant.

All the elephants in the lines jumped up as if they had been shot, and their grunts at last waked the sleeping mahouts, and they came out and drove in the picket-pegs with big mallets, and tightened this rope and knotted that till all was quiet. One new elephant had nearly grubbed up his picket, and Big Toomai took off Kala Nag's leg-chain and shackled that elephant forefoot to hindfoot, but slipped a loop of grass string round Kala Nag's leg, and told him to remember that he was tied fast. He knew that he and his father and his grandfather had done the very same thing hundreds of times before. Kala Nag did not answer to the order by gurgling, as he usually did. He stood still, looking out across the moonlight, his head a little raised, and his ears spread like fans, up to the great folds of the Garo hills.

'Look to him if he grows restless in the night,' said Big Toomai to Little Toomai, and he went into the hut and slept. Little Toomai was just going to sleep, too, when he heard the coir string snap with a little 'tang', and Kala Nag rolled out of his pickets as slowly and as silently as a cloud rolls out of the mouth of a valley. Little Toomai pattered after him, barefooted, down the road in the moonlight, calling under his breath, 'Kala Nag! Kala Nag! Take me with you, O Kala Nag!' The elephant turned without a sound, took three strides back to the boy in the moonlight, put down his trunk, swung him up to his neck, and almost before Little Toomai had settled his knees slipped into the forest.

There was one blast of furious trumpeting from the lines, and then the silence shut down on everything, and Kala Nag began to move. Sometimes a tuft of high grass washed along his sides as a wave washes along the sides of a ship, and sometimes a cluster of wild pepper vines would scrape along his back, or a bamboo would creak where his shoulder touched it; but between those times he moved absolutely without any sound, drifting through the thick Garo forest as though it had been smoke. He was going uphill, but though Little Toomai watched the stars in the rifts of the trees, he could not tell in what direction.

Then Kala Nag reached the crest of the ascent and stopped for a minute, and Little Toomai could see the tops of the trees lying all speckled and furry under the moonlight for miles and miles, and the blue-white mist over the river in the hollow. Toomai leaned forward and looked, and he felt that the forest was awake below him – awake and alive and crowded. A big brown fruit-eating bat brushed past his ear; a porcupine's quills rattled in the thicket; and in the darkness between the tree stems he heard a hog-bear digging hard in the moist, warm earth, and snuffing as it digged.

Then the branches closed over his head again, and Kala Nag began to go slowly down into the valley – not quietly this time, but as a runaway gun goes down a steep bank – in one rush. The huge limbs moved as steadily as pistons, eight feet to each stride, and the wrinkled skin of the elbow-points rustled. The undergrowth on either side of him ripped with a noise like torn canvas, and the saplings that he heaved away right and left with his shoulders sprang back again, and banged him on the flank, and great trails of creepers, all matted together, hung from his tusks as he threw his head from side to side and ploughed out his pathway. Then Little Toomai laid himself down close to the great neck, lest a swinging bough should sweep him to the ground, and he wished that he were back in the lines again.

The grass began to get squashy, and Kala Nag's feet sucked and squelched as he put them down, and the night mist at the bottom of the valley chilled Little Toomai. There was a splash and a trample, and the rush of running water, and Kala Nag strode through the bed of a river, feeling his way at each step. Above the noise of the water, as it swirled round the elephant's legs, Little Toomai could hear more splashing and some trumpeting both up stream and down – great grunts and angry snortings, and all the mist about him seemed to be full of rolling, wavy shadows.

'*Ai!*' he said, half aloud, his teeth chattering. 'The elephant folk are out tonight. It *is* the dance, then.'

Kala Nag swashed out of the water, blew his trunk clear, and began another climb; but this time he was not alone, and he had not to make his path. That was made already, six feet wide, in front of him, where the bent jungle-grass was trying to recover itself and stand up. Many elephants must have gone that way only a few minutes before. Little Toomai looked back, and behind him a great wild tusker, with his little pig's eyes glowing like hot coals, was just lifting himself out of the misty river. Then the trees closed up again, and they went on and up, with trumpetings and crashings, and the sound of breaking branches on every side of them.

At last Kala Nag stood still between two tree trunks at the very top of the hill. They were part of a circle of trees that grew round an irregular space of some three or four acres, and in all that space, as Little Toomai could see, the ground had been trampled down as hard as a brick floor. Some trees grew in the centre of the clearing, but their bark was rubbed away, and the white wood beneath showed all shiny and polished in the patches of moonlight. There were creepers hanging from the upper branches, and the bells of the flowers of the creepers, great waxy white things like convolvuluses, hung down fast asleep; but within the limits of the clearing there was not a single blade of green – nothing but the trampled earth.

The moonlight showed it all iron-grey, except where some elephants stood upon it, and their shadows were inky black. Little Toomai looked, holding his breath, with his eyes starting out of his head, and as he looked, more and more and more elephants swung out into the open from between the tree trunks. Little Toomai could count only up to ten, and he counted again and again on his fingers till he lost count of the tens, and his head began to swim. Outside the clearing he could hear them crashing in the undergrowth as they worked their way up the hillside; but as soon as they were within the circle of the tree trunks they moved like ghosts.

There were white-tusked wild males, with fallen leaves and nuts and twigs lying in the wrinkles of their necks and the folds of their ears; fat, slow-footed she-elephants, with restless little pinky-black calves only three or four feet high running under their stomachs; young elephants with their tusks just beginning to show, and very proud of them; lanky, scraggy old-maid elephants, with their hollow, anxious faces, and trunks like rough bark; savage old bull elephants, scarred from shoulder to flank with great weals and cuts of bygone fights, and the caked dirt of their solitary mud-baths dropping from their shoulders; and there was one with a broken tusk and the marks of the full-stroke, the terrible drawing scrape, of a tiger's claws on his side.

They were standing head to head, or walking to and fro across the ground in couples, or rocking and swaying all by themselves – scores and scores of elephants.

Toomai knew that, so long as he lay still on Kala Nag's neck, nothing would happen to him; for even in the rush and scramble of a Keddah-drive a wild elephant does not reach up with his trunk and drag a man off the neck of a tame elephant; and these elephants were not thinking of men that night. Once they started and put their ears forward when they heard the chinking of a leg-iron in the forest, but it was Pudmini, Petersen Sahib's pet elephant, her chain snapped short off, grunting, snuffling up the hillside. She must have broken her pickets, and come straight from Petersen Sahib's camp; and Little Toomai saw another elephant, one that he did not know, with deep rope-galls on his back and breast. He, too, must have run away from some camp in the hills about.

At last there was no sound of any more elephants moving in the forest, and Kala Nag rolled out from his station between the trees and went into the middle of the crowd, clucking and gurgling, and all the elephants began to talk in their own tongue, and to move about.

Still lying down, Little Toomai looked down upon

354

scores and scores of broad backs, and wagging ears, and tossing trunks, and little rolling eyes. He heard the click of tusks as they crossed other tusks by accident, and the dry rustle of trunks twined together, and the chafing of enormous sides and shoulders in the crowd, and the incessant flick and *hissh* of the great tails. Then a cloud came over the moon, and he sat in black darkness; but the quiet, steady hustling and pushing and gurgling went on just the same. He knew that there were elephants all round Kala Nag, and that there was no chance of backing him out of the assembly; so he set his teeth and shivered. In a Keddah at least there was torchlight and shouting, but here he was all alone in the dark, and once a trunk came up and touched him on the knee.

Then an elephant trumpeted, and they all took it up for five or ten terrible seconds. The dew from the trees above spattered down like rain on the unseen backs, and a dull booming noise began, not very loud at first, and Little Toomai could not tell what it was; but it grew and grew, and Kala Nag lifted up one forefoot and then the other, and brought them down on the ground – one-two, one-two, as steadily as trip-hammers. The elephants were stamping all together now, and it sounded like a war-drum beaten at the mouth of a cave. The dew fell from the trees till there was no more left to fall, and the booming went on, and the ground rocked and shivered, and Little Toomai put his hands up to his ears to shut out the sound. But it was all one gigantic jar that ran through him – this stamp of hundreds of heavy feet on the raw earth. Once or

twice he could feel Kala Nag and all the others surge forward a few strides, and the thumping would change to the crushing sound of juicy green things being bruised, but in a minute or two the boom of feet on hard earth began again. A tree was creaking and groaning somewhere near him. He put out his arm and felt the bark, but Kala Nag moved forward, still tramping, and he could not tell where he was in the clearing. There was no sound from the elephants, except once, when two or three little calves squeaked together. Then he heard a thump and a shuffle and the booming went on. It must have lasted fully two hours, and Little Toomai ached in every nerve; but he knew by the smell of the night air that the dawn was coming.

The morning broke in one sheet of pale yellow behind the green hills, and the booming stopped with the first ray, as though the light had been an order. Before Little Toomai had got the ringing out of his head, before even he had shifted his position, there was not an elephant in sight except Kala Nag, Pudmini, and the elephant with the rope-galls, and there was neither sign nor rustle nor whisper down the hillsides to show where the others had gone.

Little Toomai stared again and again. The clearing, as he remembered it, had grown in the night. More trees stood in the middle of it, but the undergrowth and the jungle-grass at the sides had been rolled back. Little Toomai stared once more. Now he understand the trampling. The elephants had stamped out more room – had stamped the thick grass and juicy cane to trash, the trash into slivers, the slivers into tiny fibres, and the fibres into hard earth.

'Wah!' said Little Toomai, and his eyes were very heavy. 'Kala Nag, my lord, let us keep by Pudmini and go to Petersen Sahib's camp, or I shall drop from thy neck.'

The third elephant watched the two go away, snorted, wheeled around, and took his own path. He may have belonged to some little native king's establishment, fifty or sixty or a hundred miles away.

Two hours later, as Petersen Sahib was eating early breakfast, the elephants, who had been double-chained that night, began to trumpet, and Pudmini, mired to the shoulders, with Kala Nag, very footsore, shambled into the camp.

Little Toomai's face was grey and pinched, and his hair was full of leaves and drenched with dew; but he tried to salute Petersen Sahib, and cried faintly: 'The dance – the elephant-dance! I have seen it, and – I die!' As Kala Nag sat down, he slid off his neck in a dead faint.

But, since native children have no nerves worth speaking of, in two hours he was lying very contentedly in Petersen Sahib's hammock with Petersen Sahib's shooting-coat under his head, and a glass of warm milk, a little brandy, with a dash of quinine inside of him; and while the old hairy, scarred hunters of the jungles sat three-deep before him, looking at him as though he were a spirit, he told his tale in short words, as a child will, and wound up with:

'Now, if I lie in one word, send men to see, and they

will find that the elephant folk have trampled down more room in their dance-room, and they will find ten and ten, and many times ten, tracks leading to that dance-room. They made more room with their feet. I have seen it. Kala Nag took me, and I saw. Also Kala Nag is very leg-weary!'

Little Toomai lay back and slept all through the long afternoon and into the twilight, and while he slept Petersen Sahib and Machua Appa followed the track of the two elephants for fifteen miles across the hills. Petersen Sahib had spent eighteen years in catching elephants, and he had only once before found such a dance-place. Machua Appa had no need to look twice at the clearing to see what had been done there, or to scratch with his toe in the packed, rammed earth.

'The child speaks truth,' said he. 'All this was done last night, and I have counted seventy tracks crossing the river. See, Sahib, where Pudmini's leg-iron cut the bark off that tree! Yes; she was there too.'

They looked at each other, and up and down, and they wondered; for the ways of elephants are beyond the wit of any man, black or white, to fathom.

'Forty years and five,' said Machua Appa, 'have I followed my lord the elephant, but never have I heard that any child of man had seen what this child has seen. By all the gods of the hills, it is – what can we say?' and he shook his head.

When they got back to camp it was time for the evening meal. Petersen Sahib ate alone in his tent, but he gave orders that the camp should have two sheep and some fowls, as well as a double ration of flour and rice and salt, for he knew that there would be a feast.

Big Toomai had come up hotfoot from the camp in the plains to search for his son and his elephant, and now that he had found them he looked at them as though he were afraid of them both. And there was a feast by the blazing camp fires in front of the lines of picketed elephants, and Little Toomai was the hero of it all; and the big brown elephant-catchers, the trackers and drivers and ropers, and the men who know all the secrets of breaking the wildest elephants, passed him from one to the other, and they marked his forehead with blood from the breast of a newly killed jungle-cock, to show that he was a forester, initiated and free of all the jungles.

And at last, when the flames died down, and the red light of the logs made the elephants look as though they had been dipped in blood too, Machua Appa, the head of all the drivers of all the Keddahs – Machua Appa, Petersen Sahib's other self, who had never seen a made road in forty years: Machua Appa, who was so great that he had no other name than Machua Appa – leaped to his feet, with Little Toomai held high in the air above his head, and shouted: 'Listen, my brothers. Listen, too, you my lords in the lines there, for I, Machua Appa, am speaking! This little one shall no more be called Little Toomai, but Toomai of the Elephants, as his great-grandfather was called before him. What never man has seen he has seen through the long night, and the favour of the elephant folk and of the gods of the jungles is with him. He shall become a great tracker; he shall become greater than I, even I – Machua Appa! He shall follow the new trail, and the stale trail, and the mixed trail, with a clear eye! He shall take no harm in the Keddah when he runs under their bellies to rope the wild tuskers; and if he slips before the feet of the charging bull elephant, that bull elephant shall know who he is and shall not crush him. *Aihai!* my lords in the chains,' – he whirled up the line of pickets – 'here is the little one that has seen your dances in your hidden places – the sight that never man saw! Give him honour, my lords! *Salaam karo*, my children! Make your salute to Toomai of the Elephants! Gunga Pershad, ahaa! Hira Guj, Birchi Guj, Kuttar Guj, ahaa! Pudmini – thou has seen him at the dance, and thou too, Kala Nag, my pearl among elephants! – ahaa! Together! To Toomai of the Elephants. *Barrao!*'

And at that last wild yell the whole line flung up their trunks till the tips touched their foreheads, and broke out into the full salute, the crashing trumpet-peal that only the Viceroy of India hears – the Salaam-ut of the Keddah.

But it was all for the sake of Little Toomai, who had seen what never man had seen before – the dance of the elephants at night and alone in the heart of the Garo hills!

The Firebird

retold by Felicity Trotman

The story of the firebird is based on Russian folk tales. Like Petrushka, the ballet's music was composed by Igor Stravinsky. The Firebird was the first ballet music Stravinsky ever composed – he was 28 at the time. It was one of the ballets that caused a sensation in London when Sergei Diaghilev brought the Ballets Russes to London in 1911.

Long ago and far away, in the great realm and empire of the Russians, there was a time when the kingdom was ruled by a Czar who had one son. This prince, the Czarevich Ivan, loved hunting. He knew the ways of all the birds and beasts, and how they lived. He could find the bear in its cave, or the timid deer at the wood's edge. He could track the smallest creature across the wind-blown grass of the great steppes, or through the thickest forest. His keen eyes could follow the flight of the falcon from its craggy nest to the instant when it stooped on its prey. He was only happy when he was involved in the chase, and he cared nothing for the arts of the ruler.

One day Ivan was hunting through a huge forest which he had never entered before, for it was many leagues from his home. Carrying his great bow, he walked carefully, for the trunks of the trees pressed closely together, and the forest was very dark. He looked from side to side keenly, to take note of his path, and to see if there were any signs of the game he longed to find, but there was nothing. As night fell, Ivan saw in front of him a high stone wall. This was quite unexpected, for there had been no sign of another human being in all the forest.

Was there a dwelling-place here in the depth of the forest? Or was the wall the last remaining part of some great building now fallen to ruin? The young prince decided to find out what lay beyond the wall. The stones were rough, so it was easy for him to climb over it.

In the starlight, Ivan could just see that he was in a garden. There were trees in the garden, and one in particular caught his eye, for it was covered with great golden apples.

Suddenly there was a blaze of light. For a moment, Prince Ivan was dazzled, for his eyes were accustomed to the dim starlight. When he could see again, he was amazed to find that the light came from a creature of a kind he had never seen before. Half bird, half woman, she was clad in feathers of scarlet and gold, copper and vermilion, which glowed and flickered like flames in the darkness. The light that came from her fell on the apple tree, and the gold apples shone and glittered as she swooped down and landed in the branches. It was the magical Firebird!

All the prince's hunting instincts were roused. What a

prize the Firebird would be if he could catch her! While the Firebird was busy picking the golden apples from the tree, he crept closer, then, when she came near enough to him, he leaped forward, and caught her.

The Firebird was terrified! She fluttered in his hands as she struggled to free herself, but the prince's grasp was too strong. She pleaded with him, for firebirds lose their lustre in captivity, and grow dim and drab before they die, but Ivan would not let her go. Desperate for her freedom, the Firebird made one last effort. Begging the prince for mercy, she offered him one of her scarlet breast-feathers. This was a magical talisman, for if ever Prince Ivan were in need, he could summon the Firebird to his aid through the power of the feather.

Ivan was touched by the Firebird's distress. Never before had this hunter willingly let go of his quarry, but no other creature was as beautiful or as magical as the Firebird, or had implored him so passionately as she had done. He opened his hands, and let her go.

For a moment, the Firebird hovered like a dancing flame near Ivan. Then, as the dawn began to break over the topmost branches of the trees, she flew away, leaving him alone in the garden.

As the daylight grew stronger, Prince Ivan could see that the garden was outside a huge old castle, which looked grim and forbidding in the morning light. He heard sounds, as though someone was coming, so he hid behind a tree. He peeped out, and saw thirteen beautiful young girls, dressed in white, come into the garden. They ran to the apple tree, and began to play ball with one of the apples, which they shook off a branch.

The girls were so graceful as they played, and looked so lovely, that Ivan decided they must be princesses, Czarevnas, just as he was a prince, a Czarevich. One of the girls, who seemed to be the leader of the group, was so beautiful that Ivan fell instantly in love with her. He had to speak to her! He stepped from his hiding-place.

The girls were very startled by his appearance, for they had never before seen a stranger in their garden. They clustered round him, and the girl he admired, who was indeed their leader, told Ivan their story. They were princesses, as he had guessed, but they had fallen under the spell of a wicked wizard. They were the captives of Kostchei, whose enchantments were old and powerful, and who could not be overcome because he was immortal.

Although the princess had fallen in love with Ivan as soon as she had seen him, she begged him to flee while he had time, for he was in terrible danger in Kostchei's magic garden. The wizard's domain was full of stone statues, all that remained of the princes who had dared to enter it in search of the princesses they had loved and whom Kostchei had stolen away.

Prince Ivan had faced packs of hungry wolves, and enraged and dangerous bears and wild boars, and had overcome these perils. He would not fear a wizard! Besides, now that he had fallen in love, Ivan wanted to rescue his princess and her companions. He asked her if she would dance with him, and for a while all her friends joined in, circling light-heartedly in the sunshine.

But the day went by, and the sun began to sink. The princesses had to return to their captivity in the castle, and Ivan was forced to say farewell to his love. She told him it must be farewell for ever, and begged him to escape while there was still time. He kissed her once, then, as a trumpet sounded in the distance, the girls ran through the gate into the castle, and the gate shut behind them.

Left alone in the enchanted garden, Prince Ivan started to think about how to rescue his princess. He forgot that he himself was in deadly danger. As the light faded and the shadows lengthened, there was unexpectedly a deafening noise of bells, gongs, and trumpets! In an instant the prince was surrounded by hideous monsters, which appeared from nowhere; grotesque and misshapen demons whose bodies were covered with scales, and whose mouths were filled with sharp fangs. They leaped and pranced about all around him, taunting him by tearing at him with their talons, catching him in their claws and pushing him from one to the other.

As suddenly as they had appeared, the demons stopped their wild activity, falling on the ground as their master appeared. Kostchei the deathless, old as the world, was unutterably hideous. He was tall, but bent with age, and his body was so thin it looked like a skeleton. In his skull his eyes burned with rage and hate, and on his head was a crown of gold spikes that gleamed malevolently as he moved. Surrounded by more of the frightful demons, he advanced towards Ivan, who stood frozen with horror at the sight of the dreadful apparition. Grinning with delight at capturing another fool rash enough to venture into his domain, Kostchei held out his arm, until the blackened nails of his hand were only inches from Ivan's face. He began the incantation that would turn the young man to stone.

Ivan was desperate. His bow was behind a tree on the other side of the garden, where he had left it earlier in the day. He had his knife, but Kostchei was immortal. What could he do? Then he remembered the Firebird, and her gift of a feather. He felt his body beginning to stiffen, but with his last strength he pulled the feather from his pouch. Holding it high in the air, he summoned the Firebird to his aid.

In a blaze of light, she was there, hovering in the air beside him. She began to dance. Her dance was itself a spell, and as she turned and spun the demons and monsters were compelled to do likewise. Faster and faster she moved, spinning with dizzying speed and brilliance, until the whole nightmare company fell to the ground in exhaustion. Then the Firebird danced again, this time a lullaby, until they were all asleep. Even Kostchei was asleep, overcome by the power of her magic.

Then she flew to Ivan, who was at last able to move. She told him he might defeat Kostchei, but he must be bold and quick, for she could not hold the wizard and his dreadful attendants in enchanted sleep for very long. In the roots of a hollow tree there was a golden

casket, and in the casket was an egg. Kostchei was immortal because he had put his soul in the egg. If Ivan could find the casket, and break the egg, Kostchei and all his evil enchantments would be overthrown.

Ivan ran to the tree, and began to search. It did not take him long to uncover the casket, and open it. He seized the enormous egg inside, and pulled it out. As he did so, Kostchei awoke from his charmed sleep! He saw Ivan holding the precious egg that contained his life, and screamed with fear. Ivan threw the egg into the air, catching it – once, twice – then he threw it up a third time, and let it smash into a thousand pieces on the ground!

As the egg shattered, Kostchei and his spells were destroyed for ever. A sudden darkness fell on the garden, and a wind blew through it, carrying away the last remains of the wizard and his evil.

When the light returned, the wizard's grim castle had disappeared. In its place was a city, with many domes and towers and spires. Out of its gates came all the unfortunate princes who had been trapped and turned to stone by Kostchei. They had been returned to their rightful forms when Kostchei was destroyed, and were eager to celebrate their freedom and applaud the hero who had brought it about. Then the thirteen lovely girls appeared. Ivan was delighted to see his princess, who ran to him at once.

Holding hands, they said farewell to the Firebird, who had brought them freedom and happiness. When she had flown away, they returned to the other princes and princesses, now joyfully reunited. Some days later, these friends were the chief guests at the magnificent wedding of Prince Ivan and his bride. After their marriage, they governed the lands once held in thrall by the wicked Kostchei with wisdom and justice, loved and blessed by all the people.

Polly's Farewell Party

LOUISA M. ALCOTT

Most people will know this author's Little Women *and its sequels best, but Louisa Alcott wrote several other good books for young readers. An* Old-fashioned Girl, *from which this extract is taken, tells the story of Polly Milton, the daughter of a poor country clergyman, and what happens to her when she goes to Boston to visit her friends the Shaws. They are rich, but she soon finds that they aren't happy. Polly is sensible, honest, and modest, and she finds that all these things can help her friends.*

In the story, two dances are mentioned. The redowa *is a slow waltz, and the* German *is the name given in America to the quadrille. This is a square dance made up of five separate dances, with sets made up of four couples.*

'Oh, dear! Must you really go home Saturday?' said Fan, some days after what Tom called the 'grand scrimmage'.

'I really must; for I only came to stay a month, and here I've been nearly six weeks,' answered Polly, feeling as if she had been absent a year.

'Make it two months, and stay over Christmas. Come, do, now,' urged Tom, heartily.

'You are very kind; but I wouldn't miss Christmas at home for anything. Besides, mother says they can't possibly do without me.'

'Neither can we. Can't you tease your mother, and make up your mind to stay?' began Fan.

'Polly never teases. She says it's selfish; and I don't do it now much,' put in Maud, with a virtuous air.

'Don't you bother Polly. She'd rather go, and I don't wonder. Let's be just as jolly as we can while she stays, and finish up with your party, Fan,' said Tom, in a tone that settled the matter.

Polly had expected to be very happy in getting ready for the party; but when the time came, she was disappointed; for somehow that naughty thing called envy took possession of her, and spoiled her pleasure. Before she left home, she thought her new white muslin dress, with its fresh blue ribbons, the most elegant and proper costume she could have; but now, when she saw Fanny's pink silk, with a white tarlatan tunic, and innumerable puffings, bows, and streamers, her own simple little toilet lost all its charms in her eyes, and looked very babyish and old-fashioned.

Even Maud was much better dressed then herself, and looked very splendid in her cherry-coloured and white suit, with a sash so big she could hardly carry it, and little white boots with red buttons. They both had necklaces and bracelets, earrings and brooches; but Polly had no ornament, except the plain locket on a bit of blue velvet. Her sash was only a wide ribbon, tied in a simple bow, and nothing but a blue snood in the pretty curls. Her only comfort was the knowledge that the modest tucker drawn up round the plump shoulders was real lace, and that her bronze boots cost nine dollars.

Poor Polly, with all her efforts to be contented, and not to mind looking unlike other people, found it hard work to keep her face bright and her voice happy that night. No one dreamed what was going on under the muslin frock, till grandma's wise old eyes spied out the little shadow on Polly's spirits, and guessed the cause of it. When dressed, the three girls went to show themselves to the elders, who were in grandma's room, where Tom was being helped into an agonizingly stiff collar.

Maud pranced like a small peacock, and Fan made a splendid curtsy as everyone turned to survey them; but Polly stood still, and her eyes went from face to face, with an anxious, wistful air, which seemed to say, 'I know I'm not right; but I hope I don't look very bad.'

Grandma read the look in a minute; and when Fanny said, with a satisfied smile, 'How do we look?' she answered, drawing Polly toward her so kindly.

'Very like the fashion-plates you got the patterns of your dresses from. But this little costume suits me best.'

'Do you really think I look nice?' and Polly's face brightened, for she valued the old lady's opinion very much.

'Yes, my dear; you look just as I like to see a child of your age look. What particularly pleases me is that you have kept your promise to your mother, and haven't let anyone persuade you to wear borrowed finery.

Young things like you don't need any ornaments but those you wear tonight – youth, health, intelligence, and modesty.'

As she spoke, grandma gave a tender kiss that made Polly glow like a rose, and for a minute she forgot that there were such things as pink silk and coral earrings in the world. She only said, 'Thank you, ma'am,' and heartily returned the kiss; but the words did her good, and her plain dress looked charming all of a sudden.

'Polly's so pretty, it don't matter what she wears,' observed Tom, surveying her over his collar with an air of calm approval.

'She hasn't got any bwetelles to her dwess, and I have,' said Maud, settling her ruffled bands over her shoulders, which looked like cherry-coloured wings on a stout little cherub.

'I did wish she'd just wear my blue set, ribbon is so very plain; but, as Tom says, it don't much matter,' and Fanny gave an effective touch to the blue bow above Polly's left temple.

'She might wear flowers; they always suit young girls,' said Mrs Shaw, privately thinking that her own daughters looked much the best, yet conscious that blooming Polly had the most attractive face.

'Bless me! I forgot my posies in admiring the belles. Hand them out, Tom,' and Mr Shaw nodded toward an interesting-looking box that stood on the table.

Seizing them wrong side up, Tom produced three little bouquets, all different in colour, size, and construction.

'Why, Papa! How very kind of you,' cried Fanny,

who had not dared to receive even a geranium leaf since the late scrape.

'Your father used to be a very gallant young gentleman, once upon a time,' said Mrs Shaw, with a simper.

'Ah, Tom, it's a good sign when you find time to think of giving pleasure to your little girls!' And grandma patted her son's bald head as if he wasn't more than eighteen.

Thomas Jr had given a somewhat scornful sniff at first; but when grandma praised his father, the young man thought better of the matter, and regarded the flowers with more respect, as he asked, 'Which is for which?'

'Guess,' said Mr Shaw, pleased that his unusual demonstration had produced such an effort.

The largest was a regular hothouse bouquet, of tea-rosebuds, scentless heath, and smilax; the second was just a handful of sweet-peas and mignonette, with a few cheerful pansies, and one fragrant little rose in the middle; the third, a small posy of scarlet verbenas, white feverfew, and green leaves.

'Not hard to guess. The smart one for Fan, the sweet one for Polly, and the gay one for Pug. Now, then, catch hold, girls.' And Tom proceeded to deliver the nosegays, with as much grace as could be expected from a youth in a new suit of clothes and very tight boots.

'That finishes you off just right, and is a very pretty attention of Papa's. Now run down, for the bell has rung; and remember, not to dance too often, Fan; be as quiet as you can, Tom; and, Maud, don't eat too much supper. Grandma will attend to things, for my poor nerves won't allow me to come down.'

With that, Mrs Shaw dismissed them, and the four descended to receive the first batch of visitors, several little girls who had been asked for the express purpose of keeping Maud out of her sister's way. Tom had likewise been propitiated, by being allowed to bring his three bosom friends, who went by the schoolboy names of Rumple, Sherry, and Spider.

'They will do to make up sets, as gentlemen are scarce; and the party is for Polly, so I must have some young folks on her account,' said Fanny, when sending out her invitations.

Of course, the boys came early, and stood about in corners, looking as if they had more arms and legs than they knew what to do with. Tom did his best to be a good host; but ceremony oppressed his spirits, and he was forced to struggle manfully with the wild desire to propose a game of leap-frog, for the long drawing-rooms, cleared for dancing, tempted him sorely.

Polly sat where she was told, and suffered bashful agonies as Fan introduced very fine young ladies and very stiff young gentlemen, who all said about the same civil things, and then appeared to forget all about her. When the first dance was called, Fanny cornered Tom, who had been dodging her, for he knew what she wanted, and said, in an earnest whisper:

'Now, Tom, you must dance this with Polly. You are the young gentleman of the house, and it's only proper that you should ask your company first.'

'Polly don't care for manners. I hate dancing; don't know how. Let go my jacket, and don't bother, or I'll cut away altogether,' growled Tom, daunted by the awful prospect of opening the ball with Polly.

'I'll never forgive you if you do. Come, be clever, and help me, there's a dear. You know we both were dreadfully rude to Polly, and agreed that we'd be as kind and civil to her as ever we could. I shall keep my word, and see that she isn't slighted at my party, for I want her to love me, and go home feeling all right.'

This artful speech made an impression on the rebellious Thomas, who glanced at Polly's happy face, remembered his promise, and, with a groan, resolved to do his duty.

'Well, I'll take her; but I shall come to grief, for I don't know anything about your old dances.'

'Yes, you do. I've taught you the steps a dozen times. I'm going to begin with a redowa, because the girls like it, and it's better fun than square dances. Now, put on your gloves, and go and ask Polly like a gentleman.'

'Oh, thunder!' muttered Tom. And having split the detested gloves in dragging them on, he nerved himself for the effort, walked up to Polly, made a stiff bow, stuck out his elbow, and said, solemnly, 'May I have the pleasure, Miss Milton?'

He did it as much like the big fellows as he could, and expected that Polly would be impressed. But she wasn't a bit; for after a surprised look she laughed in his face, and took him by the hand, saying, heartily,

'Of course you may; but don't be a goose, Tommy.'

'Well, Fan told me to be elegant, so I tried to,' whispered Tom, adding, as he clutched his partner with a somewhat desperate air, 'Hold on tight, and we'll get through somehow.'

The music struck up, and away they went; Tom hopping one way and Polly the other, in a most ungraceful manner.

'Keep time to the music,' gasped Polly.

'Can't; never could,' returned Tom.

'Keep step with me, then, and don't tread on my toes,' pleaded Polly.

'Never mind; keep bobbing, and we'll come right by and by,' muttered Tom, giving his unfortunate partner a sudden whisk, which nearly landed both on the floor.

But they did not 'get right by and by', for Tom, in his frantic efforts to do his duty, nearly annihilated poor Polly. He tramped, he bobbed, he skated, he twirled her to the right, dragged her to the left, backed her up against people and furniture, trod on her feet, rumpled her dress, and made a spectacle of himself generally. Polly was much disturbed; but as everyone else was flying about also, she bore it as long as she could, knowing that Tom had made a martyr of himself, and feeling grateful to him for the sacrifice.

'Oh, do stop now; this is dreadful!' cried Polly, breathlessly, after a few wild turns.

'Isn't it?' said Tom, wiping his red face with such an air of intense relief, that Polly had not the heart to scold him, but said, 'Thank you,' and dropped into a chair exhausted.

'I know I've made a guy of myself; but Fan insisted on it, for fear you'd be offended if I didn't go the first dance with you,' said Tom, remorsefully, watching Polly as she settled the bow of her crushed sash, which Tom had used as a sort of handle by which to turn and twist her; 'I can do the Lancers tiptop; but you won't ever want to dance with me any more,' he added, as he began to fan her so violently, that her hair flew about as if in a gale of wind.

'Yes, I will. I'd like to; and you shall put your name down here on the sticks of my fan. That's the way, Trix says, when you don't have a ball-book.'

Looking much gratified, Tom produced the stump of a lead-pencil, and wrote his name with a flourish, saying, as he gave it back,

'Now I'm going to get Sherry, or some of the fellows that do the redowa well, so you can have a real good go before the music stops.'

Off went Tom; but before he could catch any eligible partner, Polly was provided with the best dancer in the room. Mr Sydney had seen and heard the whole thing; and though he had laughed quietly, he liked honest Tom and good-natured Polly all the better for their simplicity. Polly's foot was keeping time to the lively music, and her eyes were fixed wistfully on the smoothly-gliding couples before her, when Mr Sydney came to her, saying, in the pleasant, yet respectful way she liked so much,

'Miss Polly, can you give me a turn?'

'Oh, yes; I'm dying for another.' And Polly jumped up, with both hands out, and such a grateful face, that Mr Sydney resolved she should have as many turns as she liked.

This time all went well; and Tom, returning from an unsuccessful search, was amazed to behold Polly circling gracefully about the room, guided by a most accomplished partner.

'Ah, that's something like,' he thought, as he watched the bronze boots retreating and advancing in perfect time to the music. 'Don't see how Sydney does the steering so well; but it must be fun; and, by Jupiter! I'll learn it!' added Shaw, Jr, with an emphatic gesture which burst the last button off his gloves.

Polly enjoyed herself till the music stopped; and before she had time to thank Mr Sydney as warmly as she wished, Tom came up to say, with his most lordly air,

'You dance splendidly, Polly. Now, you just show me any one you like the looks of, and I'll get him for you, no matter who he is.'

'I don't want any of the gentlemen; they are so stiff, and don't care to dance with me; but I like those boys over there, and I'll dance with any of them if they are willing,' said Polly, after a survey.

'I'll trot out the whole lot.' And Tom gladly brought up his friends, who all admired Polly immensely, and were proud to be chosen instead of the 'big fellows'.

There was no sitting still for Polly after that, for the lads kept her going at a great pace; and she was so happy, she never saw or suspected how many little manoeuvres, heart-burnings, displays of vanity, affectation, and nonsense were going on all round her. She loved dancing, and entered into the gaiety of the scene with a heartiness that was pleasant to see. Her eyes shone, her face glowed, her lips smiled, and the brown curls waved in the air as she danced with a heart as light as her feet.

'Are you enjoying yourself, Polly?' asked Mr Shaw, who looked in, now and then, to report to grandma that all was going well.

'Oh, such a splendid time!' cried Polly, with an enthusiastic little gesture, as she *chasséd* into the corner where he stood.

'She is a regular belle among the boys,' said Fanny, as she promenaded by.

'They are so kind in asking me, and I'm not afraid of them,' explained Polly, prancing, simply because she couldn't keep still.

'So you *are* afraid of the young gentlemen, hey?' and Mr Shaw held her by one curl.

'All but Mr Sydney. He don't put on airs and talk nonsense; and, oh! he does "dance like an angel", as Trix says.'

'Papa, I wish you'd come and waltz with me. Fan told me not to go near her, 'cause my wed dwess makes her pink one look ugly; and Tom won't; and I want to dwedfully.'

'I've forgotten how, Maudie. Ask Polly; she'll spin you round like a teetotum.'

'Mr Sydney's name is down for that,' answered Polly, looking at her fan with a pretty little air of importance. 'But I guess he wouldn't mind my taking poor Maud instead. She hasn't danced hardly any, and I've had more than my share. Would it be very improper to change my mind?" And Polly looked up at her tall partner with eyes which plainly showed that the change was a sacrifice.

'Not a bit. Give the little dear a good waltz, and we will look on,' answered Mr Sydney, with a nod and smile.

'That is a refreshing little piece of nature,' said Mr Shaw, as Polly and Maud whirled away.

'She will make a charming little woman, if she isn't spoilt.'

'No danger of that. She has got a sensible mother.'

'I thought so.' And Sydney sighed, for he had lately lost his own good mother.

When supper was announced, Polly happened to be talking, or trying to talk, to one of the 'poky' gentlemen whom Fan had introduced. He took Miss Milton down, of course, put her in a corner, and having served her to a dab of ice and one macaroon, he devoted himself to his own supper with such interest, that Polly would have fared badly, if Tom had not come and rescued her.

'I've been looking everywhere for you. Come with me, and don't sit starving here,' said Tom, with a scornful look from her empty plate to that of her recreant escort, which was piled with good things.

Following her guide, Polly was taken to the big china closet, opening from the dining-room to the kitchen, and here she found a jovial little party feasting at ease. Maud and her bosom friend, 'Gwace', were seated on tin cake-boxes; Sherry and Spider adorned the re-frigerator; while Tom and Rumple foraged for the party.

'Here's fun,' said Polly, as she was received with a clash of spoons and a waving of napkins.

'You just perch on that cracker-keg, and I'll see that you get enough,' said Tom, putting a dumb-waiter before her, and issuing his orders with a fine air of authority.

'We are a band of robbers in our cave, and I'm the captain; and we pitch into the folks passing by, and go out and bring home plunder. Now, Rumple, you go and carry off a basket of cake, and I'll watch here till

Katy comes by with a fresh lot of oysters; Polly must have some. Sherry, cut into the kitchen, and bring a cup of coffee. Spider, scrape up the salad, and poke the dish through the slide for more. Eat away, Polly, and my men will be back with supplies in a jiffy.'

Such fun as they had in that closet; such daring robberies of jelly-pots and cake-boxes; such successful raids into the dining-room and kitchen; such base assaults upon poor Katy and the coloured waiter, who did his best, but was helpless in the hands of the robber horde. A very harmless little revel; for no wine was allowed, and the gallant band were so busy skirmishing to supply the ladies, that they had not time to eat too much. No one missed them; and when they emerged, the feast was over, except for a few voracious young gentlemen, who still lingered among the ruins.

'That's the way they always do; poke the girls in corners, give 'em just one taste of something, and then go and stuff like pigs,' whispered Tom, with a superior air, forgetting certain private banquets of his own, after company had departed.

The rest of the evening was to be devoted to the German; and, as Polly knew nothing about it, she established herself in a window recess to watch the mysteries. For a time she enjoyed it, for it was all new to her, and the various pretty devices were very charming; but, by and by, that bitter weed, envy, cropped up again, and she could not feel happy to be left out in the cold, while the other girls were getting gay tissue-paper suits, droll bon-bons, flowers, ribbons, and all manner of tasteful trifles in which girlish souls delight. Every one was absorbed; Mr Sydney was dancing; Tom and his friends were discussing baseball on the stairs; and Maud's set had returned to the library to play.

Polly tried to conquer the bad feeling; but it worried her, till she remembered something her mother once said to her:

'When you feel out of sorts, try to make someone else happy, and you will soon be so yourself.'

'I will try it,' thought Polly, and looked round to see what she could do. Sounds of strife in the library led her to enter. Maud and the young ladies were sitting on the sofa, talking about each other's clothes, as they had seen their mammas do.

'Was your dress imported?' asked Grace.

'No; was yours?' returned Blanche.

'Yes; and it cost – oh, ever so much.'

'I don't think it is as pretty as Maud's.'

'Mine was made in New York,' said Miss Shaw, smoothing her skirts complacently.

'I can't dress much now, you know, 'cause mamma's in black for somebody,' observed Miss Alice Lovett, feeling the importance which affliction conferred upon her when it took the form of a jet necklace.

'Well, I don't care if my dress isn't imported; my cousin had three kinds of wine at her party; so, now,' said Blanche.

'Did she?' And all the little girls looked deeply impressed, till Maud observed, with a funny imitation of her father's manner:

'My papa said it was scan-dill-us; for some of the

little boys got tipsy, and had to be tooked home. He wouldn't let us have any wine; and gwandma said it was vewy impwoper for children to do so.'

'My mother says your mother's coupé isn't half so stylish as ours,' put in Alice.

'Yes, it is, too. It's all lined with gween silk, and that's nicer than old web cloth,' cried Maud, ruffling up like an insulted chicken.

'Well, my brother don't wear a horrid old cap, and he's got nice hair. I wouldn't have a brother like Tom. He's horrid rude, my sister says,' retorted Alice.

'He isn't. Your brother is a pig.'

'You're a fib!'

'So are you!'

Here, I regret to say, Miss Shaw slapped Miss Lovett, who promptly returned the compliment, and both began to cry.

Polly, who had paused to listen to the edifying chat, parted the belligerents, and finding the poor things tired, cross, and sleepy, yet unable to go home till sent for, proposed to play games. The young ladies consented, and 'Puss in the corner' proved a peacemaker. Presently, in came the boys; and being exiles from the German, gladly joined in the games, which soon were lively enough to wake the sleepiest. 'Blind-man's-buff' was in full swing when Mr Shaw peeped in, and seeing Polly flying about with bandaged eyes, joined in the fun to puzzle her. He got caught directly; and great merriment was caused by Polly's bewilderment, for she couldn't guess who he was, till she felt the bald spot on his head.

This frolic put every one in such spirits, that Polly forgot her trouble, and the little girls kissed each other goodnight as affectionately as if such things as imported frocks, coupés, and rival brothers didn't exist.

'Well, Polly, do you like parties?' asked Fan, when the last guest was gone.

'Very much; but I don't think it would be good for me to go to many,' answered Polly, slowly.

'Why not?'

'I shouldn't enjoy them if I didn't have a fine dress, and dance all the time, and be admired, and – all the rest of it.'

'I didn't know you cared for such things,' cried Fanny, surprised.

'Neither did I till tonight; but I do; and as I can't have 'em, it's lucky I'm going home tomorrow.'

'Oh, dear! So you are! What shall I do without my "sweet P", as Sydney calls you?' sighed Fanny, bearing Polly away to be cuddled.

Every one echoed the exclamation next day; and many loving eyes followed the little figure in the drab frock as it went quietly about, doing for the last time the small services which would help to make its absence keenly felt. Polly was to go directly after an early dinner, and having packed her trunk, all but one tray, she was told to go and take a run while grandma finished.

If Polly could have seen what went into that top tray, she would have been entirely overcome; for Fanny had told grandma about the poor little presents she had once laughed at, and they had all laid their heads together to provide something really fine and appropriate for every member of the Milton family.

If Polly had suspected that a little watch was ticking away in a little case, with her name on it, inside that trunk, she never could have left it locked as grandma advised, or have eaten her dinner so quietly. As it was, her heart was very full, and the tears rose to her eyes more than once, every one was so kind, and so sorry to have her go.

But the crowning joke of all was Tom's goodbye, for, when Polly was fairly settled in the car, the last 'All aboard!' uttered, and the train in motion, Tom suddenly produced a knobby little bundle, and thrusting it in at the window, while he hung on in some breakneck fashion, said, with a droll mixture of fun and feeling in his face,

'It's horrid; but you wanted it, so I put it in to make you laugh. Goodbye, Polly; goodbye, goodbye!'

The last adieu was a trifle husky, and Tom vanished as it was uttered, leaving Polly to laugh over his parting souvenir till the tears ran down her cheeks. It was a paper bag of peanuts, and poked down at the very bottom a photograph of Tom. It was 'horrid', for he looked as if taken by a flash of lightning, so black, wild, and staring was it; but Polly liked it, and whenever she felt a little pensive at parting with her friends, she took a peanut, or a peep at Tom's funny picture, which made her merry again.

So the short journey came blithely to an end, and in the twilight she saw a group of loving faces at the door of a humble little house, which was more beautiful than any palace in her eyes, for it was home.

The Story of Zamore

THÉOPHILE GAUTIER

Théophile Gautier was a French writer who, like Alexandre Dumas, loved animals. He wrote a book about the dogs, cats, horses, birds and reptiles that he and his sisters had kept when they were children. One of their most unusual pets was Zamore . . .

Our new dog was called Zamore. He looked like a kind of spaniel, but he had a very mixed pedigree. He was small, and his coat was black, with orange patches above his eyebrows and some fawn fur on his belly. He was not a beautiful dog. But in character, he was a remarkable dog.

He held all females in complete contempt. He would not obey them, and refused to pay any attention to them. Neither to my mother nor my sisters would he show the smallest sign of friendship or respect. He accepted their caresses and their titbits with dignity, but never showed any gratitude. There was no friendly bark for them, no tail beating on the floor, none of those signs of pleasure most dogs give generously to the people they love. He would sit very still, crouching like the Sphinx, just like a very serious person who did not want to join in the activities of frivolous people.

Zamore chose my father for his master, for he

recognized his authority as head of the family, but even to him he was cool and undemonstrative. Zamore never frisked about, or licked him. He watched Father all the time, turning his head to follow his movements, and followed him everywhere, with his nose glued to Father's heel. He was never distracted, not even by other dogs going past.

My dear father was a keen fisherman, who loved every part of the sport. Zamore would go fishing with him, and during the long night-time sessions which catching fish seems to need, he would sit right at the edge of the water, as though he wanted to see through the darkness and follow the movements of the prey. Although he would occasionally prick up an ear to listen to the thousand vague, far-off noises which can be heard in the deep silence at night, he never barked, for he understood that a good fisherman's dog must be absolutely quiet. Only when the line went tight and a fish was caught would he give a short yap; then he watched with great interest as it was brought to shore.

Who would believe that under that remote, cool surface, which scorned all pleasures, smouldered unsuspected a strange and burning passion, in complete contrast with the serious, rather sad character of this animal?

And can you guess what Zamore's hidden vice was? Was he a thief? No! Was he a rake? No! Did he like swigging brandy? No! Did he bite? Never! Zamore had a passion for dancing! In him, choreography had lost an artist.

We discovered his passion like this. One day on the Place de Passy, a little grey donkey with a skinny backbone and twitching ears appeared. She was one of those clown-like little donkeys that some artists like painting. In two baskets balanced on the protruding knobs of her spine were a troupe of clever dogs dressed up like courtiers, troubadours, Arabian princes, Swiss shepherdesses or queens of Golconda. The showman put the dogs on the ground, cracked his whip, and all the performers quickly sprang on to their hind legs. The fife and the drum began to play, and they started to dance.

Zamore was strolling sedately by. He stopped, amazed at the sight. The dogs were dressed in gaudy colours, their clothes covered in gold and silver braid, with plumed hats or turbans on their heads. They had been trained to move so beautifully they looked almost like human beings. Zamore thought they were magical. Their graceful sequences of steps, their glides, their pirouettes entranced him, but he was not discouraged. It was as though he said to himself in dog language, 'I can do that, too!' Seized with a desire to copy them, when the troupe passed in single file in front of him, he stood up, staggering a bit, on his hind paws, and tried to join them. The crowd were very amused.

The showman didn't like it at all, and cracked his whip over Zamore's flanks. Zamore was chased from the circle just like a member of the audience at a theatre who tried to get on the stage to join the ballet would be chased away.

This public embarrassment didn't discourage Zamore from following his calling. He came back to the house with his tail down and in a dream. All that day he was very silent and moody, deep in thought. That night, my sisters were woken up by a strange noise coming from the spare bedroom next to theirs. It was where Zamore normally slept on an old armchair. The sound was like a rhythmical stamping, made louder by the silence of the night. At first they thought it was mice dancing, but the noise of steps and jumps on the floor was too loud to be the feathery pitter-patter of mouse paws. The bravest of my sisters got up, half-opened the door – and what did she see in the moonlight that filled the room? Zamore, standing upright and waving his front paws in the air. He was practising the steps he had admired so much in the street that morning, as though he was at a dancing class!

And it wasn't a passing fancy! Zamore was ambitious. He worked hard and became a good dancer. Every time he heard the fife and drum, he ran out into the Place de Passy, slipping between the spectators' legs, and watching the clever dogs going through their routines very carefully, but he remembered the stinging of the whip too, and he didn't try to join in their dances again. He paid careful attention to their steps and how they held their bodies, and he practised these at night, in the quiet of his little room. During the day, though, he never changed his gloomy behaviour. Soon it wasn't enough for him to copy. He invented, he composed – it's fair to say that of all his noble race, very few dogs could outdo him. We often used to watch him through the gap in the door. He practised so energetically that each night he drank up all the water from the large bowl in the corner of his room.

When he thought he was as good as the best dancers in the doggy troupe, he decided he wanted an audience to watch him perform. Our house had a courtyard, closed in on one side by iron railings. These were wide enough apart for fairly slim dogs to squeeze through quite easily. So Zamore sent invitations to fifteen or twenty of our friends' dogs, and one morning they met around a square of well-smoothed ground, which the artist had previously swept with his tail. The performance began. The dogs seemed delighted, and showed their enthusiasm by barking *'Ouah! Ouah!'* just like the *'bravos'* from the regulars at the Opera! Everyone proclaimed Zamore a star and the best dog dancer in the world, apart from one old, very dirty dog, who looked very sour and was undoubtedly a critic. He barked something disapproving about dogs who departed from good old traditions. Zamore had performed a minuet, a jig, and a waltz. Many two-legged spectators had joined the four-legged ones, and Zamore had the pleasure of being applauded by human hands.

The dance had been such a success that he departed from his usual customs, and stood bowing, feet turned out, like an old-fashioned courtier. All he lacked was the cocked hat covered with feathers tucked under his arm.

Apart from that, he was as sad as ever, only showing interest when he saw his master picking up his stick and his hat. Zamore died of a brain fever. We think it was probably brought on by the amount of work he put into learning the schottische, which was a highly fashionable dance at the time. On Zamore's tombstone we wrote the epitaph of a dancer from ancient Greece – *'Lie lightly on me, Earth – I was so small a weight on you'.*

Grand Jeté

JEAN RICHARDSON

In this story, the author uses a true incident as part of her plot. Stephen's letter is based on a real letter written by a famous male dancer and choreographer.

S tephen had taken to going the long way home from school because there was nothing to go home to any more.

Not that Dad didn't try. But housework wasn't his thing, and on the days when Linda didn't pop in for a quick tidy, the sink stayed full of unwashed dishes sulking in deflated suds. If he felt hungry, Stephen made himself beans on toast, or butties plastered with peanut butter and jam. But most times he waited until Dad arrived home with a take-away. Luckily the local chippy did very good chips.

The long way home took him up a steep hill that had once been downland but was now avenues of large houses. Many had been turned into nursing homes for the elderly. In summer the oldies sat marooned in wheelchairs, facing a sea they could no longer hear or see.

It was dark now by four, and there were lights in most of the houses Stephen passed. Lately, as a dare, he'd begun creeping up to the lighted windows and trying to see in. He'd watched nurses having a quick ciggie before giving the inmates tea, and women in spotless kitchens with nothing to do but get supper for the grey-haired man in front of the fire. Then, just when it was becoming boring, he found a house that drew him back day after day.

He was attracted first by the sound of a piano, which reminded him of his mother. But Mum had liked soft, gentle music. This was forceful, no-nonsense playing. *Bang, bang, di bang bang.*

He edged round the side of the house, taking care to stay outside the pool of light that spilled into the garden. The windows at the back were full-length, and it was difficult to see in without being seen. He had to cross the lawn before he could hide behind some bushes. They had very sharp thorns, but the odd scratch was worth it.

It was like being at the theatre, though not at all like a pantomime. He was looking at a large room with no furniture apart from a small piano and a few chairs. At first he thought a brown bear was at the piano, until he realized that it was a woman in a knitted hat and fun-fur coat. Stephen could only see her because she was reflected in a large mirror that covered the length of one wall. Attached to it was a wooden rail, and at intervals along the rail stood girls of about Stephen's age.

They were wearing what looked like navy swimsuits, but instead of being bare their legs were encased in pink tights and long woollen socks. They all had their hair held back by pink headbands, and they all looked very serious, as though they were doing something that required great concentration.

As Stephen watched, they began sinking very slowly down to the floor before rising up just as slowly again. After they'd done this several times, they all turned and did the same thing again, this time facing the garden.

Stephen felt a touch of panic. Surely they could see him. He didn't recognize any of the girls, but once he realized that he was safe, he looked at each in turn. The one he liked best had a round face, dark eyes and curly hair that fizzed over her headband.

The class was conducted by a small woman with ugly muscled legs. She showed the class what she wanted them to do and Stephen could tell that she was a real dragon. Some of her commands were spat out in a language he couldn't understand. *Battement tendu. Battement fondu. Battement frappé.* He couldn't see any point to the movements, unless they were some kind of aerobics. Some of the stretching exercises made him wince in sympathy.

By the fourth time he'd begun to recognize the pattern of the class. Exercises at the rail, exercises in the centre, chains of steps done first by the dragon and then copied by each girl. It must be harder than it looked, he thought, because few of the girls got everything right. He could see at once when anyone made a mistake, and he longed to leap through the window and shout 'No, it goes like this.'

It was freezing in the garden, but he was afraid to stamp his feet in case anyone heard him. Once it was raining, and although he put the hood of his anorak up, he got soaked. He didn't really know why he stayed, apart from the obvious reason that it was better than going home to an empty house. Anything was better than that.

Some days the girls were different – he couldn't stand the babies on Fridays – but his favourite class was there on Tuesdays and Thursdays. He'd like to have spoken to the girl with fizzy hair, but on the day he hung about afterwards, she was whisked away in a car.

They were practising jumps now, crossing the diagonal from corner to corner as though they were doing the splits in mid-air. No one was as good as the dragon. He was waiting for the fizzy girl's turn, and willing her to do well, when suddenly, out of nowhere, a hand grasped his shoulder.

Afterwards, Stephen wondered why he hadn't shaken the hand off and run away. Instead, he let the dragon march him across the lawn and into the house.

Face to face, he saw she had flashing eyes ringed by dark theatrical lines.

'Why were you spying on us?' she demanded, coming straight to the point. 'It's not the first time, is it?'

'I-I'm sorry,' Stephen said. His brain, like his hands and feet, seemed to be frozen. 'I didn't mean any harm. I just liked watching.'

'Did you,' said the dragon. 'Well perhaps you'd like a better view.' And before he could grasp what she meant, she had propelled him into the classroom.

'Meet our mysterious prowler,' she said. Some of the

girls tittered. Stephen's face burned.

'Louise, get our guest a chair. He says he likes watching, so let's give him a grandstand view.'

The girl with fizzy hair brought a chair and put it near the piano. Stephen was trying to work out whether he could make a dash for it, but the girls had formed a maze in the middle of the room.

'Sit!' commanded the dragon.

Stephen, feeling like an obedient dog, sat.

At first he didn't know where to look. He was embarrassed by the physical nearness of the girls, their arms, legs, bottoms. Occasionally he glanced at their faces, but this was worse. At the end of the class, at a sign from the dragon, each of the girls came over and curtsied. Only later did he realize the curtsies were for the pianist.

'Now,' said the dragon, 'it's your turn.'

Stephen saw that the girls had gathered round the sides of the room.

'Fair's fair,' said the dragon. 'You've enjoyed watching us. Now it's our turn to watch you.'

'But—' Stephen saw that it was intended as some kind of punishment. He had to make a fool of himself.

'I'll do the jumps,' he said, unzipping his anorak and kicking off his shoes.

He remembered how the girls had positioned their feet and copied them. Then he spanned the room in two arcs, striding through the air, arms outstretched. The floor was invitingly springy. He made the return, surprised by how easy he found it to do the splits in mid-air. To his amazement, all the girls clapped.

'Have you danced before?' asked the dragon.

Stephen shook his head. He hadn't realized he was dancing.

'Would you like to? A boy who can dance is like gold-dust in this town.'

The girls drifted away to change, leaving Stephen alone with the dragon.

'I'll make you an offer,' she said. 'Come for the rest of the term free of charge, and if you like it, we'll take it from there. Think about it.'

Over the next few weeks Stephen was happier than he'd been for a long time. The only drawback to his happiness was that he couldn't share it with his father.

He tried to work out how to tell Dad, but there was something about enjoying dancing classes that was hard to explain. Perhaps, he thought, it would be easier if his father could see him dance, could see how good everyone said he was.

They were rehearsing for the end of term show and the dragon had arranged a special dance that showed off what she called Stephen's 'elevation'. He had to leap in through an open window, bound around the stage and then do a short dance with Louise, who was just the right height to be his partner.

The show was on a Saturday night, with a rehearsal all the afternoon. It turned out also to be the Saturday when the local football team were playing their greatest rivals. Supporters fought for tickets – and Stephen's father had two.

'I can't come,' Stephen said miserably.

'Why not?'

It was the wrong moment to explain. "Because – because I'm dancing,' Stephen said.

'Dancing!' Dad's tone said it all.

'Yes. I've been having free lessons, so I can't let them down.'

'And where does this dancing go on?'

'At the Rosen School of Ballet. It's a proper school. They do exams and things.'

'Ballet! Prancing around in a pair of tights! What's come over you, Stephen? I never thought I'd see the day when a son of mine wanted to jig around in tights.'

'It's not like that. It's hard work. You have to train, just like for football. And I'm good at it. Everyone says so.'

His father looked away. Stephen saw that he was embarrassed. 'You can come and see me dance. Will you?'

'I don't think so. If you're going to be out, I'll have a drink with the lads. It's more my scene.'

They didn't mention the match or dancing again, but Stephen could feel it there, even when they were watching TV. He felt angry and disappointed. It was as though they were strangers, because Dad didn't want to know the person Stephen had discovered that he was.

They avoided each other on the Saturday morning. Stephen rushed breakfast and then went upstairs to practise. He understood the point of the exercises now, and the routine of bending and stretching comforted him. He felt nervous, but also excited and wound up.

It was all over so quickly. He flew through the window, whirled round the stage, held Louise's hand and supported her as she twirled round. She too was on Cloud Nine.

Afterwards, changing by himself, he envied the girls the chatter of the dressing room. They'd become like a family, like sisters, some nicer than others. He heard them leaving, calling out to each other and him, 'Happy Christmas! See you next term.' But would they see him? He couldn't imagine Dad paying for lessons, and he couldn't expect to go on dancing for free.

He didn't realize at first that the woman in the corridor was waiting to speak to him.

'Congratulations! You were very good. I've had a word with Mrs Rosen and we both think you should audition for full-time training. You've got a good chance of getting a grant. Ask your parents to drop me a line at this address and I'll send the details.'

Stephen didn't know what to say. He stuffed her card into his pocket and mumbled a thank you.

When he got home, Dad was watching TV. Stephen would like to have told him about the show, about the excitement of being on stage, the applause. About how afterwards he'd done great leaps, *grands jetés*, all the way down Culford Avenue from one lamp-post to the next. But he wasn't sure that Dad would understand, was afraid that he would break the spell. So he went straight to his room. It felt very lonely.

He took off his anorak and lay on his bed looking at the card. The address was somewhere in London. It might as well have been on Mars. There was no way Dad would ever write to a ballet school.

He looked at the photo of Mum beside his bed. His mother had loved music. He was sure she would have wanted him to dance. He remembered Louise telling him she hoped to go to London for full-time training. Perhaps they could go to the same school . . . His mind raced ahead. Perhaps they could become real partners, like the dancers the dragon talked about. Fonteyn and Nureyev. Sibley and Dowell . . .

One day, he thought, when I'm a famous dancer, Dad'll see that I was right. But he isn't going to stop me. No one's going to stop me.

He got up, found a scrap of paper and began drafting a letter. *'My son loves dancing and his teacher says he is very good at it, especially his'* – he wasn't sure how to spell elevation, so he put *'jumps.'*

It didn't look like Mum's writing, but they'd never know. Even if they guessed, would it matter? It wasn't like forging someone's signature on a cheque. He wasn't trying to steal anything.

What mattered above all, he was sure, was that it was a letter written by someone who knew what he wanted. Someone who was determined to make a *grand jeté* into the future.

Acknowledgements

The compiler and publishers would like to thank the following for permission to include copyright material:

'The Rose of Puddle Fratrum' by Joan Aiken, from *A Harp of Fishbones and Other Stories*, by Joan Aiken, published by Jonathan Cape, reprinted by permission of A. M. Heath & Co. Ltd., copyright © Joan Aiken Enterprises, 1970.

'The Nutcracker' by E. T. A. Hoffmann, retold and translated by Anthea Bell, reprinted by kind permission of the publishers, Michael Neugebauer Verlag, English translation copyright © Anthea Bell, 1987.

'The Dancing Princesses', from *Told Again (or Tales Told Again)*, by Walter de la Mare, published by Alfred A. Knopf, reprinted by kind permission of The Literary Trustees of Walter de la Mare, and The Society of Authors as their representative, copyright © Walter de la Mare 1927.

'The Cutlers' Ball', from *Granny was a Buffer Girl*, by Berlie Doherty, reprinted by permission of the publishers, Methuen Children's Books Ltd., copyright © Berlie Doherty 1986.

'The Barrel-Organ' by Eleanor Farjeon, from *The Little Bookroom*, by Eleanor Farjeon, published by Oxford University Press, reprinted by permission of David Higham Associates Ltd., copyright © Eleanor Farjeon 1955.

'Dear Florence', from *A Long Way from Verona*, by Jane Gardam, published by Hamish Hamilton, reprinted by permission of David Higham Associates Ltd., copyright © Jane Gardam 1971.

'And Olly Did Too' by Jamila Gavin, from *Prima Ballerina*, edited by Miriam Hodgson, published by Methuen Children's Books, reprinted by permission of David Higham Associates Ltd., copyright © Jamila Gavin 1992.

'The Dancing Display', from *The Fantora Family Photographs*, by Adèle Geras, published in London by Hamish Hamilton Ltd., 1993, reproduced by permission of Penguin Books Ltd., copyright © Adèle Geras 1993.

'The Mega-Nuisance' by Geraldine Kaye, from *The Spell Singer and Other Stories*, compiled by Beverley Mathias, published by Blackie in association with NLHC, reprinted by permission of A. M. Heath & Co. Ltd., copyright © Geraldine Kaye, 1989.

'Toomai of the Elephants' by Rudyard Kipling, from *The Jungle Book*, by Rudyard Kipling, published by Macmillan, by kind permission of A. P. Watt Ltd., on behalf of The National Trust for Places of Historic Interest or Natural Beauty, copyright © Rudyard Kipling.

'The Tavern of the Rathshee' by Patricia Lynch, from *Strangers at the Fair and Other Stories*, by Patricia Lynch, published by Browne and Nolan, reprinted by kind permission of the Estate of Patricia Lynch, copyright © Patricia Lynch 1945.

Chicken Alley

OTHER CHILDREN'S BOOKS AVAILABLE
FROM ROBINSON PUBLISHING

__ **Horse Stories**   Felicity Trotman   £4.99   ☐

Horse Stories contains over thirty of the best stories about horses, riders and riding ever written. There are new stories by Monica Edwards, Andrew Lang and Geraldine McCaughrean as well as modern classics by such popular writers as James Herriot.

__ **Fantasy Stories**   Mike Ashley   £4.99   ☐

This anthology brings together some of the most imaginative fantasy stories of this century, written by the best authors. Many have been written especially for this book, others are already classics.

__ **Space Stories**   Mike Ashley   £4.99   ☐

Space Stories contains over thirty of the most exciting and intriguing space stories written for children. Some are set on a future earth, some in our solar system and some on worlds far away.

Robinson books are available from all good bookshops or can be ordered direct from the Publisher. Just tick the title you want and fill in the form on the next page.

Robinson Publishing, PO Box 11, Falmouth, Cornwall TR10 9EN
Tel: +44(0) 1326 317200 Fax: +44(0) 1326 317444
Email: books@Barni.avel.co.uk

UK/B.F.P.O. customers please allow £1.00 for p&p for the first book, plus 50p for the second, plus 30p for each additional book up to a maximum charge of £3. Overseas customers (inc Ireland), please allow £2.00 for the first book plus £1.00 for the second, plus 50p for each additional book.

Please send me the book(s) ticked on previous page.

NAME (Block Letters) ....

ADDRESS ....

....

....

POSTCODE ....

I enclose a cheque/PO (payable to Robinson Publishing Ltd) for

_____

I wish to pay by Switch/Credit card

Number _____

Card Expiry Date _____